1217

OSPREY
PUBLISHING

For my friend and colleague

Sean McGlynn

who originally prised open the lid of this particular
can of worms.

1217

THE
BATTLES
THAT SAVED
ENGLAND

CATHERINE HANLEY

OSPREY PUBLISHING
Bloomsbury Publishing Plc
Kemp House, Chawley Park, Cumnor Hill, Oxford OX2 9PH, UK
29 Earlsfort Terrace, Dublin 2, Ireland
1385 Broadway, 5th Floor, New York, NY 10018, USA
E-mail: info@ospreypublishing.com
www.ospreypublishing.com

OSPREY is a trademark of Osprey Publishing Ltd

First published in Great Britain in 2024

A catalogue record for this book is available from the British Library.

ISBN: HB 9781472860873; PB 9781472860897; eBook 9781472860910;
ePDF 9781472860903; XML 9781472860927; Audio 9781472860880

24 25 26 27 28 10 9 8 7 6 5 4 3 2 1

Image credit lines are given in full in the List of Illustrations (pp. 6–7).

Diagrams by Tina Ross
Family Trees by Stewart Larking
Index by Zoe Ross

Typeset by Deanta Global Publishing Services, Chennai, India
Printed and bound in Great Britain by CPI (Group) UK Ltd, Croydon CR0 4YY

MIX
Paper | Supporting
responsible forestry
FSC
www.fsc.org   FSC® C171272

Osprey Publishing supports the Woodland Trust, the UK's leading woodland
conservation charity.

To find out more about our authors and books visit www.ospreypublishing.com.
Here you will find extracts, author interviews, details of forthcoming events and the
option to sign up for our newsletter.

Contents

List of Illustrations

MAIN TEXT

Acknowledgements

One of the best things about publishing a book is being able to thank the people who helped in all sorts of ways as it came into being. I'd like to start here by expressing my gratitude to my editor at Osprey, Kate Moore, and my agent, Kate Hordern, for seeing the potential in this subject and encouraging me to explore it. Extra thanks are also due to the former for allowing me to get as nerdy as I liked with regard to details such as armour-wearing and the release velocity of trebuchet missiles.

Also at Osprey, Gemma Gardner's picture research and advice were invaluable, while archaeological illustrator Tina Ross did a fantastic job on the in-text plans. Towards the end of the publishing process I was fortunate to benefit from the expertise of copy-editor Julie Frederick, proofreader Cleo Favaretto and indexer Zoe Ross.

I'm extremely grateful to the Department of Archaeology and History at the University of Exeter for my appointment as an Honorary Senior Research Fellow, which has enabled me to benefit not only from access to research resources, but also from the wonderful collegiality of fellow medievalists at seminars and in correspondence.

A number of friends and colleagues generously gave their time to help out with specific points: Susan Brock and Andrew Buck deciphered numerous Latin abbreviations and provided translations of a passage that was causing me particular problems; Paul Webster kindly allowed me the sight of his notes on the Anonymous of Béthune ahead of his own publication on the subject; staff at Lincoln castle answered my queries about the existence and location of possible postern gates; members of the Survey of Lincoln group were happy to look into exactly which streets in the city were cobbled in 1217; and Jonathan Dean, much to my joy, found evidence of the origin of the perennially irritating myth about medieval archers needing to shoot twelve arrows per minute.

My husband James and our children have been incredibly supportive along the way, and a special shout-out this time to our eldest son Edwin, who is a mathematician rather than a historian, and who reads a lot of my writing from a non-specialist point of view so he can tell me exactly where I'm not making sense.

My great friend and fellow medievalist Sean McGlynn, an expert who has published widely on this period, is always happy to discuss everything over lunch, although we probably owe an apology to anyone who has inadvertently overheard us talking about massacres and atrocities while they were trying to eat. Sean: thanks for all the tea, the chips and the moral support, and please accept a book dedication in return.

The English Royal House

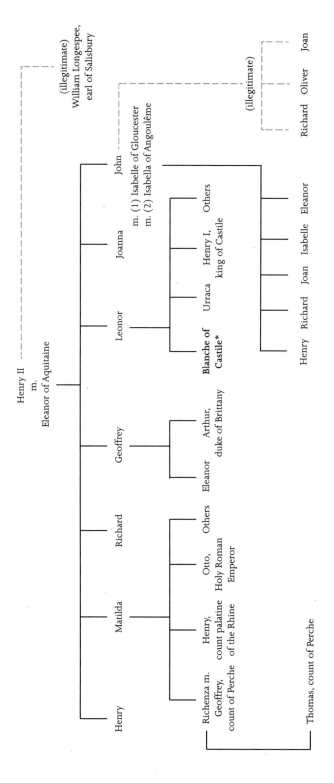

The French Royal House

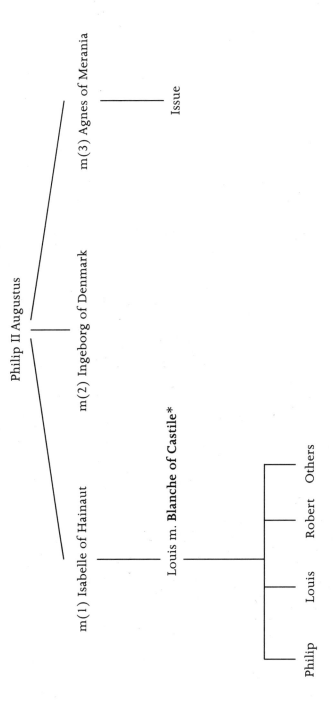

Philip II Augustus

m(1) Isabelle of Hainaut   m(2) Ingeborg of Denmark   m(3) Agnes of Merania

Issue

Louis m. **Blanche of Castile***

Philip   Louis   Louis   Robert   Others

Dramatis Personae

THE ROYALISTS

John, king of England, reigned 1199–1216

Isabella of Angoulême, John's queen

Henry (later Henry III), John's son and heir, born in 1207

Falkes de Bréauté, mercenary commander

Hubert de Burgh, England's justiciar and castellan of Dover castle

John Marshal, knight and nephew of William Marshal

Nicola de la Haye, sheriff of Lincolnshire and castellan of Lincoln castle

Oliver Fitzroy, illegitimate son of King John

Peter de Creon, member of the garrison of Dover castle

Philip d'Albini, knight and sea captain

Ranulf de Blundeville, earl of Chester

Richard of Chilham, illegitimate son of King John

William Marshal, earl of Pembroke and Striguil, later regent of England

William of Cassingham, a man of the Weald

THE REBELS

Geoffrey de Mandeville, earl of Essex, and of Gloucester by
marriage

Gilbert de Gant, knight and claimant to the earldom of Lincoln

Henry de Bohun, earl of Hereford

Isabelle of Gloucester, countess of Gloucester in her own right

Nicholas d'Albini, son of William d'Albini and castellan of
Belvoir castle

Robert Fitzwalter, knight and baron

Saer de Quincy, earl of Winchester

William d'Albini, knight and castellan of Rochester castle

THE VACILLATORS

William d'Aubigny, earl of Arundel

William de Forz, earl of Albemarle

William de Warenne, earl of Surrey (styled Earl Warenne),
cousin of King John

William Longespee, earl of Salisbury, illegitimate half-brother
of King John

William Marshal junior, heir to the earldoms of Pembroke and
Striguil

THE FRENCH

Philip II Augustus, king of France, reigned 1180–1223

Louis (later Louis VIII), his son and heir, born in 1187

Blanche of Castile, Louis's wife

Eustace the Monk, admiral and pirate

Hervé de Donzy, count of Nevers

Peter de Dreux, duke of Brittany

Robert de Béthune, lord of Béthune

Robert de Courtenay, lord of Courtenay and cousin of Philip
   Augustus

Thomas, count of Perche, related to King Philip and King John

OTHER SECULAR LEADERS

Alexander II, king of Scots, reigned 1214–49

Llywelyn the Great, prince of Gwynedd (later also prince of
   Wales), reigned 1195–1240

THE CHURCH

Pope Innocent III, reigned 1198–1216

Pope Honorius III, reigned 1216–27

Guala Bicchieri, cardinal and papal legate to England

Pandulf Verraccio, papal legate to England

Peter des Roches, bishop of Winchester

Simon Langton, priest, Louis's advisor and chancellor, brother
   of Stephen Langton

Stephen Langton, archbishop of Canterbury

THE NARRATORS

The Anonymous of Béthune, a contemporary in the household
   of Robert of Béthune

The author of the *History of William Marshal*, a contemporary

The author of the *Romance of Eustace the Monk*, a contemporary

The Barnwell annalist, a contemporary monk of Barnwell

Matthew Paris, a later monk of St Alban's

The Minstrel of Reims, a later French chronicler

Philip Mousket, a later French chronicler

Ralph of Coggeshall, the contemporary abbot of Coggeshall

Roger of Wendover, a contemporary monk of St Alban's and prior of Belvoir

William the Breton, a contemporary chaplain of Philip Augustus

Prologue

Canterbury

Late August, 1217

A buzz of excitement runs through the city. *They're on the way! It won't be long now.*

It's a bright morning towards the end of a long summer, and Canterbury's merchants, traders, craftsmen and housewives are making a token effort to go about their normal business. But nobody is getting much done, because it's just too tempting to stop and chat. The talk on every street and corner is of recent events, and of what they will soon see when the spectacle makes its hotly anticipated arrival.

The inhabitants of the south-east of England have been living through unprecedented and dangerous times. For years, a violent threat has been hanging over them – one that has caused death and destruction, and a constant, overwhelming terror that their peaceful streets might soon be echoing with screams of fear and running with the blood of their families and children. But now that threat is gone, and the relief of the citizens is palpable as they stand about in little knots, shading their eyes against the slanting early sunlight, talking it over and over. Their voices rise in excitement as they interrupt each other, wondering at their escape and speculating on what might happen next, and what they might see now, this very morning.

Shouts echo from the southern streets, where those who have opportunistically climbed up on to the city walls manage to catch the first glimpse of the jubilant party approaching the Worthgate along the road from Dover. The noise is contagious, spreading like fire as the news is passed from mouth to mouth and street to street: *They're here. Come and see!*

The riders and marchers are through the Worthgate now, crossing the castle bailey and emerging into the noise and bustle of Castle Street. The citizens crane their necks for a better view, shouting and jostling each other in the overcrowded space while children and dogs zigzag in and out and around them, getting underfoot. Those who are lucky enough to lean out of the upper-floor windows of the shops and houses have the best vantage point; they're so close to the action that they can almost touch the heads of the passing horsemen, and they add their cries to those from the street below as the trophy comes into view.

By the time the procession reaches the wider St Margaret's Street, with its market, almost the whole city has come out to watch: pushing and shoving, slipping on cobbles and into gutters, cheering and bawling as they follow the cavalcade, engulfing and carrying it along as though the horsemen were no more than twigs bobbing on the surface of a river.

When they reach the looming cathedral, the backdrop to all their lives for as long as they can remember, the crowd comes to a halt. Hats are removed and children shushed. The sign of the cross is made while prayers are said and thanks given to God for releasing the people of south-east England from the years of danger and terror. *Amen.*

And then the parade starts up again. The visiting party can't remain long in Canterbury: they have other towns to visit, because everyone wants to see what they're carrying and to know that the news is really true. So there's just one last chance for the people of Canterbury to catch sight of the prize before it disappears forever. The man charged with bearing it lifts it high with a final flourish.

The trophy is a severed head, impaled on the point of a spear.

Introduction

The procession that made its gory way through Canterbury and other towns of south-east England in late August 1217 was one of the final acts of a war that has all but been forgotten, but one which was pivotal to the development of the kingdom of England and its national identity. It was during this war that heredity overtook all the other contributing factors to become the defining criterion for the inheritance of the crown, and the Anglo-Norman and Angevin royal dynasty finally began to be seen and described as 'English', a century and a half after it had first seized the throne. It was also during this war that notions of heroism and chivalry were stretched to the limit, as those on both sides attempted to justify the unjustifiable on the basis that their cause was the right one and it was the end result that mattered.

In this book we are going to examine the series of battles and engagements that 'saved England' during this conflict – which, of course, raises an obvious question: what did England need saving from?

The Norman Conquest of 1066 is one of the best-known events in English history, but a second invasion from across the

Channel took place exactly 150 years later, during the course of which a French prince was welcomed and proclaimed king by a cheering throng in the streets of London. Have you ever heard of King Louis I of England? If not, you are not alone. The war that followed Louis's arrival was almost entirely overlooked in the history books of subsequent centuries, for reasons we will examine in due course, and few people now are familiar with it. However, at the time it was a cause of great concern and interest to the entire population of England, and it was extremely well documented by contemporaries.

The story of the invasion, and of the war that took place on English soil for seventeen months from May 1216 to September 1217, is one of military triumph and disaster, and the purpose of this book is to pay particular attention to the three principal engagements that decided the course of the campaign and the future of England. The first is a siege, the second a battle on land and the third a battle at sea. These three very different encounters played seemingly isolated roles in the war, but they actually developed from, and had a significant impact on, each other, while also being linked by events elsewhere. They were distinctive in their introduction of new military technology and the use of innovative tactics that would greatly influence future engagements, both in England and beyond.

We will investigate these developments as we go along, and we will also meet the people who planned and fought in the critical engagements. There are many individuals whose names and deeds stand out against the backdrop of the war, and they are not always the ones we might expect: we will hear of commoners and clergy as well as knights and nobles, and women as well as men. We will also attempt to track down a few of the more shadowy and elusive figures whose contributions were vital but less heralded. Those who fought in the sieges and battles would not have been in a position to do so had it not been for the clandestine resistance efforts of others they had never met, including one man who has a very good case to be the inspiration for the legend of Robin Hood.

There are heroes and there are villains, although (with one notable exception) hardly any of the protagonists can be defined solely as either one or the other – most of them were just people who were trying to do what they thought was right during difficult and desperate times. The question of what exactly constituted behaviour that was 'right', and what lengths combatants might go to in order to win the war for their side, will raise its head more than once, and we will find that there are no easy answers.

There is a great deal of primary evidence for this war. Some of it is in the form of charters, treaties, letters, financial records and so on, which give us the factual bare bones of who was where, and when, and what they agreed while they were there. But there is also a very human story to be told, and for this we will rely on the works of the chroniclers (of both sides) who documented events. Some of these were eye-witnesses who were actually living through the horrors they were narrating, and others wrote later and were able to do so in hindsight, evaluating what had passed. This mixture of viewpoints enables us to build up a rich and detailed composite picture.

We will meet many of these medieval chroniclers in person as we go along, getting to know their particular characters, foibles and prejudices as we hear what they have to say. None of them wrote in English, because that was not the language of the educated minority who had the skills to set their thoughts down in ink and parchment. Instead they composed their narratives in Latin, in Old French or in the French dialect known as Anglo-Norman. In some cases modern English versions of these texts have been published, and I have quoted from and acknowledged the work of the translators; individual citations may be found in the notes, and a full list in the 'primary sources' section of the bibliography. Other works are only available in their original language, and any quotations from these are my own translation, maintaining – I hope – not only the words but also the spirit and tone of the original.

***

The invasion and the war of 1216–17 did not appear out of nowhere; they were the product of a complex set of circumstances that had been brewing for some time on both sides of the Channel and as far away as Rome. Our story does, however, begin in England, and with the character and actions of the man generally considered to be that realm's worst ever king: John.

ONE

The French King of England

MAGNA CARTA

> We utterly reject and condemn this settlement, and under threat of excommunication we order that the king should not dare to observe it and that the barons and their associates should not require it to be observed: the charter, with all undertakings and guarantees whether confirming it or resulting from it, we declare to be null, and void of all validity for ever. Wherefore, let no man deem it lawful to infringe this document of our annulment and prohibition, or presume to oppose it. If anyone should presume to do so, let him know that he will incur the anger of Almighty God.[1]

Pope Innocent III did not beat around the bush when he issued a thunderous denunciation of Magna Carta on 24 August 1215, just a couple of months after the charter had been agreed and sealed, and as soon as he knew the details of it himself. The tone of his words might have come as a shock to some, but the unambiguous nature of the declaration gave

King John the excuse he needed to start an all-out war with his rebellious barons.

England's nobility had been increasingly divided for over a decade, split into two distinct factions. One group of lords (whom we will call 'royalists') felt that they still owed loyalty to a monarch who had been unsuccessful in almost every aspect of kingship: one who had lost Normandy to the French, failed spectacularly in a campaign to regain it, imposed huge and unjustified financial exactions on his subjects, ruled by fear, acted unjustly and mistreated and murdered various political rivals. A second group (we will refer to them as the 'rebels') had lost patience with John; they believed that he should be made aware of the error of his ways, and decided that something ought to be done to ensure he was subject to oversight. The very idea of this, at a time when kings ruled personally and with few restrictions on their authority, was so radical as to be astonishing. Certainly nothing of the kind had occurred in England since the Conquest — but then again, in all that time there had never been a king like John, and an unprecedented situation called for unprecedented measures. The rebels were firm in their attempts to impose some kind of control on the king, and John and his supporters were equally firm in resisting it.

The roots of this conflict lay deep in the past. John had been the fourth son of Henry II, which meant that as a boy and young man his expectations were low, with the family titles and territories being parcelled out among his older brothers (hence his nickname of 'Lackland'). However, the deaths of Henry II's first and third sons, Henry the Young King and Geoffrey, who was duke of Brittany in right of his wife, in 1183 and 1186 respectively, had elevated John in the hierarchy. The one other surviving brother, Richard, was childless, so the only hurdle standing between John and the English throne was the child Arthur of Brittany – born posthumously to Geoffrey's widow and therefore higher in the hereditary order than John – and, to a lesser extent, Arthur's sister, Eleanor.

As the eldest surviving son, Richard succeeded his father in 1189 without any dispute. John had to accept this, but was never exactly his brother's loyal subject, taking advantage of Richard's long absence on the Third Crusade and his subsequent imprisonment to stir up trouble and push his own claims. When Richard was released and returned to England, John was forced to come to terms with him, but he still had his eye on the main chance, and Richard's unexpected death (still with no legitimate children) in 1199 gave him the opportunity he craved. There was an immediate conflict between those who supported John and those who favoured the claims of Arthur – who was at that point twelve years old – but John emerged the victor, Arthur disappeared into a dungeon and was never seen again, and his sister Eleanor of Brittany was taken into a captivity that would prove to be lifelong.

John was in possession of the crown, but in one respect he had done himself a disservice: the manner of his accession had emphasised that the English royal succession was something negotiable and disputable. John had used his wealth, power, contacts and resources to seize the crown ahead of two candidates who had a better hereditary claim. He did not know it at the time, but this point was to come back to haunt him over a decade later.

In the meantime, many of those barons who had supported John were now coming to regret their decision, as he proved over and over again that he was hopelessly unsuited to be a king. In 1203–4 his military ineptitude resulted in the loss of Normandy, which had been linked to the English crown since 1066, as the French king Philip II Augustus swept through and conquered it, adding the duchy to his own royal domains. Philip then started to make inroads into the other Angevin-held lands in Anjou, Maine and Poitou. John made a weak and unsuccessful attempt to stop him in 1206, and later entered into an alliance with the Holy Roman Emperor (who was, as it happened, his own nephew Otto of Brunswick),* and a couple of disaffected French counts, Ferrand of Flanders and Renaud of Boulogne. However, Philip won a great victory over these allies at the battle of Bouvines, in Flanders, in July 1214, while John himself was simultaneously defeated at La-Roche-aux-Moines in Poitou by Philip's adult son and heir, Louis.

In between all these military losses John spent his time alienating his barons, making unfair and extortionate financial demands on them, assaulting their wives and daughters and generally being suspicious, paranoid, erratic, violent and cruel. He was uninspiring, ineffective, unpopular and untrustworthy, and the complaints against him piled up as the years went by.

---

*Otto was the son of Henry the Lion, duke of Saxony and Bavaria, and his wife Matilda of England, who was Henry II's daughter and John's eldest sister.

Although the idea of a rebellion was radical, under the circumstances it is perhaps not surprising that many of the barons should have come to the end of their collective tether and decided to rebel against John in an attempt to impose some kind of order and control. Indeed, the only real wonder is that there were so many who stuck by such a terrible king as long as they did.[2]

By early 1215 the situation had reached crisis point. Representatives of the two parties met in London but made little progress in negotiations, and in April the rebels reiterated their position by insisting that John agree to abide by a set of demands they had drawn up, known at that point as the Articles of the Barons. He refused. Inevitably, armed conflict ensued, and the rebels were able to take control of London. With his capital in their hands John had no choice but to agree to the demands, and on 15 June 1215 he set his seal to the Charter of Runnymede, later and now more commonly known as Magna Carta. This document has been the subject of a huge amount of analysis over the years and centuries, but the crucial point for us to note here is that it established the principle that the king was subject to the law, rather than sitting above it, and that this could be enforced if necessary.[3]

Twenty-five named barons, seven of them earls and all chosen by the rebel side, would ensure that the terms of the charter were kept. Prominent among these were a number of men we will meet again as the war develops: Saer de Quincy, the earl of Winchester; Geoffrey de Mandeville, the earl of Essex (and also earl of Gloucester in right of his wife, who was, rather awkwardly for the king, John's ex-wife Isabelle of Gloucester *); and Robert Fitzwalter, a knight and baron who, although not holding the rank of earl, was among the rebel ringleaders. Chief among the royalists remaining loyal to the king at this point were William Longespee, the earl of Salisbury (who was John's illegitimate half-brother); William de Warenne, the earl of Surrey (John's cousin); William d'Aubigny, the earl of Arundel; Ranulf de Blundeville, the earl of Chester; and Hubert de Burgh, a man of non-noble birth who had risen to prominence under John in a variety of administrative positions. One family managed to have a foot in both camps: William Marshal, the earl of Pembroke and Striguil and England's elder statesman, supported John, while his eldest son and heir William Marshal junior was named on the baronial side.† Whether or not the two William Marshals were genuinely opposed to each other, or whether they simply wanted to ensure that someone in the family ended up on the winning side no matter what happened, is a question that has never been satisfactorily settled. Finally, the position of the Church was made clear by the fact that ten

---

* Isabelle of Gloucester, countess of Gloucester in her own right, had been betrothed to John for many years when he was younger. She was the means by which Henry II intended to provide a title and lands for his youngest son, although John put off the wedding as long as possible in order to keep his options open. Richard had forced the marriage through in 1189, upon his own accession, to curb any ambitions John might have for an influential foreign alliance, but John had more or less ignored Isabelle, and his first act as king had been to use the well-worn excuse of consanguinity to divorce her.

† Given the large number of earls and noblemen in England at this time who were called William, and the restricted range of other forenames in use, for disambiguation purposes we will refer to these men where necessary either by their titles (e.g. Arundel, Salisbury), or by surname (e.g. Marshal) where these are more commonly used and recognisable.

clergymen, including Pandulf Verraccio, the papal legate to England, were named as John's counsellors, while the barons' list was entirely secular.

The Church had not always been on John's side. He had experienced a rocky relationship with the institution during the previous decade, and this would have a huge influence on the course of subsequent events. In 1205 a disputed election to choose a new archbishop of Canterbury, in which John had preferred one candidate and the canons of Canterbury another, had resulted in the pope overruling both sides and appointing Stephen Langton (an English cardinal then in Rome) to the position. John had refused to accept this, and barred Langton from entering England, whereupon Innocent placed England under an interdict in 1208 and then excommunicated John personally in 1209. Just to clarify the difference, an *excommunication* was a decree against an individual which suspended him – or, more rarely, her – personally from full communion with the Church. It also meant that the individual could neither be buried in consecrated ground nor be admitted to heaven if they died while still under the sentence, so it had serious implications for a person's immortal soul. An *interdict*, meanwhile, was more widely applied and prohibited various Church services from taking place over a whole kingdom or region, encompassing all that area's inhabitants. It was thus the case that from March 1208 to May 1213 nobody in England, no matter how innocent or unconnected with John's conflict they were, could receive the sacraments or bury their dead with the correct rites in consecrated ground. As we might imagine, this did very little to improve John's popularity, but he seemed completely unconcerned, and indeed his main response was to confiscate Church lands and to use their incomes for his own benefit. By early 1213 the pope's counter-response was to consider attempting to depose him.

However, as John found himself in deeper and deeper trouble with his barons and under threat of invasion from France, he realised that he needed the Church onside. In a dramatic climb-down, in May 1213 he not only submitted to Innocent and allowed Archbishop Langton to enter England, but astonishingly ceded the whole of England as a papal fief – that is, John would officially hold it as a vassal of the pope, rather than as an independent monarch. In March 1215 he even took the cross; he probably had very little intention of ever actually going on crusade, but swearing the oath gave him and his lands an entitlement to Church protection. All of this meant that John's standing with the pope improved immeasurably, and Innocent could be relied upon to take John's part in any future dispute with the barons.[4]

John had agreed to Magna Carta, but he had not done so willingly; one thirteenth-century commentator tells us that afterwards his fury was such that 'he gnashed his teeth, rolled his eyes, grabbed sticks and straws and gnawed them like a madman, or tore them into shreds with his fingers'.[5] This exhibition of emotional instability, while possibly exaggerated, does go some way towards demonstrating why some of the barons did not want John to have sole and unrestricted power over them and over England. Even those who were more measured in their criticism of the king were clear that John had no intention of keeping his word and that he knew Innocent would be his best ally. 'Shame and anger at his vassals' arrogance filled his heart,' wrote a contemporary, 'and he began to think about revenge.' And this, as the same writer continues, is where John's recent papal reconciliation began to pay dividends:

> He saw clearly that he could never get this [revenge] except through the power of the pope. Very privately he summoned his envoys and sent them to go quickly to Rome. He told the pope that as his lord he should for God's sake have mercy on him and consider his affair, for his vassals were behaving to him in such a way and had forced such a peace on him as he could see in this letter and as his envoys would fully inform him.[6]

John asked the pope to annul the charter, and Innocent responded in no uncertain terms, as illustrated by the quote from his proclamation that opens this chapter. In a separate papal letter addressed to them directly, the rebellious barons were denounced for their actions, which Innocent 'abominate[d] as a crime' and which were, in his opinion, 'illegal and unjust' and deserved to be 'universally rejected'. The leading rebels were excommunicated. Archbishop Stephen Langton – who had attempted to be a moderate voice in the dispute and who had helped to draw up the charter – was suspended from his position and summoned back to Rome, where he would be obliged to remain for several years.[7]

With such robust and unambiguous papal authority behind him, John immediately sprang into action, bolstering the resources at his disposal by summoning mercenaries from his remaining French lands in Aquitaine and from Flanders. He organised additional provisions and strengthened the garrisons in his own strongholds, then began a siege of the castle of Rochester in Kent, which was at that point in the hands of the rebels. He was evidently in this for the long haul, prepared to do whatever it took to re-impose his authority and instigate violent reprisals against those who had humiliated him.

All of this left the opposing barons with only one realistic choice. They had signally failed to control John, even when they had thought victory was within their grasp, and they were now justly afraid of his desire for revenge — the only possible remaining option, therefore, was to overthrow him. But this, of course, created an urgent question: who would take his place on the vacant throne of England? The rebel barons were not radical anti-monarchists, seeking to destroy the concept of kingship as a whole; they merely wanted a better king than John, so they would have to find one from somewhere.

As it happens, the rebels had already come up with an answer to that question. And the issue that would cause the forthcoming war to be not only one of rebellion but also of nascent national feeling, a war of English independence, was the identity of the candidate they had lined up.

LOUIS

Unsurprisingly, one of the main beneficiaries of the internal conflict in England had been the king of France. This was Philip II Augustus, who had acceded back in 1180 when he was still only in his early teens, and who had been doing everything he could since that time to increase the authority of the

French crown. During his long and authoritative reign he had already seen off rival kings Henry II and Richard I, successfully encouraged discord within every part of the English ruling family, and wrested Normandy from the hapless John to add it to his own royal domain.[8] Philip was the latest king in the long and stable Capetian line, which had occupied the French throne in undisputed direct father–son succession since the accession of Hugh Capet in the year 987. This was in marked contrast to the chaotic situation in England over the same period, where the Anglo-Danes and Anglo-Saxons had struggled with each other over several generations before the realm had been conquered by the Normans, who had only managed a line of three kings (William the Conqueror, and his sons William Rufus and Henry I) before another almighty succession dispute broke out, resulting in the short-lived rule of the house of Blois (King Stephen) and then the succession of the Angevin Henry II. Henry II derived his right to the throne from his mother, Empress Matilda – the daughter and only surviving legitimate child of Henry I – but his father was the count of Anjou, hence him and his dynasty being known as Angevin.[*]

These twists and turns had all added grist to the mill of the idea that the English throne was not held by hereditary right but was rather up for grabs every time it fell vacant, and that anyone who could get the crown put on his head could

---

[*] Henry II's father, Geoffrey of Anjou, was also known by the nickname 'Plantagenet' due to his habit of wearing a sprig of broom (*planta genista*) in his hat. Although his family are often referred to by this name in modern works, it was not used by contemporaries and only came into wider use when re-adopted by Geoffrey's descendant Richard, duke of York, in the fifteenth century as part of his bid to wrest the throne from the house of Lancaster.

be the king, regardless of who he had been beforehand. One contemporary remarked on the great contrast with the French royal line, noting that in England 'we have seen rulers, not succeeding each other by lineal descent, but rather through inversion, acquiring violent domination by killing their own and slaughtering their relatives', while in France 'these [the Capetians], always following their father's reign in hereditary sequence and by natural right, preserve balance and moderation and mercy towards their subjects […] reigning long both prosperously and tranquilly'.[9]

In the summer of 1215, as the struggles over Magna Carta were taking place, Philip celebrated his fiftieth birthday and seemed perfectly content to reign over his peaceful and enlarged French kingdom, secure in the knowledge that England was imploding and would be no danger to him for the remaining years of his life. In fact Philip's biggest issue, given the lack of external threat, was that he had an adult son and heir, the twenty-seven-year-old Louis* – and if his tussles with the Angevin royal family had taught him anything, it was that restless and ambitious sons could be dangerous. Henry II had allowed his sons very little autonomy and then seen them rebel against him, and this was not a model that Philip wished to follow. It would therefore be in his best interests to find something for Louis to do, preferably something that did not

---

*In modern works Louis is sometimes incorrectly referred to as 'the Dauphin', but this title was not used for the heir to the French crown until the mid-fourteenth century, following the acquisition of the Dauphiné of Vienne in 1350. Louis referred to himself in his charters as *Ludovicus domini regis Francie primogenitus*, or 'Louis, eldest son of the lord king of France'.

involve Philip having to cede any of his own power as king of France.

Louis did in fact have something of a claim to the English throne via his marriage, and this was, ironically, a situation of John's own making. As we saw earlier, when Richard the Lionheart had died in April 1199, there had been two contenders to succeed him as king of England and duke of Normandy: his youngest and only surviving brother, John; and their young nephew Arthur, duke of Brittany, who was the son of Geoffrey, the deceased brother who had come between Richard and John in age. At first Philip Augustus had supported Arthur's claim, but the French king had later come to terms with John, and the Treaty of Le Goulet of May 1200 set out the terms of the arrangement between them. As was common when such treaties were made, it was proposed that a marriage alliance be formed to seal the deal. Philip was able to put forward his then twelve-year-old son and heir, Louis, as one half of the union, but John had at that time no children of his own.* He was obliged, therefore, to find a niece suitable for the purpose, and (aided by his mother, Eleanor of Aquitaine, who travelled over the Pyrenees in person to make the selection), his choice had fallen on Blanca, the third daughter of his sister Leonor and her husband Alfonso VIII of Castile. Blanca, or Blanche, as she was from that point known, was just coming up for twelve herself, and she was sent to

---

*That is to say, John had as yet no legitimate children. As we will see later, he had several who had been born out of wedlock, but they could not be put forward for a marriage alliance of this magnitude.

France, where she and Louis were married forthwith.[10] For various reasons – her youth at the time, the fact that she spent her formative teen years at the French court, the warm welcome and protection she received from Philip and her growing emotional bond with Louis as they faced life together – Blanche became whole-heartedly Capetian in outlook. She had started her married life as a helpless pawn offered up by John, but, as we will see later, she would grow up to be Louis's greatest asset.

The young Arthur of Brittany, meanwhile, continued to be seen as a rival to the English throne until his capture in 1202, at the age of fifteen. He was taken into John's custody and never heard of again, widely (and plausibly) reported to have been murdered at John's order. His sister, Eleanor, was considered less of a danger but still carried a hereditary right to the English throne which might be claimed by any man who married her; she would spend the rest of her life in captivity to prevent this from happening. In addition, she had become duchess of Brittany in her own right following Arthur's assumed death, but given Brittany's precarious position, stuck both geographically and politically between France, Normandy and England, its nobles decided that her captive status made her ineligible, so they declared her younger half-sister Alix duchess instead. Alix was the daughter of Constance of Brittany – who had also been duchess in her own right – by her third marriage and therefore no relation (and no threat) to the English royal house. Alix was married off at a young age to Peter de Dreux, a member of a cadet branch of the Capetians, who became duke in his wife's name; we will meet him later.[11]

Great estates and titles such as that of Brittany could be claimed by a man in a manner known as *jure uxoris*, 'in right of his wife', if she was an heiress, and this had occasionally also applied to kingdoms. The former Holy Roman Emperor Henry VI, for example, had within living memory also been king of Sicily (1194–7) via his marriage to Constance of Hauteville, heiress to the crown there in her own right; and John's own great-grandfather Fulk of Anjou had earlier been king of Jerusalem in right of his wife Queen Melisende. The idea that a kingdom might be inherited *jure uxoris* was the reason for Eleanor of Brittany's lifelong captivity, which was certainly unfortunate for her, but in 1213 it had come in handy for Louis.

At that time the pope had reportedly been considering John's deposition, so Philip Augustus had started to prepare an invasion fleet, with the ultimate goal being Louis's accession to the English throne in John's place.[12] This would have been something of a win-win situation for Philip, getting Louis out of his hair and also ensuring a lasting peace with England, while simultaneously eliminating the last remaining adult male of the Angevin ruling dynasty. This could not justifiably be achieved by simple conquest, though; Louis would need some semblance of a legitimate entitlement to the English throne. As it happens, he was actually a direct descendant of William the Conqueror,* but this was not mentioned anywhere in his claim, which referenced instead his more immediate right by marriage.

---

*Louis's paternal grandmother was Adela of Blois, the granddaughter and namesake of William's youngest daughter.

Louis's marriage to Blanche, and her close blood relationship to the English royal family, featured heavily in the reasons given for Louis's candidacy, although her hereditary claim was tenuous at best: even discounting the superior entitlement of Eleanor of Brittany, Blanche had a younger brother and two older sisters of her own who would normally take precedence. Moreover, her mother Leonor had been the second of Henry II's daughters, meaning that the children of Leonor's elder sister Matilda, the late duchess of Saxony, could be considered as having a better claim.

None of this prevented Louis from being a very plausible candidate for the English throne — which had, after all, been passed uncontested from father to eldest surviving son only once since the accession of William the Conqueror a century and a half previously.* All that was really needed was some semblance of a credible right plus the determination and the military resources to back it up. As the case of Arthur of Brittany and King John had shown, a better claim in strictly hereditary terms could be trumped by effective baronial support, more money and a greater ruthlessness.

However, while Philip and Louis were moving forward with their plans on this basis, the situation in England changed. John's submission to the pope and subsequent ceding of England as a papal fief in May 1213 had, of course, changed Innocent's mind on the question of deposition, and he had performed a swift U-turn: he cancelled all his criticisms of John and threatened

---

*Award yourself a bonus point if you knew this occurred in 1189, when Henry II was succeeded by Richard the Lionheart.

Philip with excommunication if he continued his invasion plans. At the time Philip had only recently been reconciled with the pope himself following an excommunication due to his irregular marital affairs, and he had reluctantly acquiesced to Innocent's decree so as not to provoke another conflict.* To add insult to injury, Philip's fleet was then destroyed in May 1213 when the earl of Salisbury, crossing the Channel with ships of his own, found it almost unguarded at Damme because the crews were ashore. He was able to set fire to most of it before Philip could get there with his army to drive him off.

Not unnaturally, Louis had been disappointed by the pope's decree and Philip's decision to acquiesce to it. His father was in robust health and likely to live a good many years yet, so the French crown was not an immediate prospect and he was left kicking his heels, having thought that he was about to embark on an exciting adventure with the English throne at the end of it. By 1215 Louis was in his late twenties, the prime of life, and itching for something to do. His future prospects were secure and serene: he had been recognised as the heir to the French throne since the moment of his birth, and could not possibly be unseated by any rival candidate. He was happy in his family life too – he loved his wife, and although he and

---

*Philip's first queen (and Louis's mother), Isabelle of Hainaut, had died in childbirth in 1190. Philip had married again in 1193, taking as his wife Ingeborg of Denmark, but – for reasons that have never been fully understood – he repudiated her the day after the wedding. He later 'married' for a third time, to Agnes of Merania; but as the pope had never recognised Philip's attempted divorce of Ingeborg and considered them still married, he held that Philip's third union was bigamous and the children born of it illegitimate. Philip spent twenty years contesting this, long after Agnes had died, and only consented to restore Ingeborg to her rightful place as queen in early 1213; it was this act that had reconciled him with the pope.

Blanche had tragically already lost three children in infancy, they had two surviving sons and every hope of more. He was pious and respectful of his father, but at the same time aggressive and warlike, with a marked predilection for military pursuits, and he wanted something to do now. Fortunately for Louis, the barons of England had not forgotten about his candidacy, and he would shortly receive a very appealing proposal.

With regard to a replacement king, the choices available to the rebel barons were threefold. First, they could install one of John's children on the throne. He had by this time (August 1215) four or five legitimate children, all by his second wife, Isabella of Angoulême, and all very young: Henry was seven, Richard six, Joan five, and Isabelle probably between one and two. A third daughter, Eleanor, had either just been born or would shortly arrive. This idea does not seem to have been seriously considered at all – or, if it was, it was discarded quickly enough to make no impression on contemporary writers. The most likely reason for this would seem to be that a young child of John's would be nothing more than a puppet controlled by John, and that the status quo would therefore not change. John also had a dozen or so illegitimate children, of whom at least two, Richard of Chilham and Oliver Fitzroy, were grown men, but again there does not seem to have been any discussion at all of one of them being crowned.*

---

*John giving the same name to two different sons was not helpful to later historians, especially when combined with the tendency of contemporary chroniclers to refer simply to 'the king's son Richard', which led to confusion in some later translations and accounts of the war as to which son was meant in some circumstances. At least one notable nineteenth-century historian managed to dismiss the contribution of Richard of Chilham to the war because he thought

The second choice available to the barons was to elevate one of themselves, but this would require some measure of royal blood. Two men among the nobility were related to the Angevin royal family, but they were both at this point still staunch adherents of John, which would cause difficulties, and in any case they were both tainted by illegitimacy: the earl of Salisbury was an illegitimate son of Henry II, and Earl Warenne was the son of Henry II's illegitimate half-brother.* Neither of them, therefore, was a credible proposition. Meanwhile there was nobody among the rebel barons who could claim, even distantly, to be 'royal', and this precluded their attempting to take the throne. The institution of the monarchy had to be respected even if the individual who was the present incumbent was considered unsuitable.

The third option, and the one that was taken by the rebel barons, was to find a contender who was already of royal birth, who was connected to the Angevin ruling family, and who (crucially) was strong enough to take on the challenge and stand a chance of winning. Here the field was not exactly teeming with suitable candidates. John was the last survivor of his sibling group and, as we have just seen, his children were

---

a contemporary account was referencing the younger, legitimate Richard, and he found this implausible given the boy's age. However, having repeat names in the same family was not uncommon, and we should have no problem in this book differentiating between the legitimate (born in 1209) and the illegitimate (born c. 1190).

* Earl Warenne is generally styled thus (rather than 'earl of Surrey') in contemporary records, a convention we will follow. His father, Hamelin of Anjou, was the illegitimate son of Henry II's father, Geoffrey of Anjou. Although this made Hamelin Henry's half-brother, he had no royal claim at all, because Henry derived his right to the throne not from their shared father but from his mother, Empress Matilda.

not considered. Only one of his legitimate brothers, Geoffrey, had left surviving children, a son and a daughter, but Arthur was already dead and Eleanor was in captivity. Theoretically anyone who could break her out of prison and marry her could claim the English throne in her right, but this was not attempted. That left the children of John's sisters. Two of Matilda's sons were at this point still alive, but Henry was Count Palatine of the Rhine, busy with his estates in Germany and with no interest in England, while Otto, having once risen to the dizzying status of Holy Roman Emperor, had been soundly beaten at the battle of Bouvines in 1214 by Philip Augustus, and subsequently deposed by a rival. He was now living in disgrace and seclusion in the Empire and was certainly not a fit candidate for the English throne.[13]

John's next sister, Leonor, had died in 1214, leaving several children. Her one surviving son was just eleven years old and already the king of Castile, under the regency of his eldest sister, who was separated from her husband; neither of these would be of much use to the barons in a military campaign. Next in line were the second sister, Urraca, who was the queen of Portugal by marriage, or the third, Blanche, who was married to the heir to the French throne.

From a purely practical point of view it was probably Blanche's marriage to Louis that made her claim look in any way plausible, rather than the other way round. If she had not been the wife of a man of royal blood, who was a keen and able warrior and who had the might and resources of the French crown behind him (or so the barons thought at the time) then she would almost certainly have been overlooked like the others. Rather, the fact that her family links gave Louis – the barons' *actual* preferred candidate – at least a fig-leaf of justification was a point in her favour.

All of this had already been decided by the time the fateful moment arrived. Innocent's condemnation of Magna Carta followed by John's immediate recourse to violence merely sped up the inevitable, and in the autumn of 1215 a party led by Robert Fitzwalter and the earls of Winchester and Hereford sailed for France.

THE OFFER

When the party of English rebels arrived in Paris, they did not get quite the response they were expecting. Louis, as might be imagined, was extremely keen to take up their offer that 'if he decided to pack his cloak and come to England, they would give him the kingdom in good peace and would make him their lord', but King Philip was markedly less enthusiastic.[14] Various reasons have been put forward for this over the years, including Philip's unwillingness to jeopardise his reconciliation with the pope, or concern for the reputation of the French crown if it should become involved in the affair (and particularly if it should all end unsuccessfully), or fear that Louis, if crowned king of England, would be his equal and no longer subject to his authority. The most plausible explanation seems to be that Philip was actually playing a double game: he would not support the campaign overtly, in order to stay on the right side of the pope, but nor would he forbid it; and, indeed, he would back it clandestinely. Although Philip's ever-loyal chaplain and biographer, William the Breton, stoutly claimed that Louis acted 'against the wishes of his father', another well-informed contemporary, the Anonymous of Béthune, tells us that Philip 'publicly made it appear as though he did not want to be involved because of the truce he had granted [that is, making peace with the pope]; but privately, it was believed that he had advised him'.[15]

Officially, Louis would have to put his case to a council of nobles (the French monarchy's custom of consultation was another reason why Louis was an attractive prospect for the English barons), and this would not happen until the following spring. Unofficially, he accepted the offer straight away and sent an advance party of 140 knights across the Channel in December 1215.

Arguably, this was the point at which the rebellious barons lost the moral high ground and damaged their own cause. They were dissatisfied with the way the kingdom was being run and unhappy with the personal rule of the man on the throne: fair enough. They had every right to seek reform, even to the extent of enforcing Magna Carta. But offering the throne and control of the kingdom – in perpetuity, as far as anyone knew at the time – to a member of a foreign dynasty was of an entirely different order of magnitude. There were now French troops on English soil who, although 'invited' by some, were representative of an invasion force.

Did the rebel barons know what they were getting themselves into? There is an interesting discussion to be had here as to whether they were simply thinking in the short term, blinded by their dislike for John and desperate to do anything to get rid of him, and by their own ambition, or whether they were genuinely happy with the prospect of long-term Capetian rule over England. Given their actions, the latter seems more probable. The stability demonstrated by the Capetian line was certainly an attraction: it had occupied the French throne since before the turn of the millennium, and its last six kings (including Philip Augustus himself) had each reigned for more than a quarter of a century before passing the crown uncontested to a son and designated heir. All of this compared very favourably with the turmoil that had attended virtually every change of monarch in England during the same timeframe, and the weary rebel barons – most of whom had lived through the reigns of three kings and plenty of vicious royal disputes already – might have been willing to swap their notions of 'Englishness' for a bit of peace and stability. 'Englishness' was in any case a very nebulous concept among the nobility at this time. Although the majority of the population of the kingdom (those who actually spoke English and who tilled the soil, tended the animals and baked the bread) could claim that it had been their ancestral home for generations, the nobility was made up of Anglo-Normans whose first language was a dialect of French, and who had many ties and deeper roots in France.*

It was not much more than a decade since John had lost Normandy, and most of these 'English' barons had grown up in

---

*Interestingly, this class-based linguistic divide can still be seen in modern English, which, unlike most languages, has different words for domestic animals and the meat of those animals. The people who stood in cold, muddy fields tending the livestock called them cows, pigs and sheep; but those who had the meat cooked and dished up to them in their banqueting halls called it beef (boeuf), pork (porc) and mutton (mouton). Similarly, many modern English words relating to power and authority, such as parliament and government, have French roots.

a cross-Channel, Anglo-Norman realm in which many families held estates on both sides. When Normandy fell, they had been forced to jump one way or the other and choose between their two sets of lands. Some had given up one set completely, in loyalty to either John or Philip, and had been compensated accordingly by their chosen king with estates confiscated from those who had made the opposite choice. But other families had hoped that the breach would only be temporary and had therefore divided the estates between different family members, meaning that some of the English barons had close relatives in Normandy. Only one nobleman of note, incidentally, had personally retained his lands in both places: William Marshal. This meant that John was his overlord in England and Philip was his overlord in Normandy, a point to which we will return later. But to everyone else whose ancestral holdings had been lost or split, the idea of being able to reunite their estates on both sides of the Channel under one king would have been of some interest.[16]

That is not to say that there would necessarily be only one king in the future. If Louis were successful in claiming the English throne, and then later inherited the French one as well, he would be king of both realms; but when he died, he would have the choice of leaving both to his eldest son – in which case they might feasibly be amalgamated in the future – or he might leave France to his eldest and England to his second, in the same way that William the Conqueror had bequeathed Normandy and England to different sons. Although a patrimony (the ancestral estates passed down the male line) was by custom inherited by a family's eldest son,

46

it was acknowledged that any further lands or titles gained by marriage or conquest could be disposed of differently, with younger sons benefiting. In this particular case the political difference would be slight, because either of the possible inheritance scenarios would result in close ties between England and France for the foreseeable future, and the rebel barons must have been aware that this would be the eventual result of their actions. They do not appear to have spent much time wondering how their plans might suit the rest of the population of England – either the opposing lords or the largely ambivalent lower classes – and there were certainly others among the nobility who felt differently. These royalists now reiterated their support for the beleaguered John and his dynasty while they watched developments across the Channel.

THE WINTER OF 1215–16

John had remained at Rochester castle for the entirety of the siege – seven weeks, from mid-October to early December – directing operations personally. Such was his determination to crush the rebels that this was the longest he ever spent continuously in one place during his whole reign.[17] He was eventually successful and the castle fell, at which point he wanted to have the entire garrison executed as an object lesson. He was talked out of it, though, and in the end only one man (a crossbowman who had previously been in John's own service) was hanged; the rest were imprisoned, including the castle's commander, William d'Albini. With business at Rochester concluded, John departed on 6 December, but by this time Fitzwalter and his companions had already spoken to Louis in

Paris, and the advance party of French knights was or would shortly be on its way to London.

The most sensible thing for John to do at this point, and probably the option a bolder king would have chosen, was to capitalise on his victory at Rochester and make a decisive attempt to recapture London. It would have been much easier for him to plan his response to the expected invasion if the capital were once more under his control, and it might also encourage any waverers back to his side. However, he did not. On 20 December 1215 he got as near to it as St Albans, but during a council there he decided to split his forces: one part, under the earl of Salisbury and an experienced military commander named Falkes de Bréauté,* was to remain in the south in order to contain the French and rebels in London (but not to attempt to retake it), while John himself would head northwards on a punitive ravaging operation through the lands held by rebel barons. This was a more immediately satisfying and lower-risk option than beginning a siege of the capital, though it would be less effective in the long run. It would provide him with one short-term advantage, however: money. John needed a great deal of ready cash in order to pay his hired mercenaries, but with London and much of the kingdom in rebel hands, his normal revenue-collecting systems were not generating income at the rate he needed. Plundering the lands and estates of his

---

*Falkes de Bréauté was a rare example of a man of less-than-noble birth who had risen to prominence in the secular world. He was probably the illegitimate son of a Norman knight, but after entering John's service he had been rewarded with knighthood and promotion. By this time he was one of John's most trusted lieutenants, having acquired both a great deal of wealth and a reputation as the king's ruthless enforcer.

enemies would therefore serve the dual purpose of teaching them a lesson and swelling his own coffers.

On Christmas Day 1215 John was at Nottingham; after that he made his way to Newark, Doncaster, York, Durham and Newcastle, his men licensed to plunder any lands held by rebel barons as they went, much to the dismay of local populations who did not really care who sat on the throne as long as they could live, work and trade in peace. John's methods could be brutally direct. Belvoir castle (on the Leicestershire–Lincolnshire border) was held by Nicholas d'Albini, whose father William had commanded the rebels at the siege of Rochester and who was now in John's custody; John ordered Nicholas to surrender, threatening to starve his father to death if he did not. This was something the king had done before, so it was a credible threat and Nicholas had no choice but to yield.*

By mid-January John was in Berwick, where he 'burnt and destroyed' the luckless town. The seventeen-year-old Scots king, Alexander II, had made some speculative raids south of the border, but he now retreated before John's onslaught.[18] Elsewhere, Llywelyn the Great of Wales was also making incursions into English-held territory, probably with similar motives to Alexander's: he did not like John and supported the rebels because it was to his own advantage.† William Marshal,

---

*It was well known that John had previously allowed people he held captive to starve to death – most notably twenty-two knights captured fighting for Arthur of Brittany in 1203, and, more recently, the noblewoman Matilda de Briouze and her son in 1210.

†This was despite the fact that Llywelyn was John's son-in-law. His wife, Joan, lady of Wales, was John's illegitimate daughter (this Joan, born c. 1191, should not be confused with John's legitimate daughter of the same name, who was born in 1210). She was often tasked with the

whose lands lay in the west of England and in south Wales, was dispatched to deal with this (along with Ranulf de Blundeville, the earl of Chester, another major adherent of John, whose lands lay along the Welsh border) but he was pinned down while the Welsh made gains.[19] This kept Marshal neatly away from John and any association with the brutal tactics the king was using, while also enabling his contemporary biographer to gloss over any possible conflicts of loyalty.

This anonymous writer — whose work is one of the major sources for the period and one we will refer to frequently in later chapters — is always keen to present his protagonist in the best possible light. This is not surprising, given that he was commissioned by Marshal's family after the latter's death, but it does mean that some of his details need to be taken with a pinch of salt, and that his omissions are almost as illuminating as his inclusions. Of the period immediately after Magna Carta and over the winter of 1215–16, he says cryptically only that 'I must pass over in silence the war [...] for there were many incidents which it would not be profitable to relate; indeed to do so might result in harm to myself'. A few lines later he reiterates Marshal's loyalty to the king almost to the point of absurdity:

The marshal at least, a man of loyal and noble heart, stayed with him [John] in hard and difficult circumstances; he never left him, he never changed that steadfast heart of his,

difficult mission of mediating between her husband and her father, although generally to little avail given their political differences.

serving him in good faith as his lord and king. Not once did
he leave him […] he was always with him or his men, being
the worthy and loyal man he was. It is true, it is a proven fact
[…] he never abandoned him for anyone.[20]

The strategic problem with John's campaign in the north was
that he could not spend too long there, lest the situation further
south get even more out of hand. So, after deciding against
chasing Alexander deep into Scotland, he turned and made
his way back, reaching Bedford by the end of February 1216.
He had seized enough booty to replenish his coffers but had
made no real long-term gain, as he could not afford to leave any
men behind to hold lands in his name. These estates, although
plundered and with stores depleted, were thus still owned by
the rebel lords, who would benefit from their revenues once
they recovered.

John's other problem was that, in taking his revenge against
the rebels, he had attacked his own subjects. Moreover, he
had used foreign mercenaries to do so, which (at least in the
eyes of those subjects who saw their homes burned and their
livelihoods destroyed) made him just as bad as any invader.
Contemporaries were not impressed, blaming these foreigners
for the atrocities they witnessed:

The whole surface of the earth was covered with these
limbs of the devil like locusts, who assembled from remote
regions to blot out everything from the face of the earth,
from man down to his cattle; for, running about with drawn
swords and open knives, they ransacked towns, houses,

cemeteries and churches, robbing everyone, and sparing neither women nor children; the king's enemies wherever they were found were imprisoned in chains and compelled to pay a heavy ransom. Even the priests whilst standing at the very altars, with the Cross of the Lord in their hands, clad in their sacred robes, were seized, tortured, robbed and ill-treated.[21]

Meanwhile, the earl of Salisbury and Falkes de Bréauté had been acting on John's behalf further south. Not content with simply pinning down the French and rebels in London, they had also carried out brutal raids in Essex, Hertfordshire and Cambridgeshire, sacking the cathedral city of Ely, where a contemporary noted that 'they made great slaughter, as they did everywhere they went, sparing neither age, nor sex, nor condition, nor the clergy'.[22] Throughout their raids they 'collect[ed] booty and indulg[ed] in rapine; they levied impositions on the towns, made prisoners of the inhabitants, burnt the buildings of the barons, destroyed the parks and the warrens, cut down the trees in the orchards, and having spread fire as far as the suburbs of London, they took away an immense booty with them'.[23]

John's principal antagonist had not even arrived yet, but already much of England lay in charred ruins. The smoke from the buildings burned by the earl of Salisbury and Falkes de Bréauté could be seen from London and was no doubt intended as an incentive for the inhabitants and their guests to rethink their loyalties, but they did not. They knew that Louis would soon be on his way.

THE INVASION

The original party of 140 French knights had been in London since December, and they were joined by a second advance group in January 1216. They were not able to begin any major military operations, due to a combination of the blockade on the capital and the fact that they were waiting for Louis's own arrival, but they did engage in some training and 'team-building' exercises with their new allies. Unfortunately, the initial consequence of this was the loss of a key figure: Geoffrey de Mandeville, the earl of Essex and Gloucester, was accidentally killed by a French knight during a tournament. He had no children so the earldom of Essex went to his brother, William de Mandeville. The vast Gloucester estates were left without a male leader, although the widowed Isabelle of Gloucester, countess in her own right, continued to support the rebels in opposition to her ex-husband King John – which gives us some insight into the nature of their personal relationship.[24]

Louis, meanwhile, had been preparing his case to put before the council of French nobles, which occurred in April at the Assembly of Melun. Louis spoke personally and was also represented by a team of legal advisors led by Simon Langton, an English cleric and lawyer who had been educated in Paris. Simon was the younger brother of Stephen Langton, the archbishop of Canterbury, and was an experienced international negotiator who had acted as an envoy between King John and the pope during the period of the disputed Canterbury election. In 1215 he had himself been elected archbishop of York by the canons there, but John protested and the appointment was quashed by Innocent III, who, in his usual no-nonsense style, accused Simon of 'insolence', 'intrigue' and 'presumption'.[*25] Simon then returned to Paris and entered Louis's service, much to the pope's chagrin, and at the assembly he was vehemently opposed by Guala Bicchieri, the papal legate. King Philip presided over the council, but he remained ostentatiously neutral, intervening only where the arguments of either side intruded on his own interests.

Louis's hereditary claim, via his wife, was weak. But he also made a case that he could claim the English throne by right of election, having been invited to do so by the rebel barons. This was interesting, as the same could technically be said of John himself, who had been crowned in 1199 with the support of most of the nobles despite Arthur and Eleanor of Brittany being higher up the hereditary queue. Earlier post-Conquest kings, notably Henry I and Stephen, had also claimed election, so there was ample precedent. Guala's main case for the opposition was that John had taken the cross, so his lands were under the protection of the Church, and that he held England as a papal fief and could therefore be deposed by nobody except the pope. The legate threatened King Philip with excommunication unless he forbade his son from invading England – a threat that did not endear him to the assembled counts and lords, as Philip was popular with his nobles.

The results of the council were predictable. The French lords wholeheartedly supported Louis and dismissed Guala's arguments; Guala departed in anger and headed for England,

---

*If Simon's election had been ratified, the concurrent archbishops of Canterbury and York would have been brothers, an event unique in English history.

where he issued a sentence of excommunication against Louis; and Philip continued to walk a tightrope between dynastic ambition and papal approval. He would not officially support Louis's invasion, but he would not forbid him from going, either. All three of these outcomes of the assembly were to have a crucial influence on the progress of the forthcoming war, as we will see.[26]

With the backing of the council of nobles, Louis began to prepare his invasion in earnest, and a fleet of ships was assembled at the Channel ports of Wissant, Gravelines, Boulogne and Calais. However, Philip's public refusal to support the campaign meant that this was not an undertaking of the French monarchy, and that Louis was therefore not able to call officially upon all those who owed service to the crown. Instead he was obliged to recruit privately, and although he did succeed in attracting a good number of volunteers, he had a much smaller number of troops than he would otherwise have done. His invasion force would not be of sufficient size to attempt a real conquest, but under the circumstances he should not need to: once he landed in England he would be joined by the existing rebel forces, he would persuade the remaining nobles to come over to his side, and he would be acclaimed and crowned king without the need for any fighting other than that required to mop up any small pockets of resistance.

Or so he thought.

The fleet was to be commanded at sea by a notorious figure known as Eustace the Monk. He was, as his name implied, a renegade monk, who had for a number of years operated as a pirate from a base in the Channel Islands. In 1205 or 1206 he had sold his services to King John, but he switched sides in 1212 and had been working for Philip Augustus ever since, making himself extremely unpopular in England by attacking English ships and raiding coastal towns. His was the ship on which Louis and his chief advisor Simon Langton sailed, with the rest of the fleet comprising around 1,200 knights and an unspecified (but almost certainly much larger) number of non-knightly combatants and all the necessary engineers, grooms, servants and administrators. They set sail on 20 May 1216.

Most of this was already known in England: it would have been impossible for the 800 or so vessels to be gathered in secret. John had therefore assembled a fleet of his own that was meant to sail to Calais and engage Louis's ships there, preventing them from crossing the Channel at all. However, a storm had prevented them from putting to sea, so they never left England and the French fleet departed unharmed. The same storm then scattered them, but almost all the ships survived and they were soon able to rendezvous at Sandwich. John was by this time at Sandwich himself, with his army, and he now had to make one of the biggest decisions of his life: would he engage the French invaders as soon as they landed, or not?

There were good arguments for and against either course of action. The attraction of an immediate battle was that if John were to be victorious, the invasion would be over before it had the chance to start. If Louis were dead or in captivity this would put John in an enormously strong position, and the rebel barons in London and elsewhere would either be persuaded to surrender or they would be easier to pick off because they were isolated and could expect no further help to arrive. But the all-or-nothing result of a pitched battle was precisely the reason why they were generally avoided by twelfth- and thirteenth-century commanders – the risks were simply too great. Anything could happen, and the merest stroke of bad luck could ruin months' or years' worth of careful campaigning. Moreover, John had been defeated by Louis at La-Roche-aux-Moines during an abortive campaign to regain his French lands only two years previously, and the simultaneous shattering defeat of his allies by Philip Augustus at the battle of Bouvines had resulted in a re-orientation of power in western Europe that would last for decades.[27] This, perhaps understandably, gave him pause. Another significant point was that many of the men under John's command were French mercenaries, who had been happy to engage in the ravaging expedition in the north of England, but who might balk, or even change sides, if ordered to take up arms against the heir to the French throne. All battles were risky, but a battle in which a commander could not be sure of the loyalty of his own men was almost certain to be disastrous.

The counsel of John's advisors, seemingly according with his own inclination, was therefore not to attempt to give battle at this stage. Naturally, this decision was interpreted differently by the various contemporary chroniclers depending on their own points of view: John 'did not dare' face Louis; or he 'lost heart [...] and made a very poor showing'; or he merely 'chose to retreat for a time, rather than to give battle on an uncertainty'; or, rather more damningly, 'despite having three times as many men as Louis, he abandoned his camp and, forgetting his promise and his royal pride, preferred to flee rather than to fight'.[28]

From Sandwich John withdrew first to Dover, but he did not want to end up trapped in one place, so he left the castle there in the capable hands of Hubert de Burgh and moved further west towards Guildford and Winchester, being joined at some point on his journey by the papal legate Guala. Given that John had declined battle, the next phase of the war seemed certain to be characterised by a series of sieges, so he did what he could in terms of re-supplying and re-garrisoning the castles that held out for him. He also took precautions to protect the future of his dynasty by having his heir, the eight-year-old Henry, placed under close guard in the very defensible castle of Devizes, while second son Richard was lodged separately in the equally formidable Corfe. The invasion had not been stopped in its tracks, but John had lived to fight another day and his campaign had regrouped.

Meanwhile Louis, perhaps to his surprise, landed unopposed. This left him facing a major decision of his own: should he attempt to take Dover castle, the principal stronghold in the region, now, or should he ride straight for London? He opted for the latter, and the rebel barons in the capital were able to ride out to meet him on the way: Robert Fitzwalter, William Marshal junior and the earls of Winchester, Essex, Norfolk and Oxford, among others, met him at Rochester and paid homage to him as their new king. As a show of unity they assailed the royalist-held Rochester castle together, and it fell to them swiftly, not having yet been properly repaired from John's siege of the previous autumn.

Louis and the combined party of French and rebels left Rochester and headed for London, where Louis was proclaimed king on 2 June 1216:

> He then went to London, and was there received with great joy by all the barons; he then received homage and fealty from all of them, and from the citizens who had been awaiting his arrival there, whilst he himself swore on the holy gospels that he would grant good laws and restore their inheritances to each and all of them.[29]

It is difficult to overstate just how momentous an occasion this was: a Capetian, a representative of the ancient French royal house, the son of the reigning French king, cheered and acclaimed in England's capital as England's king. The reaction of the Londoners is not altogether surprising, of course. They had suffered under John's rule and wanted to get back to a situation where they could trade in peace and prosperity, so they were pleased that a change of regime had been achieved with minimal violence – and not overly bothered that their new king was a Frenchman, because this would make little difference to their lives. Others of higher rank, meanwhile, were caught out by the swift and almost bloodless nature of Louis's success, and some former staunch royalists were intimidated into changing sides before it was too late. Among those who came over to Louis in June were four notable Williams: the earls of Albemarle, Salisbury, Arundel and Warenne, who between them provided huge additional resources in terms of castles and troops. Louis wrote to Alexander of Scotland and to all the remaining royalist barons, 'ordering them to make their fealty to him, or to retire with all speed from England.'[30] John was now a deposed fugitive in his own kingdom, and the situation looked very bleak indeed for him and his remaining loyal supporters.

A NEW KING?

Fortunately for John, his dynasty and anyone else who did not want to see England under perpetual Capetian control, the royalists now benefited from an enormous stroke of luck, because the next thing Louis did was to make a catastrophic mistake: he failed to have himself crowned.

There were a number of reasons for this. First and foremost, a coronation was a Church rite as well as a secular one, and Louis was currently under sentence of excommunication and thus unable to participate in any religious service. Added to this were the facts that neither the traditional coronation site (Westminster Abbey, which had closed its doors to him due to the excommunication) nor the traditional celebrant (the archbishop of Canterbury, currently in Rome and suspended from his position) was available. Any coronation at this point would thus run the risk of being declared invalid at a later date, or would at the very least be the object of ongoing suspicion. The legate Guala might have lost his argument at the Assembly of Melun, but his actions after departing from it had resulted in profound consequences for the kingdom of England, because if Louis had been crowned in a valid ceremony at this point, then it could well have been game over for the Angevin dynasty. Indeed, if Louis had been as politically astute as his father (or if he had benefited from better advice), he might have pressed ahead with the rite anyway, despite the impediments, on the basis that any coronation was better than none and they could argue about the details later on. But he did not, preferring instead to leap straight into a military campaign.

This decision was of critical importance, because at this time it was the act of coronation that turned an ordinary mortal, no matter how royal their blood, into a king or queen. The person next in line to the throne upon the death of their predecessor, even if formally designated as the heir, did not become the monarch until they had been crowned; and, conversely, once someone was crowned, they were the monarch no matter who they had been before. This is the principal reason why John was the king of England and Arthur of Brittany was not. There had been other such instances in England in the last century and a half, resulting in Kings William Rufus, Henry I and Stephen rather than King Robert Curthose, Queen Matilda or King Theobald.* Henry the Young King (John's eldest brother), on the other hand, was considered by contemporaries to have been a king because he had been crowned, even though he pre-deceased his father and never reigned in his own right. What this all meant in the present situation was that Louis, despite his invitation and his acclamation, remained merely

---

*Robert Curthose was William Rufus's elder brother, irrevocably displaced when Rufus was crowned. He later endured the same experience a second time when another younger brother, Henry I, rushed to organise a coronation for himself only days after Rufus's death. It is relatively common knowledge that Stephen of Blois usurped his cousin Empress Matilda, but less well known that he actually had an elder brother of his own: Theobald, count of Blois. Stephen thus also raced to get the crown put on his head as soon as he heard of his predecessor's death, in order to trump any claims of superior heredity.

a *claimant* to the English throne, while the only crowned and anointed king in the realm was John. This gave John a superior, God-given status, and was the slender thread that kept his cause alive.[31]

Staying alive – literally rather than metaphorically – and at liberty was now John's principal short-term goal. This meant that he needed to remain mobile, so he engaged in a cat-and-mouse game with Louis across south and south-west England.

Louis divided his forces into three parts, one staying in London and one ranging through the counties of Essex, Norfolk and Suffolk while he himself pursued John towards Winchester. But he could not head straight there, as he was obliged to stop and take every castle in his path so as not to leave a string of hostile strongholds behind him. John expected this to slow down the French campaign quite considerably, but things did not quite go according to plan. Louis encountered no resistance at all at Reigate (owned by Earl Warenne, who had the gates left open for him), and he was not long delayed at Guildford or Farnham. Thus it was still only 14 June when he reached Winchester, meaning that John left in rather more of a hurry than he had anticipated, ordering the suburbs to be burned behind him. There were two castles in Winchester, a larger royal one and the smaller Wolvesey Castle owned by the bishop of Winchester, who was at this point Peter des Roches, a staunch adherent of John. Setting up a dual siege and capturing both castles would surely take some time, so initially John moved only 50 miles south-west to Corfe. In the two weeks it took Louis to subdue Winchester, John was able to order the reinforcement of the garrison at Corfe, as well as the royal castles of Wallingford, Wareham, Bristol and Devizes, and to arrange for additional arms and provisions to be brought in. Then, as Louis once more approached his position, he moved further west, with Falkes de Bréauté at his side.

In one respect John was fleeing before his enemy, but another way of looking at the situation was that he was obliging his opponent to spread his resources very thinly. Louis had only a third of his overall force with him (a force that was, in itself, not as great as he would have liked), and they were now strung out all the way along the south coast, leaving him vulnerable to a potential attempt to cut him off from the capital. He therefore took the decision to return to London, leaving John with a breathing space and the chance to press back towards the midlands.[32]

The great strength of the royalist cause, as John himself realised, was the castles that still held for him. These were dotted around the kingdom in various strategic locations, but the most important of them, at this stage, was the mighty fortress of Dover under its castellan Hubert de Burgh. It was Dover that now became Louis's objective; a hostile fortress still holding out in an otherwise subdued area was an immense danger, and Louis could not consider his base in south-east England to be secure until he had every last part of it under his control.

Dover castle was described by one thirteenth-century chronicler, with good reason, as 'the key to England', and it was now to be a key venue in the fight to keep England out of French hands.[33]

Dover, July to October 1216

THE IMPORTANCE OF CASTLES

Nearly all western European conflicts of this period were characterised by series of sieges rather than pitched battles, with the sieges having a significant influence on the final outcome. To give a recent example, the catalyst for the conquest of Normandy by the French in 1204 had been the capture of a string of castles, culminating in the fall of Château Gaillard, the supposedly impregnable fortress built by Richard the Lionheart; its loss left a gaping hole in Normandy's defences and allowed Philip Augustus to sweep through the entire duchy with an army at his back. Castles were of paramount importance, and every king, earl, count and lord who could afford it poured time, energy and money into building and maintaining them.

The defensive properties of castles were obvious: they were a stronghold and a retreat that conferred a distinct strategic advantage on anybody who owned one. The lord (or, occasionally, lady) of a castle was protected behind stone walls, with a roof over his head and – if he had planned correctly — plenty of troops to defend him and supplies to keep them all going. In fact he did not even need a particularly large garrison: a castle could be held by a relatively small number of men against a much larger attacking force, as Louis himself had recently discovered. During his campaign in the south of England in the early summer of 1216, the French prince and his army had been held up for a fortnight at Odiham castle in Hampshire, but when the garrison finally surrendered and emerged, it turned out to comprise only thirteen men: three knights and ten soldiers.

Of further advantage to the defenders was that capturing a castle was difficult, time-consuming, expensive and dangerous, so the holder might simply be able to wait until an opponent gave up — a besieging army encountered difficulties of supply and sanitation, and could not remain in place forever. Even if all else failed, a castellan would generally be able to negotiate a settlement that saved lives, and sometimes also possessions, in return for handing over the fortification.

Less well known is the fact that castles also served an important offensive purpose, and this was why it had been so important for Louis to capture all of those in his path as he chased John during the summer of 1216 and sought to impose himself on England. When not being actively besieged, the garrison of a castle could range around the local countryside at will during the day, protecting the local population (and the food they were growing) and mounting attacks on any hostile forces, before returning to safety behind their walls and locked gates at night. This meant that the circle of influence of a castle was around half a day's ride – approximately 10–15 miles in any direction, allowing time to get out and back before dark – and that a series of castles built close enough to each other for their circles to overlap was an extremely effective asset. The conquest of a region was therefore never complete until every castle in it had been captured, because if any were ignored and bypassed, the invading force would find itself subject to lightning counter-attacks from behind, which would cause casualties, halt its advance and potentially isolate it from its main base.[1]

The problem was that setting up a siege, particularly of a large castle, involved a huge investment of time and resources, and (as had been demonstrated by John at Rochester the previous year) it meant remaining static for long periods of time. When Louis had first landed in Kent, therefore, he had judged that the potential gain of taking Dover castle was worth less than the loss of momentum involved, when he needed to head straight for the capital and have himself declared king. But since then Dover had become more of a thorn in his side, providing protection for guerrilla attacks on his forces and continuing to dominate the region. In July 1216 Louis weighed his options again and decided that the likely loss of time, money and lives was now a fair price to pay if it meant he would have the whole of the south-east unequivocally under his control, and a safe harbour in which to land more troops from France as and when he could get them. This was no mean undertaking, because Dover castle was a particularly impressive specimen, one of the finest and most defensible in England, and indeed in the whole of western Europe.

DOVER CASTLE

The Strait of Dover was (and remains to this day) the shortest crossing of the Channel, and in the early thirteenth century it was both an important hub for communication with the rest of Europe and a pivotal location for the defence of the English realm. There is surviving evidence of building work on the castle site from Roman times, on top of an earlier Iron Age hillfort, followed by continuous occupation through the Early Medieval period, probably in the form of a burh or fortified settlement. In 1066 William the Conqueror spent eight days at Dover 'fortifying it where it was weakest' – although we do not know precisely what the existing fortifications or weaknesses were – and left it in the hands of his half-brother Odo, bishop of Bayeux.[2] From that point onwards it was a royal castle, held for the crown by a series of castellans.

Just over a century later, in the 1180s, Henry II began significant work on Dover in order to develop and strengthen its fortifications, to such an extent that he virtually started from scratch, sweeping away most of what was already there in favour of a more modern design. It was he who built the massive and elaborate square keep that can still be seen today, with its four corner turrets and thick stone walls. This keep was, along with other domestic buildings, set within an inner bailey; the curtain wall that enclosed it boasted fourteen mural towers, and its two entrances, to the north and the south, were protected by stone gatehouses, the northern one with an additional barbican.*

Once all this was complete, Henry moved on to an additional concentric layer of defence, in the form of a much more extensive outer curtain wall, also featuring mural towers and intended to reach southwards down the site as far as the cliffs that towered over the sea. This wall appears to have been incomplete at the time of his death in 1189, but work on the castle was continued by his sons. Financial records indicate that in total Henry II spent the enormous sum of £6,400 on Dover during his reign (averaging about one twentieth of the crown's total annual income every year during the 1180s), with Richard spending another £725 and John a further £1,000.[3]

By 1216 Dover was a formidable castle indeed and one that would be very difficult to besiege. From the south it could only be approached by sea, with the cliffs preventing direct access. On the landward side it stood high on a hill above the town, making the approach difficult for attackers, who would then have to fight their way through successive layers of defence: a temporary wooden barbican which had been built to the north-west outside the stone outer gatehouse; then the outer and inner curtain walls, both designed for effective cross-fire and exhibiting no weak points; and finally, the keep itself.

---

*A barbican was a supplementary outwork to a castle, built as an additional layer of defence for a gate or gatehouse. It might be semi-permanent or permanent and built of stone, or sometimes temporary and constructed from wood.

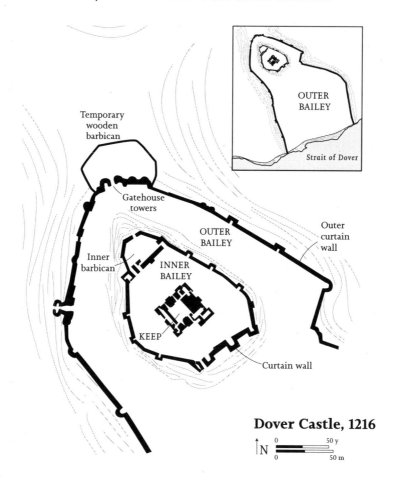

Dover Castle, 1216

The keep was 25 metres (four floors, around 80 feet) high, 30 metres square (just under 100 feet on each side) and had walls up to 6 metres (20 feet) thick. The entry door was set above ground level, accessible only by a staircase, and there were only arrow-slits for windows. The castle garrison would be able to mount a multi-stage defence, falling back behind successive walls as and when any one concentric layer was breached, and remaining in the keep for as long as their stores held out.

The building would not be the most pleasant place to spend a great deal of time, admittedly, the arrow-slits letting in very little light and making it grim and gloomy inside, but it was otherwise very well designed.* Importantly for the purposes of nutrition and sanitation – always an issue during long sieges – the keep had an inbuilt water system which collected clean rainwater on the roof and stored it; there was even a piped water supply to flush out the latrines.[4]

It was essential for Louis to take Dover castle, and it was equally essential for John to hold on to it. There was nothing more that the king could do in the short term with regard to additional fortifications, but he was able to re-supply and re-garrison it, and he had left it in the hands of an extremely capable castellan.

HUBERT DE BURGH

Hubert de Burgh was probably in his mid-forties when he was appointed castellan of Dover in 1216, having earlier held the position for a short time during the previous decade. He was not a scion of one of the great noble families, hailing rather from a background of minor gentry in Norfolk, and he seems to have entered John's service in the late 1190s, when John was merely the count of Mortain and had no immediate expectation of ascending to the throne. Hubert was John's chamberlain (the official in charge of his household and finances), and remained so in the short term after the latter's accession, which gave him a rather significant and unexpected promotion to the post of

---

*Almost every facet of castle design was a trade-off: what was more defensive was less comfortable, and vice versa.

chamberlain of the royal household. After that he was moved on and held a number of positions in fairly quick succession – including castellan of Dover, member of an embassy to Portugal, sheriff of Dorset and Somerset, and custodian of the Welsh marches – while accumulating various manors for himself and working his way up the social ladder.

In 1202 Hubert's duties switched from partly administrative to entirely military and he was sent to France, where he was the castellan of Falaise castle in Normandy at the time John's nephew and rival Arthur of Brittany was imprisoned there.[*] Later he was moved to Chinon in Touraine, which he held stoutly while John's ancestral lands collapsed and fell one after the other into the hands of Philip Augustus. The surrender of Rouen, the Norman capital, to Philip on 24 June 1204 meant that the French king had conquered Normandy, Maine, Anjou and part of Poitou, and that the only two castles still holding out against him in Touraine were Chinon and Loches. Hubert refused every offer to surrender and held out for an entire year until June 1205, expecting every day that help would soon arrive from John. John, by that time back in England, did begin to muster forces with the intention of sending them across to France; however, there was a distinct lack of support from his barons for another overseas campaign and he was obliged to cancel the whole plan, leaving Hubert and his men to their fate.

---

[*] It is interesting to speculate on whether one of the reasons why Hubert de Burgh rose so high in John's service is that he knew what really happened to Arthur, and therefore had to be kept on side in case he decided to tell all.

By the laws and customs of war at the time, receiving notification that no assistance was to be forthcoming from his overlord entitled Hubert to surrender with honour. But he did not. Loches fell to King Philip soon after this, at which point the entire French royal army descended upon Chinon, which was already battered and with a weakened garrison after their long defence. Under further bombardment the walls sustained so much damage that the castle was rendered indefensible, but still Hubert would not surrender. After burning his remaining stores so that they would not fall into the hands of the French, he took the only other course of action open to him and charged out with his men in an attempt to cut through French lines and escape. Given the disparity in numbers (and also in health and strength, after such a long siege) between the parties, this enterprise was doomed from the start. Hubert was badly wounded and taken prisoner.[5]

Hubert's captivity was to last two years, until 1207, but at least John assisted in the payment of his ransom as a reward for his loyalty – something he had refused to do for others whom he felt had surrendered too easily, and which was another action that later rebounded on him. Robert Fitzwalter and his kinsman Saer de Quincy, the earl of Winchester, had in 1203 surrendered Vaudreuil to Philip without a blow being struck, and John's consequent refusal to pay anything towards their ransom no doubt contributed to their later dissatisfaction with him and their unwavering commitment to Magna Carta.

Upon his release Hubert returned to England, but by 1212 he was back in France as the seneschal of Poitou, ruling the remaining lands that John still held there in his position as duke of Aquitaine.* Hubert also continued to amass lands and wealth; by 1213 he held more than fifty knights' fees scattered across England, which gave him an annual income similar to that of an earl, despite being nowhere near that rank by birth. He remained in Poitou until John mounted his disastrous campaign of 1214, but following the defeats at Bouvines and La-Roche-aux-Moines there was not much left to be seneschal of, so he returned once more to England. Hubert was one of the royalists listed in Magna Carta in June 1215 as standing for John and advising him to agree to the charter. In the document Hubert is referred to as the seneschal of Poitou, but by the end of the same month he was being styled 'justiciar', the highest administrative position in the land, albeit one that had waned a little in significance recently.†

By now Hubert de Burgh was an experienced administrator, a hardened military veteran, the renowned defender of Chinon and – importantly – John's proven loyal man, and it was with all this in mind that this 'energetic and faithful soldier' was appointed castellan of Dover. There can have been few of

---

*A seneschal, in thirteenth-century France, was the officer appointed by the crown to oversee the administration of a designated region. Although John was the king of England, not France, Poitou was part of his French holdings so the appointment of a seneschal was appropriate and a procedure familiar to local lords and knights.

† The post of justiciar had been established under the Anglo-Norman and Angevin kings, as they ruled England and extensive lands in France, which necessitated them spending a great deal of time on the continent; the justiciar was the king's representative who acted on his behalf in England while he was away on the other side of the Channel. Following John's defeats in France he was expected to spend most or all of the remaining part of his reign in England, which gave rise to questions about the purpose and future of the post of justiciar, and whether he actually needed one at all.

John's men better suited to defend it against Louis and his French army.[6]

SOURCES FOR THE SIEGE

The siege of Dover is our first opportunity to meet in person those chroniclers who provide the vivid details of the war's engagements. These men – and in this instance they are all men[*] – are a mixture of English and French, monastic and secular, contemporary and later, and between them they spin the many separate threads that we can weave into a rich narrative tapestry.

Some pay more attention to the siege of Dover than others. The engagement is recorded only briefly in the narratives of the English writers Ralph of Coggeshall, Roger of Wendover, Matthew Paris and the anonymous Barnwell annalist (and not at all by the biographer of William Marshal, who unsurprisingly passed over an engagement at which his hero was not present), and also the French chroniclers William the Breton and Philip Mousket. Of these, Matthew Paris and Philip Mousket were writing two or three decades later and were thus in possession of valuable hindsight; the rest are contemporary or almost contemporary to the siege, but told at second hand by authors who received their information from others. We are, however, extremely fortunate in the survival of a wonderful eye-witness account.

---

[*]This is not to say that there were no female scholars. A number of women writers were active at this time, both in England and in France, but they tended to be cloistered in convents (which were centres of female literacy) and to focus on religious matters. Additionally, a very few secular women wrote literary texts or poetry, but the chroniclers who wrote of governance, politics and war, and especially those who were eye-witnesses, were men; they had greater opportunities to travel and experience events themselves, or to interview the key participants later on.

The author of this first-hand description of the siege is known only as the Anonymous of Béthune – generally referred to as 'the Anonymous', as though that was actually his name. As is evident from this, we do not know exactly who he was, but he was a member of the household of Robert de Béthune, one of the French lords who had come across with Louis and who was present at Dover. The Anonymous wrote two different works, oddly from slightly different points of view: his *History of the Dukes of Normandy and the Kings of England* and his *Chronicle of the Kings of France* cover some of the same ground but, as their titles imply, focus on different people and priorities. Both of his narratives are rich in detail, describing not only the major events of the siege but also the deeds of various named individuals. Of course, because he was a member of the assailing army, his story of the siege is told from the outside; however, by using his information, and that of others, in conjunction with what we know of other accounts of being besieged, we can also extrapolate something of the experiences of de Burgh and his garrison on the inside.[7]

The tale that follows is woven together from the works of all of these writers, who would be surprised – and perhaps proud – to know that there were people living unimaginably different lives eight centuries in the future who were eager to hear what they had to say.

LATE JULY: LOUIS ARRIVES

A large besieging force was not able to approach a castle by stealth, so Hubert de Burgh and his garrison of 140 knights and a larger number of men-at-arms were well aware that Louis was on his way, and they were safely ensconced behind their walls when he arrived somewhere between 22 and 25 July 1216. The siege train must have been quite a sight, stretching out for miles on the road as the mounted lords and knights were followed by columns of foot soldiers, crossbowmen, engineers, servants, cooks and grooms, with wagons carrying baggage and disassembled siege machinery rumbling along behind.

The would-be king of England was not in any particular hurry to start the assault, preferring instead to spend a few days after his arrival in careful reconnaissance and planning. He lodged initially in a priory in the town, quartering some of his men there and in the surrounding dwellings while others made a tented encampment. Unfortunately we have no information on how the civilian population of Dover reacted to this, but in fact the lack of any accounts of uprisings or violence is in itself illuminating, leading us to suppose that the inhabitants simply tried to keep their heads down and stay out of the way. Like most of the 95 per cent of the population of England who were of sub-baronial and sub-knightly rank, they were not overly concerned with the identity of the man on the throne as long as they could live and trade in peace. Just to expand on those demographics for a moment: the higher nobility made up only a very tiny fraction of England's population, with the lower nobility, knightly and gentry families between them comprising around 1–2 per cent and members of religious communities (priests, monks and nuns) another 3–4 per cent. The rest – the vast majority of the population – were predominantly involved in agriculture or trade and were unlikely to have had much personal interest either in the contents of Magna Carta or the reasons for the war.[8] A swift end to hostilities, with peace both established and enforced, was therefore more important to them than the identity of the victor.

The besieging army soon found that they had one significant topographical advantage, which was that there was a hill to the north of the castle, in front of the outer gatehouse; this would give them higher ground from which to attack and from where Louis could direct operations with clear lines of sight. He therefore left some of his men in the town, to the west of the castle, while the rest moved to this hill and began to erect their siege machinery.

It was clear to those inside that the main assault could not begin until the construction of these machines was complete, so they took advantage of the lull to launch offensives. 'Time and again the men in the castle sallied out through the gates,' says the Anonymous. 'They had a barbican outside the gate defended by Peter de Creon, well protected by oak fascines* and also by a good ditch surrounding it [...] the castle's defenders often came out in front of this barbican, fully armed, and the besiegers could see them plainly.'[9] Peter de Creon is a rather shadowy figure in the contemporary sources, but the fact that the Anonymous names him specifically indicates that he must have been of some importance. He was probably the Peter

---

*A fascine is a long cylindrical bundle of thin pieces of wood, tightly bound (the original Old French term in the text here is *roulleis de caisne*, or 'pieces of oak rolled up'). Many of them placed closely together would have formed an effective defensive barrier, and they could also be used to fill in ditches or pits. Given that this temporary barbican had been erected at relatively short notice, it might have been quicker to put fascines together than to fell whole trees to make a palisade.

de Craon or de Croun (spellings of names could vary from document to document), 'our loyal man', who in May 1216 had been confirmed by John in possession of all the English lands previously held by 'his father Maurice'. Maurice II de Craon had been a lord in Mayenne, in Anjou, and a loyal retainer of Henry II, so it would make sense if his younger son had sought advancement in England.[10]

Hubert's show of confidence in making sorties led to some sporadic individual encounters, with French crossbowmen coming forward to shoot at the garrison, although one apparently got too close and was captured and dragged off inside; his fate thereafter is unknown. Meanwhile the engineers continued their work, constructing siege machinery. In the contemporary sources these are generally referred to as 'petraries and mangonels', and for many years the received wisdom was that these were two distinct types of engine, the former working by balance and traction – men pulling down on ropes in order to fling the other arm of a lever in the air and release the missile – and the latter by the torsion of twisted ropes. This was based on the fact that torsion machines had been in common use during the Roman and Late Roman eras in western Europe, and it was assumed that the technology had survived into the Middle Ages. More recent research, though, has cast doubt on whether they existed at all at this time. Of course, it is quite difficult to prove the *absence*, rather than the presence, of any particular type of weapon, but it is certainly significant that there are no surviving detailed contemporary descriptions of torsion engines in action, and that all the illustrations we have of siege machinery from the twelfth and thirteenth centuries are of balance engines. The earliest extant pictorial representation of a torsion machine in England dates from c. 1326.[11] It seems likely, then, that our chroniclers (most or all of whom were clerics and not military specialists) used 'petraries and mangonels' as a kind of generic term for 'machines that threw stones', perhaps engines of different sizes.[*]

Whatever the exact nature of these machines, they appear to have been relatively modest in scale, and although the French had enjoyed success with them at some smaller castles such as Odiham and Winchester, these devices would be markedly less effective against the mighty walls of Dover. Louis had already thought of this, and before taking the road to Dover he had written to his father – a noted besieger and breaker of castles – to request that he send a newer type of machine, one that had never yet been seen on English soil. This was the trebuchet, which acted in a similar way to existing engines in that it used a balance beam in order to throw stones. However, instead of using traction it used a counterweight: that is, instead of pulling down on ropes at one end of the beam to release the missile at the other, the men operating the machine would instead pull down on the sling end itself, in order to lift up a large counterweight (for example a box filled with earth and/ or rocks), which could then be fixed into place at its highest point. Once this counterweight was released, it travelled

---

[*] If it sounds implausible that medieval chroniclers could use two such distinct-sounding terms as 'petraries and mangonels' in such a generic way, consider the number of modern people who might use phrases such as 'kith and kin', 'flotsam and jetsam', 'goods and chattels', etc, without knowing the precise difference between the words.

downwards at a great rate, thus releasing the missile rapidly from the sling end.

A counterweight trebuchet had several marked advantages over the smaller traction machines. It could throw heavier missiles and they were released with greater force, meaning that they could travel further and do more damage to walls, gates or personnel. Expert calculations show that, depending on the length of the beam and the mass of the counterweight, a missile of 70 kilograms (154 pounds) could be propelled between 100 and 250 metres (320 and 820 feet), while a smaller 30-kilogram (66-pound) projectile could reach even further, up to 345 metres (1,100 feet) – thus allowing the operators to remain out of the range of any archers inside the castle.[12] Moreover, once the trebuchet was set up and correctly calibrated it could throw each stone in exactly the same direction with exactly the same amount of force (as opposed to the use of traction, where the manpower was inconsistent), so one specific area of wall or gate could be targeted with greater accuracy.

The design, construction and operation of trebuchets was complex and required a great deal of engineering skill, meaning that engineers, generally of lowly birth, were much prized and were as important or even more so than armed fighting men during a siege. And, happily for us, the novelty of it all meant that a specific and distinct term was used, so when chroniclers refer to a 'trebuchet' we can be relatively confident that this is the type of siege engine they mean.[13]

King Philip, despite his avowed intention of not publicly supporting his son's campaign, dispatched just such a machine.

Some accounts tell us that it was called *Malvoisine* or 'Bad Neighbour', a common nickname for trebuchets throughout the Middle Ages.* Louis benefited from the delivery twice over: he was able to erect the trebuchet on the hill overlooking the gatehouse, and once his ships had unloaded their cargo they were set to patrol at sea (out of reach of any weapons in the castle) in order to prevent any reinforcement or re-provisioning from that direction. Dover castle was completely surrounded, and the garrison would be able to rely on nobody but themselves.

The time was fast approaching when Hubert and his men would face a direct assault, but they were as well prepared as they could be. The fortifications were formidable. The garrison was of a precisely calculated size, enough to defend such a large stronghold but not so many that they would run out of provisions too quickly. There were no civilians accidentally trapped inside, no children or elderly people who would need feeding without being able to fight; everyone in the castle was there deliberately in order to defend it or (in the case of cooks, grooms and so on) to support the needs of those who were fighting. They were ready for whatever the French might throw at them in the days, weeks and months to come.

JULY AND AUGUST: INITIAL ASSAULTS
It will not have come as a surprise to the garrison that the principal point of attack would be the northern outer gatehouse

---

*To give two recent examples, the name *Malvoisine* had been given to trebuchets at the siege of Acre in 1191, during the Third Crusade, and at the siege of Minerve in 1210, during the Albigensian Crusade in southern France.

and its wooden barbican. At the end of July Louis began the assault with various traditional siege methods: his stone-throwing machinery, plus 'a very tall castle', or siege-tower, made of wattle.[14] This last was a means by which besiegers could gain height and therefore be at the same level as, or even above, the defenders on a castle wall, meaning that they could loose arrows or crossbow bolts across or down at them rather than having to shoot upwards, which was less effective. Alternatively, the tower could be moved close to the wall so that attackers could cross straight over to the battlements without needing to climb ladders. In this particular case, the hill on which the French were positioned and the steep slope up to the gatehouse made it more likely that the tower was used for the former purpose. In a longer-term strategy, Louis also set his miners, under cover of a protective device known as a 'cat',* to work on the ground under the wooden barbican wall. We will hear more of their efforts in due course.

Such tactics were standard fare, and as an experienced castellan, Hubert de Burgh would have been ready for them. In these early stages the walls held firm against the French missiles, so it was a case of staying calm, dealing with each day and each incident as it came, and maintaining the morale of

---

*A cat was a covered roof on wheels that sheltered men who were beginning mines (before they got deep underground), or as they were working on the surface to attack the base of a wall with picks, from missiles launched by those inside the castle. The roof would be made of thin woven branches, so it was not too heavy to move, and might be covered in hides to make it as fire retardant as possible. The origin of the name is obscure but probably derives from the device looking like a cat sheltering kittens underneath it; it was sometimes also known as a 'sow', presumably for similar reasons.

the garrison now they knew that they really were going to be trapped for quite some time.

The psychological pressures of being under siege are not often mentioned, and perhaps were not properly understood, by contemporary chroniclers – partly as they did not really have the vocabulary to do so, and partly because they were in general concerned with glorifying the experience or the bravery of the participants. But these pressures should not be underestimated. The men of the garrison were likely to suffer feelings ranging from disquiet to outright fear, while experiencing the claustrophobia that comes with being trapped in a dangerous situation; and all made worse by being able to see, day by day, the progress and development of the siege works that were hemming them in ever more tightly. Once the bombardment started, further feelings of inadequacy and helplessness might set in, and the longer the siege went on the more likely it was that the defenders might fly into sudden and desperate actions in an attempt to relieve the tension and to feel as though they were actually *doing* something. The commander of a castle under siege had his work cut out to maintain strict discipline and to prevent his men from doing anything too foolhardy.[15]

In this particular case, the members of Dover garrison were also aware of the fate of Rochester castle, a mere 40 miles away and besieged and broken only the year before while its defenders were 'exposed to the danger of death, and enduring all kinds of misery':

[The assailing army] did not allow the besieged in the meantime any rest day or night; for amidst the stones hurled from the petraries and slings, and the missiles of the crossbowmen and archers, frequent assaults were made by the knights and their followers, so that when some were in a measure fatigued, other fresh ones followed them in the assault; and with these changes the besieged had no rest. The besieged too, despairing of any assistance from the barons [i.e. their allies], endeavoured to delay their own destruction, for they were in great dread of the cruelty of the king. [...] The siege was prolonged many days [...] the provisions of the besieged failed them, and they were obliged to eat horses and even their costly chargers.[16]

The Rochester garrison, exhausted, starving and forced back by successive assaults into a desperate defence of one part of the keep, had eventually surrendered; King John had at first ordered their immediate execution, and had only narrowly been persuaded against it. The Dover garrison might believe that they would not be so lucky if their castle fell to the French invaders, and it would not be surprising if such thoughts preyed on their minds.

Hubert de Burgh faced a stiff task, then, to keep up the spirits of his men, and he succeeded admirably – partly by pre-empting any rash deeds by organising two proactive courses of action himself, both well suited to the situation. First, he stationed crossbowmen on the walls as snipers, able to pick off any of the besiegers who strayed within range. This, of course, had been how Richard the Lionheart met his death back in 1199, and it was a hugely valuable tactic for castle defenders, carrying very little risk but with enormous potential gains: if by any chance one of the Dover crossbowmen could manage to hit and kill Louis, the siege would be over very quickly. In the popular imagination the crossbow has sometimes suffered by comparison with the simple bow (later the longbow), because it was cumbersome and had a much slower rate of fire, but it was ideally suited to a defensive siege situation: unlike a bow, which had to be released as soon as it was drawn back (the draw weight being too great to be held by muscle power alone for more than a fraction of a second), the crossbow string was held in place with a catch once it was at full draw, meaning that the operator could take as long as he liked to aim. The additional time it took to reload was also not a problem during the long and seemingly endless days of the siege.[17]

Hubert's second proactive tactic was to have the garrison make frequent sorties: they charged out on horseback in lightning raids, killing and wounding groups of attackers, and then turned to retreat back behind the castle walls before a counter-attack could be mounted. In this way he kept his fighting men busy and their horses exercised while also inflicting casualties on the attackers, all of which would have helped the garrison's morale.

Several weeks elapsed in this fashion. Every day that passed was a small victory, of sorts, for Hubert and a loss for Louis, who grew frustrated at his lack of progress and the simultaneous depletion of his forces. Some of these were killed or wounded by the sorties of the garrison, but others were mercenaries who got bored or decided they were not being paid enough, and simply disappeared. More worryingly for Louis, some were his own French lords who decided that their period of military service was up. It was usual for such nobles to promise forty days of service, which, in the present instance, if taken to start on the day of embarkation on 20 May, would actually have expired before the siege of Dover even started. Any of Louis's lords or knights who were already impatient that the English campaign was taking so long – and who might have signed up in the expectation of swift glory, coronation and the distribution of new lands and incomes – would have grown even more frustrated after several weeks spent sitting around outside Dover, subject to sporadic attacks and with little opportunity to retaliate.

One of the problems with sieges, from the attackers' point of view, was that lords and knights had very little to do. Their idea of warfare, and the one for which they had spent many years training, was to fight in hand-to-hand combat on horseback; but sieges, particularly in the early stages, needed the work of common men – engineers, siege-machine operators, miners, archers, crossbowmen and so on. It was only if and when a breach could be made in the walls that knights could really get into the action. Some of Louis's retainers therefore decided, after several weeks of inactivity, that they had better things to do and other places to be. As Louis had been obliged to recruit for his campaign privately, and not in the name of the French crown, he had no official leverage and there was little he could do about it except become angry. His ire was partly directed at the departing French troops themselves, but mainly at the defenders for being so stubborn: he was 'greatly enraged and swore he would not leave the place until the castle was taken and all the garrison hung'.[18]

In another tactic (or perhaps out of sheer boredom) the French also tried a few psychological manoeuvres. In order to 'strike terror' into the garrison, they 'built a number of shops and other buildings in front of the entrance to the castle, so that the place appeared like a market; for they hoped that they would, by hunger and a protracted siege, force them to surrender, as they could not subdue them by force of arms'.[19] They were perhaps not aware of just how well stocked the castle was; the amply provisioned garrison simply ignored this attempt at provocation.

In mid- to late August, Louis received a political boost. King Alexander of Scots had been agitating in the north of England for some time, both on his own behalf and on Louis's, and the news now came that he had left the siege of Carlisle and – astonishingly – marched unopposed the entire length of England in order to meet Louis in person and recognise his claim to the throne. Louis left Dover temporarily to meet Alexander at Canterbury, and then, 'with great joy', brought him back to Dover, where Alexander 'did homage to him for the right which he ought to hold from the king of the English'.[20]

This is not to say, incidentally, that Alexander gave homage to Louis for Scotland itself (which was a separate, independent realm owing allegiance to nobody); rather, it was for the lands that he held in England. However, it was still recognition for Louis and his right to the English throne from a crowned monarch. We do not have the precise details of the ceremony, but, given that Louis specifically asked Alexander to travel on from Canterbury to Dover for it, it seems very likely that it took place in the open, in full view of the castle defenders, in order to affect their morale. If Louis's cause was so far advanced that another king was recognising him, if he had control over so much of England's geographical area that his allies could march right through it with no trouble, Hubert de Burgh might like to reconsider his position as John's adherent and throw in the towel while there was still time to get something out of it for himself.

Once again Hubert declined to surrender. But the longer the siege went on, the higher the stakes became: how much longer could Louis afford to spend in one place, and what might his next steps be in his determination to subdue Dover and its garrison?

AUGUST AND SEPTEMBER: BREAKTHROUGH AND FIGHTBACK

Once his homage was rendered, Alexander left Dover to head back north. Louis had received a political boost from the occasion, and in late August he also made the military breakthrough he had been waiting for.

The idea of making a direct assault on castle walls or gates during a siege was one that had to be carefully considered. If it worked, the gains might be swift and considerable, but even if it did – and certainly if it did not – the cost in lives could be horrendous. Louis now weighed his options, no doubt taking into account his lack of progress thus far and the dissatisfaction of his bored knights, and decided that he would launch an attack on the wooden barbican.

It is not clear from the sources whether this move took the defenders by surprise, or whether it was simply that a temporary wall made of wood could not withstand such an assault, or whether the work of Louis's miners had any significant effect, but in any case the attack was successful. Peter de Creon, who was in charge of the barbican's defence, was fatally wounded in what seems to have been a bloody hand-to-hand engagement, along with a number of his men, and the rest of the barbican's defenders had to flee back through the main gatehouse to the safety of the castle's stone outer curtain wall.[21] The French now had direct access to the castle walls and the outer gatehouse, and the miners were moved from where they had been tunnelling under the barbican fence and set to work on the gatehouse itself. Mining was an exceptionally skilled task: those engaging in it needed not only to dig and prop a long, deep tunnel that would not collapse on them prematurely, but also to ensure that it was engineered such that it would fall when they needed it to – and that in the meantime they had sufficient ventilation to survive. All of this might be complicated by the nature of what they had to dig through, with many castles being built on solid rock. Here, though, the ground was of chalk, which was relatively soft and easy to work, and they made good progress.

All of this meant that Hubert, now pushed one layer backwards in his defence, had to change his tactics. It seems likely that he was aware of the mining going on; even if the French took pains to try to conceal all the basketloads of chalk they were digging out and carrying away, they would not have been able to disguise the noise they were making or the attendant vibrations in the ground. Arguably they might even have made no attempt at concealment at all, allowing the defenders to know of the mines as a psychological tactic.

There is some evidence that Hubert tried to counteract the French mines; a number of small tunnels survive in the chalk that might be the remains of counter-mines from the period.[22] If this was attempted it was a risky course of action, as it might further endanger the walls and the gatehouse; but if the defenders could meet and kill the French miners while they were still underground, the work would be stopped, the mines filled in or otherwise made safe, and the underground threat eliminated.

Hubert also had to count the cost of his losses in men, as well as the area enclosed by the barbican. He would certainly not be able to get any reinforcements, and the disparity in the ratio of defenders to attackers was exacerbated when he was able to see that Louis did receive some. A fresh contingent arrived directly from France, headed by Louis's second cousin Peter de Dreux, the duke of Brittany (he who had married the younger half-sister of Arthur and Eleanor of Brittany), and by Thomas, the count of Perche. Perche was a very young man – around twenty or twenty-one years of age – but he was already an accomplished warrior and a veteran of the battle of Bouvines, where he had fought for Philip Augustus while still in his teens. His very complex family tree is emblematic of the way in which the French and the English (both royalists and rebels) were often closely intertwined: he was Louis's second cousin, John's great-nephew and also a kinsman of William Marshal.*

---

*Thomas's father was Geoffrey III of Perche, who was Philip Augustus's first cousin, thus making Thomas Louis's second cousin. His maternal grandmother was Matilda, duchess of Saxony, King John's eldest sister, making him John's great-nephew (and technically therefore also a claimant to the throne of England with a better hereditary right than Louis, although he never attempted

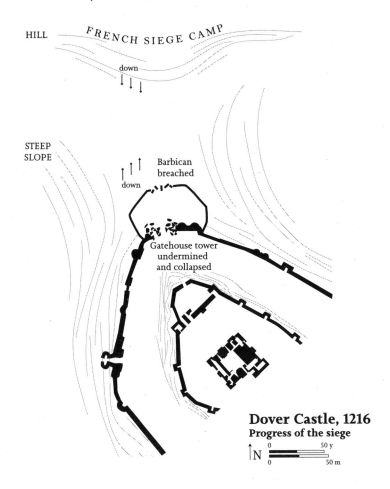

HILL

FRENCH SIEGE CAMP

down

STEEP
SLOPE

down

Barbican
breached

Gatehouse tower
undermined
and collapsed

Dover Castle, 1216
Progress of the siege

0   50 y

↑N

0   50 m

The situation for Hubert and the Dover garrison was not yet desperate, but it was certainly worse than it had been. An attack on the gatehouse itself could be expected at any time, with the

---

to press it). And finally, one of Thomas's great-grandmothers had been the sister of William Marshal's mother, making him Marshal's first cousin twice removed. Thomas held lands in both England and France, but his primary estate was the county of Perche, his patrimony, and his primary loyalty was to the French crown. Peter de Dreux's royal connection was much simpler: his paternal grandfather had been the younger brother of Louis VII, Philip Augustus's father.

consequent danger that a further withdrawal might be necessary. There was also, of course, the threat hanging over them that they would be executed if the castle fell: Louis might or might not have been completely serious in his vow that he would not leave Dover until 'the castle was taken and all the garrison hung', but there was certainly a great difference to be expected in the treatment of a defeated garrison depending on whether they had surrendered or whether the castle had been taken by storm. If a surrender had been negotiated and the fortification handed over intact, the deal normally included the lives and limbs of the garrison, and possibly also their possessions. Something similar might also be offered to a castellan who had surrendered at a later date after initial resistance, on the basis that the attacker might still be willing to offer mercy if it meant he achieved his main goal without further loss. However, if all offers were declined and the castle taken by storm, the fate of the defeated men was entirely at the discretion of the victor, and massacres were not unknown.[23]

The inevitable day came early in September, when, despite any attempts that might or might not have been made to stop them, the French miners achieved their aim. They had dug a tunnel under one of the gatehouse towers and propped up the roof with timbers; now they withdrew, setting the timbers alight, and when the wood burned through, the tunnel could no longer take the weight of the stone above it. The whole edifice collapsed and the gatehouse tower came crashing down due to the lack of support underneath it. 'At this,' writes the Anonymous of Béthune – somewhat laconically, given the dramatic situation – 'a large section of Louis's force entered the castle.'[24]

The frustrated French knights, who had spent so long sitting around out of the action, poured energetically through the breach with their swords drawn.

This was the most crucial moment to date in the defence of Dover. If the garrison could not hold their position now, they would be forced back from the outer curtain wall into the much smaller confines of the inner bailey and the keep, allowing the French to surround them completely and bring their siege machinery close enough to cause devastating damage. The likelihood of them being able to hold out for any length of time in such circumstances would be slim. The fate of Dover, and perhaps the kingdom itself, hung in the balance, and the garrison had no time to plan or to strategise. Instead they threw themselves into the breach, packing it so tightly that there was barely room to swing a sword. A desperate, hacking hand-to-hand combat ensued, as they used their bodies as a wall to prevent the French from getting through.

Fortunately, the defenders had one advantage which they could exploit: that of height. The French had come down off the high ground to the north and were having to make their way up the hill on which the castle stood – which was steep and slippery – to the broken gatehouse, so the defenders were above them. The situation of the garrison was desperate, but they kept fighting and, slowly, they were able to drive the besiegers back.

Finally the French were pushed right out of the gap and back down the slope, and immediately the garrison 'made good the place where their wall had fallen with large timbers, heavy cross beams and great oak fascines'.[25] This detail is significant, because it speaks to the level of preparation that Hubert had overseen. There were no trees to fell inside the castle enclosure, so in order to get their hands on 'large timbers' or 'heavy cross beams', the garrison must either have laid them in ready before the siege started, or sourced them by dismantling the domestic or other less defensible buildings inside the castle. It is possible that the latter was carried out in the expectation of attack following the earlier fall of the barbican.

The French assault had been repelled; the gap in the wall was filled and would be closely guarded from now on. There was now a little time for Hubert and the garrison to breathe, recover and tend to their wounded. Most of them had lived to fight another day.

SEPTEMBER AND OCTOBER: STALEMATE AND TRUCE

Louis had by now remained in one place for more than two months. This was, in effect, a victory for the royalists, because it had bought John the time to regroup and it had halted the initial momentum of Louis's campaign, which, if allowed to continue unabated, might have seen him sweep to a complete victory before the summer was over.

The question now was: how much longer was the French prince prepared to remain at Dover? His troops, even after collapsing one of the gatehouse towers, had not been able to force their way into the castle, so the only real progress they had made in nine or ten weeks had been the capture of the temporary barbican. The Dover garrison were still protected by their keep and two sets of high stone walls, so to dislodge them would require either a very large offensive indeed or a concerted attempt to starve them out. The problem with the first course of action was that Louis did not have a sufficient number of troops at his disposal, and, although he had the best siege machinery available, it would not be enough. For decades there had been a kind of ongoing race between defensive architecture and the offensive weaponry needed to break it down, each developing in response to improvements in the other, and at the moment the architecture was definitely winning.

There were also several issues with the second option. Keeping the castle surrounded and isolated from any possibility of re-supply would require a great deal of manpower for a long time, given how well provisioned it was (and that the garrison, following its losses, now comprised fewer mouths to feed, meaning their stores would last longer). Moreover, maintaining a siege camp through the winter was difficult; the besiegers might actually run out of food before the garrison did, and they were also more liable to sickness from being in an outdoor camp in the cold and the wet, rather than inside a sturdy building that had its own fresh water supply.

One option might have been for Louis himself to quit the siege and return to London, leaving the rest of his force at Dover to try to grind the castle into submission. But what would this achieve? Only one third of his army, or a little less, was in the capital; one third was here and the remaining part further north. And, given the previous depletions over the summer, it was far from sure that all of his retainers would actually remain in so dour a situation anyway. No, Louis either needed to stay here and somehow find more troops to join him, or, if he were to move, he would need to take the entire besieging force with him in order to deploy it more usefully elsewhere. There seemed to be nothing for it. A truce was declared between Louis and Hubert de Burgh on 14 October, and Louis departed, reaching London a couple of days later.[26]

Hubert had won this round. His efforts had kept Dover castle, the key to England, in royalist hands, and he had also ensured that John's party retained control of one port in the south-east – which was of crucial importance given that Louis controlled all the others from the mouth of the Thames round to Portsmouth. Moreover, Hubert and his garrison had helped the royalist cause more widely. Earlier in the year, when Louis had looked as though he would sweep all before him in a very short space of time, many wavering barons had defected to him. Now, though, the determined resistance and possible resurgence of the royalist cause meant that the vacillators hesitated again. 'Many of them,' we are told, 'thought of returning their allegiance to King John; but they were afraid that, on account of the many and great injuries by which he had been provoked to anger against them, he would not receive them though penitent.'[27]

The problem, then – as ever – was the person of King John. The waverers might have cooled in their support for Louis and the French invasion, and they might now be more sympathetic to the royalist cause as a whole, but they simply could not stomach the thought of going back to John and his catastrophically bad kingship, which effectively put them right back at square one. What they needed was another option.

Fortunately for them, events were about to take an unexpected turn.

THREE

Death and Revival, October to December 1216

THE DEATH OF KING JOHN

Once he could be confident that Louis was going to be mired at Dover for the foreseeable future, John could move out of his bolthole in the West Country, and in late summer of 1216 he turned his attention to the midlands and the eastern counties. As he went, he issued a series of public letters confiscating the lands of the barons, but at the same time he seemed intent on destroying everything in those lands, so that there was very little left to be given up. In the midlands he spent some time 'besieging and taking the castles of the barons [...] all which he ordered to be razed to the ground; and the cruel destruction which he caused amongst the houses and crops of the said barons afforded a pitiable spectacle to all who saw it'.[1] This was in late August and September, which was harvest time, so the destruction of crops would inflict great hardship on the people (not just the barons) of those regions for at least the whole of the next year. Then John made his way further east, where he continued the terror: the Barnwell annalist, who was on the spot in Cambridgeshire, tells us that 'wherever in this journey he found the lands of the enemy, he plundered and burned them, feeding them to the flames; never was such burning seen in our age'.[2] By the end of September John had reached Lincoln, where he held a meeting with the castellan of the castle, an occasion we will explore more fully in the next chapter.

Once again, however, John's campaigning had little effect. Yes, he had taken some measure of revenge on those who had defied him, but his attacks on their lands merely made them even more determined to stand against him and did little for his own cause in the long term. His unforgiving nature was plain for all to see, and he was simply too toxic and unpopular for most of the rebel barons to want to reconcile with him personally.

In the second week in October John was in East Anglia. He was welcomed, given gifts and feasted by the townspeople of Lynn,* but while there he fell ill. He was probably suffering from dysentery, although various chroniclers tried to make out that his illness was caused by his own over-indulgence ('his sickness was increased by his pernicious gluttony [...] he surfeited himself with peaches and drinking new cider') or even that it was the result of poisoning.[3] He left Lynn on 11 October, aiming to get to Swineshead abbey via the Wash, and it was there that some kind of incident occurred involving his baggage train. Of course, this gave contemporaries ample opportunity to exaggerate and use the event as an omen, as in this dramatic retelling by Roger of Wendover:

---

*To what extent the welcome was genuine is an interesting question: they might really have been pleased to see John, or they might have offered him gifts and a feast in order to prevent their town from being looted and burned, as they were well aware had happened elsewhere.

He lost all his carts, waggons, and baggage horses, together
with his money, costly vessels, and everything which he had
a particular regard for; for the land opened in the middle of
the water and caused whirlpools which sucked in everything,
as well as men and horses, so that no-one escaped to tell the
king of the misfortune. He himself narrowly escaped.[4]

It seems unlikely that the situation was anywhere near as serious
as portrayed here, because if it had been then it would have
been mentioned in more detail by other sources. The *History of
William Marshal* merely mentions 'terrible misfortune', and then
only in relation to John's illness, while Ralph of Coggeshall
writes more coolly that an accident befell part of the baggage
train when some packhorses were mired in quicksand 'because
they had hastily and incautiously set out before the tide had
receded', resulting in the loss of some household effects.[*5]

Regardless of how or why this incident happened, or how
many of his possessions John actually lost, he was aware that
he was seriously and dangerously ill. He rested at Sleaford on
14 and 15 October, from where he wrote to the pope (by now
Honorius III, Innocent III having died in July) to ask him to
'take our heir into your protection' and 'ensure the succession
of our heir to his father's inheritance'.[6] By the time John reached
Newark on 16 October, he could no longer sit in his saddle and
was having to be carried on a litter; he was put straight into bed
when he got there.

---

*The likelihood that only a few items were lost has not, of course, prevented generations of
treasure-seekers from scouring the area in search of rich plunder.

While bedridden and in pain, and knowing that his time was short, John made a will. Unsurprisingly, given the circumstances, this is a relatively brief and hurried document, although its official status was not in doubt. John, being 'overtaken by a grievous sickness', was 'incapable of making a detailed disposition of my goods', so he simply stated that he left everything in the hands of his executors and would 'ratify and confirm whatever they shall faithfully ordain and determine concerning my goods'. John also made clear – as did many repentant medieval kings on their deathbeds – that he wanted to 'make satisfaction to God and the Holy Church for the wrongs I have done [...] and distribute alms to the poor and to religious houses for the salvation of my soul'. On the subject of the crown he was specific that he wanted to ensure for his sons 'the recovery and defence of their inheritance'.[7] His named executors, not all of whom were present, included those to whom the various spiritual, political and military facets of the royalist cause would now be confided: the papal legate Guala; Peter des Roches, the bishop of Winchester; William Marshal, the earl of Pembroke and Striguil; Ranulf de Blundeville, the earl of Chester; and Falkes de Bréauté, John's military enforcer.

After the will was complete John could do little more. It was customary for the dying to make a last confession so they could be forgiven their sins before they had to face the Almighty, but it would appear that none of the clergymen named in John's will were actually with him. The abbot of nearby Croxton was therefore summoned to hear the king's confession and administer the last rites, which he did just in the nick of time; John died that same night, 18–19 October 1216.

Despite everything, John's death was a moment of profound shock. He was only forty-nine, so in the normal course of events he could have expected to live much longer;* moreover, his illness had been so sudden that there had not been time to gather all his remaining loyal supporters to his bedside, nor for anyone to consider properly what was to come next.

The first and most urgent question was what to do with John's body. Interment at Westminster Abbey was not an option: it was in French and rebel hands, and besides, it was not yet the recognised resting place for England's royalty (Edward the Confessor was the last king to have been buried there; none of the Anglo-Norman or Angevin kings were). John's own earlier wish had been to be laid to rest at Beaulieu in Hampshire, a Cistercian abbey of his own foundation, but Hampshire was at this time also under Louis's control. In his will, therefore, John stipulated that he should be buried in Worcester cathedral. Based on this instruction, much has been made of the king's supposed devotion to St Wulfstan, whose shrine was at Worcester, but one of our best-informed contemporary writers, the Barnwell annalist, is clear that the dying king chose the location 'not because he himself had chosen to be buried there, but because that place seemed more secure at the time'.[8] The funeral cortege set out from Newark to travel the 100 miles south-west to Worcester, where John's body (minus its entrails, which had

---

* It is often erroneously thought that fifty must have been considered a great age at this time, because the 'average' age of death was so low. However, this 'average' includes a very high level of infant mortality, which skews the statistics; if we look only at those who reached adulthood in the first place, we can see that a significant proportion of them lived into their sixties, seventies and sometimes even eighties.

been removed soon after death to avoid decomposition and buried at Croxton) was laid to rest on 27 October.

The second question, and the one that had profound implications for the future of the kingdom, was who was to succeed John on the English throne. Those who were with him at the last, and those who had been informed most swiftly, now had to decide what they were going to do next. Would they throw in their lot with Louis, who had already been proclaimed king and who seemed likely to win the war? Or would they continue to support the royalist cause in the person of someone else? Were they, in short, fighting only for John himself, or also for his dynasty, the line of Henry II and his ancestors, and for the very idea of an English realm separate from France?

The answers to all of these questions seem to have been obvious to John's supporters, and did not require a great deal of discussion: they immediately declared their support for the late king's eldest son and heir, Henry.

In one respect this was completely unsurprising, because father–son inheritance was an accepted norm. Nevertheless, it was not quite as straightforward as it might seem to the modern eye. Among the nobility, the hereditary accession of a minor to a title was accepted, and his or her lands were placed under the guardianship of a regent until the title-holder came of age (or until she married, if she was female, at which point everything passed to her husband; this had been the case lately in Brittany). But there was no recent precedent in England for this happening at kingly level, and indeed the convention had generally been that the claims of an adult man to the crown would take priority over those of a woman or a child, even if that man's hereditary claim was weaker than theirs. This, after all, had been one of John's arguments for taking precedence over Arthur and Eleanor of Brittany, and it was also one of the reasons why the claims of Louis, through his wife, had been preferred ahead of those of Blanche's younger brother. There had been no child king, or at least not a reigning one, in England since the Conquest. Excluding Henry the Young King (who was crowned as junior king at the age of fifteen but never ruled, as he pre-deceased his father), six of the seven men crowned since 1066 had been in their thirties at the time, with the exception, Henry II, being twenty-one. The last child kings of England had occupied the throne back in the mists of time in the 970s, and their story had not ended well.[*]

If Henry III had been close to his majority, or even in his mid- to late teens, the situation might have been different; Philip Augustus, after all, had become sole king of France when he was fifteen and had ruled in his own name right from the outset. But the state of affairs in England in October 1216 was very different. In making their choice the royalist barons were signing themselves up to many years of uncertainty – of uncharted waters, governmentally speaking – and of vicious power struggles among themselves, because little Henry had only just celebrated his ninth birthday.

---

[*] Edward the Martyr was around twelve years old when he was crowned in 975, and he reigned for only three years before being murdered. He was succeeded by his younger half-brother, Æthelred (the Unready), then also around twelve, who later famously lost his kingdom to a foreign invader. These were not really the sort of exemplars that young Henry's supporters were looking for.

THE NEW KING

At the time of John's death Henry was being kept safe in Devizes castle, along with his mother, the widowed queen Isabella of Angoulême. Both of them now emerged to travel north under protective escort to Gloucester, which the royalist nobles had reached after riding the short distance southwards from Worcester after John's funeral.

On what grounds Henry was to be proclaimed king, when there was already another claimant at hand, was another serious question that had to be considered. Some thought was given by the royalist barons to 'electing' him, to avoid any danger that John's alleged deposition might also debar his son from inheriting the crown. However, there were a number of issues with this. One was that Louis was also basing part of his claim to the throne on election, which would only put Henry on a par with his rival. Another was that, of all the possible grounds, this was the one most easily disputed.[9] What the royalists needed was a solid justification that would elevate Henry above Louis and put his claim to the throne beyond doubt, and the obvious answer to that was hereditary right. John might have been a terrible king, but he was a crowned and anointed monarch — one supported by the pope and the Church — and he had died with that status still intact. Henry was undisputedly his eldest legitimate son and heir, and Louis could not possibly trump that part of his claim. The royalists, therefore, declared Henry king solely on the grounds that he was the son and heir of the previous incumbent.

This was the point, then, at which heredity became the defining trait in the transmission of the English crown, as it has remained to this day.* All future claimants would need to prove that they held their right by birth, rather than merely asserting that they had been chosen by invitation or popular acclaim; and in order to dismiss rivals they would need to show that those rivals had a lesser birth right or had somehow been removed from a superior place in the birth order. As it transpired, this new defining criterion of heredity was tested and proven at the very next change of monarch, because when Henry III died in 1272 his heir, Edward I, was out of the realm on crusade. Edward did not return to England for over a year – which, previously, might have caused a scramble for the throne and a challenge from a rival. However, Edward had been proclaimed king by hereditary right immediately after Henry was buried, and nobody attempted to dispute his inheritance, for how could they? It was for this reason that Edward was the first English king to date his reign from the day of his accession rather than of his coronation, a custom which has continued ever since.

This was all in the future; in the challenging circumstances of October 1216 the royalists needed to back up Henry's hereditary right to the throne with the coronation that would seal the deal. As we noted earlier, it was the rite of coronation that turned a mere mortal into a monarch, and this was something Louis had not done. As it happened, some of the same impediments that had hindered him were also

---

*The questions of female succession or succession via the female line would raise their heads more than once during the centuries that followed, and absolute primogeniture replaced male-preference primogeniture as recently as 2011, but all the systems that have been in use since 1216 are based on some form of hereditary birth right.

in Henry's path, in that neither Westminster Abbey nor the archbishop of Canterbury was available. However, the royalists were aware of what Louis evidently was not, which was that half a coronation was better than none, and Henry also had the great advantages of being in full communion with the Church and having the pope's representative on hand to confirm his position. The royalists, therefore, pressed ahead with their plans in rather a hurry, and with good reason: once they had a crowned and anointed king on their side (no matter how irregular the ceremony) they could once again use that fact against Louis, who held no such status and could be dismissed as a foreign invader.

Events then moved very quickly. Henry was met on his way to Gloucester by William Marshal and nearly all his other major supporters, the exceptions being the earl of Chester, who was en route from further north, and Hubert de Burgh, who was still at Dover. It is at this point that the almost-contemporary biography of William Marshal becomes one of our major sources: having glossed over much of the earlier part of the war in order to minimise either Marshal's adherence to the hated John, or possibly his wavering, the author now becomes loquacious as Marshal begins to move into his years of greatest glory. Here he describes the meeting between the old man and the young boy on the road:

The Marshal came forward to meet him [Henry] and greeted him, and the well-brought-up child said to him: 'Welcome. I wish to tell you truly, that I give myself to God and to yourself, so that in God's name you may take charge of me. And may our true God, the protector of all that is good, grant that you so manage our affairs that you may take good care of them.' The Marshal replied: 'Fair lord, I can tell you sincerely, and may God protect my soul, that I will be yours in good faith and will not neglect you as long as I have the power to do so.' The King wept, and those standing round him wept tears of compassion, and the Marshal likewise wept pitifully.[10]

It is hardly surprising that Henry should have cried; the shock and stress of all this happening to a nine-year-old boy, coming hard on the heels of months and years of feeling himself under threat and in danger, should not be underestimated. But he was the king and his dynasty's last hope, so he would have to learn to act with a gravity and courage beyond his years.

The coronation would take place as soon as the party, turning back towards Gloucester, reached the cathedral there – on the very day after John's funeral, despite the fact that it was a Friday rather than the more traditional Sunday, which added to the air of urgency. The royalists did not want to wait even two more days, in case Louis seized the opportunity to have himself crowned at Westminster in the interim, thus enhancing his own status and positioning him as the only crowned and anointed king in England, and a grown man to boot. As one royalist baron apparently put it, 'The sooner the better, for, upon my faith, there is no question of waiting; if we wait too long, we might end up with nothing.'[11]

There was, however, another obstacle to overcome before the coronation could proceed. A king was the military leader of his people as well as the head of government (which was one of the reasons why an adult male was generally preferred for the position), and he therefore needed to be a knight. Despite the seeming absurdity of the situation, then – despite his age, his complete lack of training in the military arts or in leadership, and his apparent inability even to ride a horse by himself* – Henry was to be made a knight. The description of the event actually emphasises, rather than seeks to play down, his youth: the barons 'dressed him in his child-sized robes of state', he was a 'fine little knight', and after he was dubbed 'the high-ranking men there carried him between them to the cathedral'.[12] There the coronation took place, with the papal legate Guala singing the Mass, and Peter des Roches, the bishop of Winchester, placing the crown on the new king's head.

In a childlike, high tone – for his voice must have been unbroken at that age – Henry swore a very particular set of coronation oaths:

In the presence of the clergy and people, he [Henry] swore on the holy gospels and other relics of the saints that he would observe honour, peace, and reverence towards God and the holy church and its ordained ministers all the days of his life; he also swore that he would show strict justice to the people entrusted to his care, and would abolish all bad

---

*Henry had arrived at the meeting on the road with Marshal sitting in front of the saddle of one of his escorts, supported in the man's arms, rather than on a horse of his own. A boy of his age would normally have begun some kind of training, but possibly he was learning to ride on a much smaller mount that would not have been able to keep pace with the haste of the main party.

laws and customs, if there were any in the kingdom, and would observe those that were good, and cause them to be observed by all.[13]

Another description then gives further evidence of the new king's youth and tiny stature:

Once he had been crowned and anointed, and the service had come to an end, the knights had no desire to follow the slow pace of a child of such tender years. Instead, those inside the cathedral carried him out in their arms [...] They carried him into the chamber to divest him of his robes of state, and they were right to do so, for they were very heavy.[14]

A nine-year-old king could not, of course, take the reins of power into his own hands: a minority meant a regency of some description. The most obvious candidate to act for a small boy in such a situation would be his mother, something that was considered perfectly natural, for who else could possibly be more dedicated to their offspring's cause? There was royal precedent here, too: in the previous century Philip I of France had inherited his throne at the age of eight, his mother acting as his regent until he came of age. More recently, both Philip Augustus and Richard the Lionheart had left their mothers in charge of their kingdoms when they set out on crusade in the 1190s, easily within living memory of many of those surrounding Henry now.

In this instance Isabella of Angoulême would take no such role. She appears to have been completely ignored by the royalist nobles, her name not even mentioned in discussions (or in John's will, for that matter), and in fact she left England not many months after Henry's coronation, never to return.* On the basis of this she has been accused by various later commentators of 'abandoning' her children, but in truth she had been sidelined by John for nearly all of his reign, never given the sort of authority that other queens consort enjoyed, and having all her children taken away from her as mere toddlers or even babies. Little wonder that she chose to cut her losses and start a new life for herself.[15]

The problem with naming anyone other than a child king's mother as regent was the danger of investing too much power in one man alone, because he might get ideas of pushing his young charge aside in order to rule in his own name.† So it was sensibly decided, by what appears to have been common consent, that this would not happen. Instead a council of three men was formed to take the royalist cause and the realm forward: William Marshal would be the king's regent, governing in his name, but the bishop of Winchester would be the king's personal guardian, while both of them (bearing in mind that,

---

* Isabella returned to her homeland and married again, bizarrely to the son of the man to whom she had originally been betrothed before she married King John. She would bear her new husband nine children in very quick succession, to add to the five she had by John. In another clue as to the nature of John's personal relationships, it is noticeable that Isabella never mentioned his name again in any of her charters or official documents, not even to offer prayers for his soul.

† The early thirteenth century was a dangerous time to be a child monarch with ambitious male relations. A recent and tragic case in point was King Ladislaus III of Hungary, who was born in 1200, inherited the crown in 1204, died in suspicious circumstances in 1205, and was succeeded on the throne by his paternal uncle and erstwhile regent.

according to the royalists, England remained a papal fief) were to be subject to the pope as represented by the legate Guala. Hubert de Burgh would retain his post as justiciar for the time being, although the question of whether the king needed both a justiciar *and* a regent would raise its head later on.

The greatest loser in all of this was Ranulf, the earl of Chester: he was one of the realm's most powerful landowners, a loyal servant of King John, and aged in his mid-forties, a quarter of a century younger than William Marshal, so he might justifiably have expected to become regent, or at least a member of the regency council. But he was not present at the discussion and thus was unable to put forward his own case or to influence his friends to do so. The *History of William Marshal* depicts Ranulf arriving later to hear of the *fait accompli*, raising no objection and saying that he 'regard[ed] what is done as very well done', but we would not really expect Marshal's biographer to say anything different, and this convenient acquiescence of Ranulf's is not mentioned by any other contemporary.[16]

Suspicion seems to have been the order of the day, either within this regency committee or felt by its members towards others, because various other measures were put in place to stop any one man having too much influence over the king or using the unusual situation to enrich himself. When a new royal seal was created for Henry it was stipulated that its use while he was underage was only temporary, and that 'no charter, no letters patent of confirmation, alienation, sale or gift, or anything else that can be granted in perpetuity, shall be sealed with our Great Seal until we are of full age'.[17]

The emphasis on Henry's youth in the contemporary sources is almost certainly deliberate, for two reasons. First, the author of the *History of William Marshal* was keen to stress the king's helplessness in order to magnify his own protagonist's heroism in taking on so difficult a task. He did so in some style, however, depicting a rousing speech of Marshal's that took place soon after the coronation and which has echoed down the ages as a declaration of loyalty. Suppose, one of the other royalists says to him, that everyone were to desert Henry and defect to Louis — what would he do then? 'By God's lance!' exclaims Marshal in reply:

'If all the world deserted the young boy, except me, do you know what I would do? I would carry him on my shoulders and walk with him thus, with his legs astride, I would be with him and never let him down, from island to island, from land to land, even if I had to look for my daily bread.'[18]

This excuse to glorify Marshal is understandable, and perhaps even predictable, in his biographer. But the decision to emphasise Henry's tender years also served another purpose, in that it highlighted that the royalist cause now had exactly what it needed: a figurehead of surpassing innocence. They had a crowned king who could not be blamed for the sins of his predecessor, and who would necessarily be subject to the advice, counsel and guardianship of his loyal retainers. It was, in effect, exactly what the rebels had avowedly been wanting when they pushed through Magna Carta, and Henry's new close advisors would be able to use this to their advantage to turn the tide of the war in political terms.

But politics was one thing: there was still a very big military challenge ahead, and Dover remained the pivotal point on which the course of the war might turn.

CONTINUING DEFIANCE AT DOVER

John's death and the accession of Henry III had significant implications for the defence of Dover, where Hubert de Burgh was still holed up with his garrison, of whom the majority had survived the siege. Our sources vary as to whether Louis was still there, only leaving after he heard of John's death, or whether he had already departed; the latter seems more probable, as our eye-witness account by the Anonymous of Béthune states clearly that Louis 'had left Dover as soon as the truce was made between the defenders and himself, and gone to London'.[19] He cannot have been in the capital very long before the crucial news reached him, and it would appear that Hubert had not yet emerged from behind the castle walls, presumably cautious until he knew that Louis's departure was not simply a ruse. We do not have the exact wording of the agreement that had been made, but any truce would have involved the complete cessation of hostilities – however, deception in such circumstances was not unknown, and Hubert was right to be wary.

Unsurprisingly, one of the first things Louis did when he heard of John's death was to send messengers to Dover to order Hubert to give up the castle, on the grounds that the cause he had been fighting for was now lost. We have differing accounts of this embassy. One is relatively anodyne, merely telling us that Hubert's reply was, 'Although my lord is dead, he has sons and daughters, who ought to succeed him', and that he refused to surrender.[20] The more detailed (and possibly embroidered) version of Matthew Paris has the embassy headed on Louis's behalf by the earl of Salisbury, John's half-brother, who brought with him the captive Thomas de Burgh, Hubert's brother, who had been taken prisoner by the French at an earlier encounter.

Salisbury was evidently authorised to offer both carrot and stick:

'Listen to my advice, Hubert, and obey the will of our lord Louis, and he will give you, as an inheritance, the counties of Norfolk and Suffolk, and you will also become his chief counsellor and friend; but, if you do not do this, your brother Thomas will be hung, and you in a short time will suffer the same punishment.'

Hubert's reply was stirring, first in his castigation of the earl for his lack of loyalty:

'Earl, wicked traitor that you are, although King John, our lord and your brother, be dead, he has heirs, namely your nephew, whom, although everybody else deserted him, you, his uncle, ought not to abandon, but ought to be a second father to him; why then, base and wicked man that you are, do you talk thus to me?'

Then, 'casting a scowling look' on Salisbury, he continued: 'Do not speak another word, because by the lance of God, if you open your mouth and say anything more, you shall all be pierced with numbers of arrows, nor will I even spare my own brother.' Salisbury took this threat seriously and withdrew. When Louis heard of the conversation, we are told, 'although he was sorry and enraged, he greatly applauded the firmness of Hubert'.[21]

Of course, the record of the conversation as it appears in the chronicle is not verbatim; Matthew Paris wanted to portray Hubert giving an inspiring oration, so he put the necessary words into his mouth. However, there is no doubt that – whatever he might actually have said – Hubert did indeed ignore every offer and threat, and continued to hold Dover in the name of both the old king and the new.

With the truce still in effect and Louis safely in London, Hubert was finally able to leave Dover, and he travelled to Bristol for the first meeting of the new king's council. And it was there, on 12 November, that the royalists pulled off a masterstroke: they re-issued Magna Carta in Henry's name. This was a move that was both unexpected and significant. It was unexpected because it meant that the royalists had made a complete U-turn and were now voluntarily agreeing to uphold a charter that John had gone to war to prevent; and it was significant because it completely undermined the cause of the rebels and left them standing on very shaky ground. They had wanted to get rid of John; John was dead. They had wanted Magna Carta to be implemented; now it would be. They had wanted a new king who would work with, rather than against, his barons; now they had one. So what, the royalists asked, were they still fighting about?[22]

William Marshal followed up the public announcement with letters 'to all the sheriffs and castellans of England, enjoining them each and all to obey the newly crowned king, and promising them possessions and many presents besides'.[23] This left the rebels, and any vacillators, in a sticky situation. Their rationale for being in revolt against the crown was effectively gone, but they had already proclaimed Louis king, and of course he still held the upper hand militarily and seemed very likely to win the war. With a few notable exceptions, the main priority of all the barons was now to ensure they ended up on the winning side, regardless of which side that was.

There was a mass outbreak of indecision:

There was a great deal of wavering amongst the barons of England, to which ruler they should entrust themselves, whether to the young Henry or to Louis [...] [Louis] had retained in his own possession the lands, possessions, and castles of the said barons, which he had subdued with their help, and had placed foreign knights and people in charge of them. On the other hand, it seemed a disgrace for them to return their allegiance to a king whom they had renounced, lest they should be like dogs returning to their vomit; and, being thus in difficulty in every way, they could not mend the broken reed.[24]

Two things are important to remember at this point. First, it was the defiance of Hubert de Burgh and the Dover garrison that had bought John enough time to begin to re-energise his campaign when all seemed lost. And second, although John had not used that time particularly wisely – choosing the easy route of devastating the lands of his subjects rather than attempting to fight directly against the invader, his actual rival for the throne – he had done something incredibly useful for the royalist cause.

That useful something was, to put it bluntly, that he had died.

Clearly that sounds counter-intuitive – how could dying possibly be in his favour? But it depends on whether we view John's cause as being solely about him, a mission to keep him personally on the throne no matter what the cost, or whether it should be seen instead as a quest to ensure the survival of his dynasty as a whole. If the royalist cause was intended to support only John, then it failed, because he was not in control of his kingdom when he died. But if its purpose was to keep the crown in the hands of the Angevin royal line and away from the Capetians, if it was to ensure that England was not to be controlled by or subsumed into France, then John's death was the most useful thing that could possibly have happened.

When Louis invaded, he was seen (or was able to be portrayed by his supporters) as the hero coming to the rescue of the beleaguered barons and people of England, to save them from a tyrant king. John's death transformed Louis's image, at a stroke, to that of a foreign bully who was trying to wrest the crown from the head of an innocent child.

The sacrifices of Hubert and the Dover garrison had therefore not been in vain. They showed that there were still those who were willing to take up arms for the royalist cause even when the situation was at its bleakest, and they kept that cause alive long enough for it to be rejuvenated. Even the French chronicler Philip Mousket grudgingly recognised that the Dover garrison had acted as 'loyal, worthy men' and that Hubert in particular had defended the castle valiantly.[25] There was still a very long way to go, though, and Dover would be the scene of further conflict during the following year.*

In the meantime, the focus of the war shifted elsewhere. The Dover garrison had shown a great deal of courage, but they did not have the monopoly on it; heroism was also being exhibited in abundance in other parts of the kingdom, and by some quite unexpected characters.

---

*We will explore this more fully in Chapter 5.

FOUR

Lincoln, December 1216 to May 1217

NICOLA DE LA HAYE

In 1216 Lincoln castle was in the hands of a castellan who had led a remarkable life. We do not actually know when that life started, because Nicola de la Haye's year of birth is not recorded anywhere; the best we can come up with is that it was sometime between 1150 and 1156, and probably towards the earlier end of that range. This uncertainty is not surprising, given that the lower nobility (to which her family belonged) and even the great lords and royals were markedly less interested in the births of daughters than those of sons, and often did not bother to document them formally.

Nicola was the eldest child of Richard de la Haye, a Lincolnshire landowner, and his wife Matilda Vernon. Perhaps they rejoiced in a quiet way at the safe arrival of their little girl, and hoped for a boy next time. But Nicola was followed only by sisters, so when Richard died in 1169 it was she who inherited his position as castellan of Lincoln castle and sheriff of Lincolnshire. A sheriff was the senior administrative and judicial official in a county, who was appointed by the king (some shrievalties, such as this one, had by tradition become hereditary, but they could still be revoked by royal order) and who fulfilled a range of duties such as keeping the peace, overseeing the county court and collecting the annual shire payment that was due to the king. Sometimes royal favourites were catapulted into such positions and could hold several at once – as had been the case with Hubert de Burgh during his earlier career – but other shrievalties were in the hands of loyal and responsible families who enjoyed the respect of the local people. The de la Hayes fell into the latter category.[1]

Nicola's hereditary position, and the opportunities it would afford a husband, naturally meant that she was considered a great marriage prize, and at some point – we do not know exactly when – she contracted a union with one William fitz Erneis, by whom she might or might not have had a daughter before he died in 1178. Still young, Nicola married for a second time sometime before 1185, to Gerard de Camville, by whom she had a son, Richard, and possibly also a daughter.

As was customary, while Nicola was married her titles and positions were held by her husbands, who acted jure uxoris. Technically this meant that Nicola herself had no part to play except that of supplying the opportunities in the first place and then bearing an heir to succeed to them, but in fact she played a much more extensive role than might be expected in managing her estates and even in military matters. She was absolutely loyal to Count (later King) John throughout his chequered career, as one representative episode demonstrates. In 1191, while his brother King Richard was on crusade, John became embroiled in a dispute with William de Longchamp, the justiciar Richard had left in charge of England during his absence. Nicola and her husband sided with John, and while Gerard left Lincoln to travel with and support John personally, Nicola defended the castle during a siege by the justiciar's forces that lasted for over a month, leading a contemporary to write that she acted 'without thinking of anything womanly' and that she 'defended the castle like a man'.[2] This use of language is interesting: generally, the only positive epithets that thirteenth-century chroniclers use for women are those that relate to their nobility, beauty, fertility and so on; they do not appear to have had the vocabulary to praise a woman for courage or military endeavour. Thus the only way they could think to portray a woman as brave was to say that she acted like a man – a double-edged compliment if ever there was one.

When King Richard returned to England in 1194 he had Gerard removed from the posts of castellan and sheriff, but the offices were restored as soon as John acceded to the throne in 1199: a sure sign of whose side Gerard and Nicola were on, and of whom John knew he could trust. They continued to hold the castle and the county of Lincoln in the new king's name for over a decade.

Gerard de Camville died in 1215, after a marriage that had lasted at least thirty years, at which point Nicola was somewhere in her early to mid-sixties. Widows enjoyed a great deal more autonomy than either married or unmarried women, and she opted not to marry again, instead taking on the position of castellan herself – despite the fact that by this time her son Richard was an adult, and she could have resigned the position in his favour (something which contemporaries, and probably Richard himself, might have expected). Nicola remained a staunch royalist throughout the Magna Carta disputes, and was still holding Lincoln castle when Louis arrived in England in May 1216. In the summer of that year, while Louis was busy with his campaign in the south of England, he sent a party further north under a rebel baron named Gilbert de Gant, who had a familial claim to the earldom of Lincoln because his uncle and namesake had briefly held the title under King Stephen. The elder Gilbert had died in 1156 with no son to succeed him, so the earldom had reverted to the crown and had been in abeyance ever since, which meant it was now in the gift of the king of England. Louis's naming of the younger Gilbert as earl thus benefited both of them, as it emphasised Louis's claim to the throne (and therefore his right to dispense royal patronage) as well as ennobling Gilbert. The appointment was, of course, not recognised by King John, so it was going to be in the best interests of the new 'earl' to make sure that it was the French prince who ended up with the crown on his head.

Nicola was aware that Louis's invasion represented great danger, but she was not yet in a position to fight off a concerted attack. She thus negotiated with Gilbert and succeeded in buying him off for the time being by offering money in return for a truce.[3] As an experienced castellan and politician, Nicola would have known that the peace she had purchased would only be temporary, but she had gained enough of a breathing space to make sure that Lincoln castle was defensible, well garrisoned and well supplied.

It was while King John was engaging in his campaign through the eastern counties in September 1216 that he met with Nicola in Lincoln, as we mentioned briefly above. The scene was recalled in local records some years later: she went out to meet John via the castle's east gate (the one leading into the city) and, perhaps rather performatively, offered him the keys, saying she was elderly and unable to continue in her office any longer. John replied by calling her his 'beloved Nicola' and reiterating that he wished her to remain castellan.[4] This was one of the few sensible moves he made during the last stages of his reign, as there were not many people around who had demonstrated such sustained loyalty to him over such a long period as she had. Indeed, the king went further: one of the letters he sent out only hours before his death a few weeks later was to appoint and confirm Nicola in her position as sheriff of Lincolnshire.

The appointment of a woman to a shrievalty in her own right (rather than as a hereditary position passed on to a husband or son) was extremely unusual, and it showed the regard in which John held her. Of course, we need to remember that the field of candidates was smaller than it might have been, because some of the male contenders were at that stage siding with the French and rebels, but there is no doubt that a man might have been found if John had considered it necessary – again, Nicola's son Richard would have been an obvious choice. But it was she who was appointed; and sensibly so, given not only her own loyalty to John, demonstrated over many years, but also the esteem in which she was held by the local landowners after her decades of service in Lincolnshire. John was by this stage rather short of experienced, reliable deputies, and in Nicola he had someone he could trust absolutely, regardless of her age and her sex. She was not only dedicated and loyal but also tenacious and effective; a French chronicler of the war calls her 'a sly, bad-hearted, vigorous old woman', which, under the circumstances, she might well have taken as a compliment.[5]

It was shortly after confirming Nicola in post that John died, leading to the uncertainty in the final months of 1216 when many of the barons, faced with the choice between a young boy king and his adult French opponent who looked more likely to win the war, did not know which way to jump. This gave Gilbert de Gant, with Louis's backing, the opportunity to try his luck at Lincoln once more. Nicola, unsurprisingly, had declared for Henry III, but with the castle and county resting in the hands of an elderly woman, Gilbert might have thought that there would be easy pickings.

He was wrong.

LINCOLN

In the early thirteenth century Lincoln was one of England's largest cities. It was situated on a steep hill, with the north end being some 60 metres (200 feet) higher above sea level than the south, where the River Witham ran outside and parallel to the south wall. Lincoln comprised two distinct areas: the upper city, or 'Bail', to the north, and the lower city to the south. The whole was rectangular in shape and defended by walls that contained gates leading out of the city to the north, south (known as the Stonebow), east and west. These walls were not particularly easy to defend: they might or might not have been in good repair all the way round, and in enclosing the whole city they were very long, meaning that large numbers of men would be required to patrol and defend them effectively.

The cathedral stood in the city's north-east quadrant and the castle towards the north-west (that is, in the south-west corner of the Bail); at their closest points they were only around 200 metres (650 feet) from each other. There was some open space immediately in front of the cathedral, but most of the city was made up of narrow, tightly packed streets lined on either side with houses and shops. Lincoln's wealth was mainly based on the weaving trade and the export of fabric and wool,* and the majority of the population were civilian merchants and traders – the only soldiers around were those in the castle garrison.

The castle enclosure stood immediately adjoining Lincoln's west wall, just to the south of the main west gate, and several sources note that it had a postern in the wall on that side that led out to open ground outside the city.†The castle had separate strong defences within the city walls. It consisted – unusually – of two mottes, each with its own keep, surrounded by a bailey that was encircled by a curtain wall, which was in turn defended by a deep ditch outside it. The castle was in a prime

---

*'Lincoln green', as worn by the legendary Robin Hood and his men, was a specific type of woollen cloth manufactured in the city.

†A postern, sometimes also called a sally-port, was a lesser entrance to a castle, often on the opposite side of the site to the main gatehouse and functioning as a kind of back door. A postern was generally small, so even where it opened directly on to open ground it was not a great security threat; if breached, it would admit only one or two men at a time, on foot, who could then be easily dealt with by the defenders. Trying to pinpoint this particular gate at Lincoln from clues in the modern castle is difficult: there is a small bricked-up postern that might date from the early thirteenth century, but it is in the north wall, while the gate on the western side (where the castle and city walls run together) is of the right date but is probably too big to be called a postern.

position, allowing the garrison to look out over the valley of the Trent to the west, to dominate the significant intersection of routes (the old Roman roads of Ermine Street and Fosse Way met here) and to command the steep descent inside the city walls down as far as the river. The only entrances were the postern, and the main gate on the eastern side of the castle that led out into the city.[6]

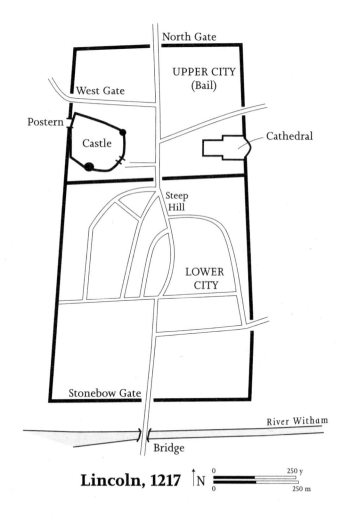

North Gate

UPPER CITY
(Bail)

West Gate

Postern

Castle

Cathedral

Steep
Hill

LOWER
CITY

Stonebow Gate

River Witham

Bridge

Lincoln, 1217 ↑N

0   250 y

0   250 m

Gilbert de Gant had left Lincoln following the truce bought by Nicola de la Haye, but towards the end of the year, in the new political situation brought about by John's death, he and his troops returned and mounted an intensive attack. The civilian inhabitants – merchants and traders as they were – were unprepared and untrained to defend themselves against such an assault, and by Christmas the city, with the exception of the castle, was in French and rebel hands. Over Christmas and into the first part of 1217 there was a general truce in the war,* but once this was over the French and rebels set about trying to subdue the castle by every means at their disposal. Siege machinery was brought in, and the castle endured heavy bombardment for weeks throughout late March, April and early May. Nicola de la Haye and the garrison held out bravely, but they were aware that their resistance could not last forever.

In early May a tipping point was reached, when the French and rebels felt that one more concerted push would see the castle fall into their hands; and, as it happens, a large party of additional troops was able to come to help them. A force under the triple command of Thomas, the count of Perche, Saer de Quincy, the earl of Winchester, and Robert Fitzwalter had been sent north from London on 30 April to relieve the siege of Mountsorrel (a castle in Leicestershire, around 40 miles southwest of Lincoln), which was then in rebel hands but under attack from Ranulf de Blundeville, the royalist earl of Chester. He, under the mistaken impression that Louis was approaching in person with the whole of his army, retreated, leaving

---

*We will hear more of this truce in Chapter 5.

Fitzwalter, de Quincy and Perche with a bloodless victory and time on their hands.[7] They were therefore very amenable to the invitation that reached them from Gilbert de Gant and his compatriots in Lincoln, so they moved to swell the French and rebel ranks there. This meant that the castle, with its garrison already exhausted and starving following months of siege, was in more danger than ever.

A RELIEF FORCE IS MUSTERED

The defenders of Lincoln were in much direr straits than their compatriots at Dover had been the previous year. Their castle was smaller, they had been under siege for longer and their enemy was much closer. At Dover the besiegers had been obliged to concentrate their initial efforts on the barbican, gatehouse and outer curtain wall; at Lincoln they were already inside the city and had been able to erect their siege machinery close enough to attack the single curtain wall and even to send missiles over it into the bailey itself. The exact size of the garrison at Lincoln is unclear, but it was certainly smaller than that of Dover, meaning that there were fewer men to take on the continual shifts necessary to defend the castle twenty-four hours a day.

It was in March 1217, shortly after the siege began, that Nicola de la Haye suffered an enormous personal loss: her only son and heir, Richard, died. We know nothing of the event other than the month in which it took place, so it is not clear whether he was inside the castle and perished as a result of the siege, or whether he was elsewhere and died of other causes. But in either case it must have been a terrible blow, leaving his grieving mother very much alone as she oversaw the defence of her castle, organising and commanding the garrison as they manned the walls, loosed arrows, crossbow bolts or stones at any attackers who came within range, dodged the continual missiles and dealt with the damage caused to buildings and personnel. And all with little sleep, against a backdrop of fear and uncertainty and the constant pressure of being trapped in a confined and dangerous space.

Then the French and rebel reinforcement party arrived, which only made matters worse. The action intensified: 'At length they arrived at Lincoln, and the barons then made fierce assaults on the castle, whilst the besieged returned their showers of stones and missiles with stones and deadly weapons with great courage.'[8] There was no chance of escape, and by mid-May stores would also have become something of a problem: regardless of how brave the garrison were, and how stoutly they defended themselves, courage could not prevent starvation. Moreover, the siege machinery of the French and rebels had done a great deal of damage, and at some point it was inevitable that the walls would become indefensible and the castle would fall.

Nicola had no reliable way of communicating with the outside world, or even with the city, where the inhabitants were unable to mount any definitive resistance and were simply keeping their heads down hoping to survive the war with their lives and businesses intact. All she could do was to continue the defence as long as possible while hoping that the new royalist regime would realise how desperate the circumstances had become.

Fortunately, the members of Henry's council were aware of the importance of the situation. Lincoln was an island of royalist resistance in a sea of French- and rebel-held territory, and losing it would give Louis the chance to surge further north, perhaps fatally for the royalist cause. So when news reached William Marshal of the supplementary force led by Robert Fitzwalter, the earl of Winchester and the count of Perche that had been diverted to Lincoln, he knew that he had to act. This, as it happens, would be easier to organise now that he did not have to manage John's military ineptitude or work around the late king's predilection for battle avoidance. As an experienced campaigner Marshal was aware that battle should be avoided where possible, but he also knew when battle, conversely, became the best option available. In this instance he might additionally have been goaded into action by the earl of Chester, who was a pugnacious man and perhaps smarting at being given no role in the regency council, while the elderly Marshal, many years his senior, had the prestige of acting directly in the king's name. Marshal could not afford to prevaricate or to be seen as too old to take decisive action when it was required, so he held a council at Northampton on 12 May at which he urged his compatriots to take up arms.

Roger of Wendover, a clerical chronicler of whom we shall hear more in a moment, focuses on the fact of the new king's youth and innocence as the reason why the royalists should engage their enemies, as well as the religious aspects of the conflict. He notes specifically that the papal legate was among those gathered, along with 'many other prelates of the kingdom [...] to assail with prayers as well as arms these disobeyers of the king, and rebels against their lord the pope; for it appeared to them they had a just cause of war, especially as he [Henry] was innocent, and a stranger to sin, whom his enemies were endeavouring in their pride to disinherit'. He also notes that the royalists wished to 'engage with the excommunicated French, and also to fight for their country'.[9]

William Marshal's biographer continues and expands on this latter theme. Naturally he depicts his hero giving an uplifting oration on the occasion, but interestingly the thrust of the speech seems to be about national pride. They will be fighting, he says:

> in order to defend our name, for ourselves and for the sake of our loved ones, our wives and our children, and **to defend our land** and win for ourselves the highest honour [...] We shall be a lily-livered lot if we do not now take revenge on **those who have come from France to take for themselves the lands of our men** [...] They seek our total destruction; so, in God's name, let us play for the highest stakes, for, if victory is ours, we must truly bear in mind that honour will accrue to us, and that **our heritage will be defended**, for us and our descendants, which they shamefully wish to deprive us of.[10]

The enemy, as depicted here, is no longer the rebel English barons but rather the French invaders, so the call is to nationalism rather than royalism. The framing of the war has shifted subtly from it being a civil conflict to one that is about defending England, 'our land', against foreign incursion and conquest.

If Marshal really did give a speech along these lines, then it worked. A combination of national, royal, religious and personal pride brought all the remaining royalists flocking to the banner, along with some of the previous waverers: two notable (re-)defections shortly before the muster were those of William Marshal junior and the earl of Salisbury. Their erstwhile companions Arundel and Warenne did not yet re-declare their allegiance, but both were notable by their absence from either side at this point, taking no part in the fighting at Lincoln at all; a sure sign that they, too, were reconsidering their position. As a final incentive King Henry was at the muster in person, in order to raise morale and show the royalists what they were fighting for. He would, of course, take no active part in the engagement due to his tender age, but the mere sight of the small, dignified child who was their figurehead must have been a moving experience for the men of all ranks who were about to risk their lives.

The muster took place on 17 and 18 May at Newark, the site of King John's death, which was 15 miles south-west of Lincoln. There was a main road that led directly from there to Lincoln, but this would bring the army to the city from the south, meaning they would have to cross the River Witham via the one bridge (which would cause a bottleneck) and then enter via the south gate and fight their way uphill through the streets in order to reach the castle. This would make life unnecessarily difficult, so Marshal decided to take a different route, and on Friday 19 May the army bypassed the city and instead marched to Torksey, around 10 miles north-west of Lincoln.

The non-combatants Henry and Guala left the host at Torksey in order to retreat to the comparative safety of Nottingham; before he went, Guala excommunicated Louis (again), together with 'all his accomplices and abettors, and especially all those who were carrying on the siege of Lincoln against the king of England'.[11] For good measure he now added to his list all the clergy and citizens of Lincoln and the surrounding area, on the grounds that they had not fought hard enough against the invaders. This was a harsh judgement and one that was to have profound and tragic consequences only a day later.

The French and rebels, meanwhile, now found themselves in a perilous position. They had held the upper hand while they were freely besieging the castle, but now they were going to be sandwiched in between two hostile forces, which was never advantageous. Moreover, they were not as numerous as they would have liked; following their reinforcement they evidently felt that they had sufficient strength to take the castle, but to take the castle *and* fight off a relieving army arriving behind them at the same time was going to be a tall order, especially considering that the rest of Louis's army was elsewhere and could not be sent to aid them. An armed engagement now seemed inevitable, however, and the lack of any siege machinery in the approaching royalist host indicated that they were not intending to settle in for the long haul: there was to be a battle, not a siege. But it was also clear that this was not going to be the 'normal' sort of battle – given the situation, both sides were necessarily going to end up with an unorthodox formation.

The encounter was going to be short, sharp and decisive, and everyone was going to have to improvise.

ARMOUR, WEAPONS AND FIGHTING TECHNIQUES

All knights, whether they were of simple knightly rank or of the middle or higher nobility, had spent their lives training for armed combat. But the *type* of armed combat they were prepared for was a relatively narrow one, with specific requirements in terms of armour, weapons and horses, so it might be useful to provide some details here in order to know what the combatants at Lincoln were letting themselves in for.

Their basic defensive garment was the gambeson, a knee-length, long-sleeved quilted item made of tough fabric such as canvas (possibly lined with silk or linen to make it more comfortable to wear next to the skin) and stuffed with coarse material such as tow or rags. The purpose of the gambeson was twofold: to absorb the shock of a blow from a weapon, and to prevent the knight from being damaged by his own mail armour,* the links of which would be driven into his flesh when hit by an opponent if there were no padding underneath it. Gambesons provided an effective defence against death or serious injury, but they were by no means 'breathable': the wearer would need to be very fit in order to deal with the profuse sweating, loss of fluids and fatigue caused by wearing it for any length of time.

Over the gambeson the knight would wear his hauberk, a single piece of mail armour shaped like a tunic, which covered his body from shoulder to knee and his arms down to the wrist, with either integral or removable mail mittens for the hands. A coif or mail hood was by the early thirteenth century also integral, covering the knight's head over a padded cap and

---

*The correct term for the type of armour worn at this time is 'mail', not 'chain mail', a pleonasm which appears to have been first used in the late eighteenth century. The French word *maille*, from which the English term derives, means 'mesh' or 'chain' anyway, so the addition is unnecessary.

under his helm. Chausses, or mail leggings, were put on each leg separately and were held up by being tied to a belt around the waist. Mail was made of thousands of small interlinking rings and was extremely flexible, but it was nevertheless heavy – a full set of harness weighed some 35 kilograms (77 pounds), hence the need for training from childhood to be able to fight while wearing it – and the weight and bulk meant that fine motor skills were restricted.[12] The knight's hearing was impeded by the layers covering his ears, and his vision was also limited. The earlier 'nasal helm', as worn at the time of the Norman Conquest, had gradually developed, first with the nasal becoming wider and wider until it formed a sort of mask across the whole face, and then by the early thirteenth century into the great helm that enclosed the entire head except for eye-slits and a few breathing holes. The major issue with helms, and indeed with armour more generally, was that anything that offered greater ease of movement or a wider field of vision was of less protective value, and vice versa, so armour design and development was a continual series of trade-offs. Nobody would put on a great helm until the last possible moment; indeed, in literature of the period, 'having one's helm laced' was a synonym for 'was imminently about to engage in combat'.[13]

The major part of the knight's training was for combat on horseback, not on foot. He would learn to ride at an early age, starting on a small pony and gradually working his way up to the warhorse, known as a destrier, that was bred and trained for combat. Contrary to popular modern opinion, incidentally, destriers were not very large animals. A horse needed great size in order to be able to pull a heavy weight (such as a loaded cart), but it needed strength rather than size in order to carry weight, so being compact was an advantage. Recent archaeological research has confirmed that in the twelfth and thirteenth centuries warhorses in England were on average just 13 to 14 hands tall – not much bigger than a modern pony.[14] They were, however, bred to be fierce and powerful, which meant that the knight required a significant amount of training in order to be able to control such a mount with his knees alone, because he would couch a lance under his right arm while his left would be used to hold a shield. The lance was the knight's primary weapon; only once its use was impracticable (because it was broken, for example, or because he was too close to his opponent) would he draw his sword and fight at closer quarters.

The combination of stamina, horsemanship and weapons training needed by a knight in order to fight with the required skill was enormous. Training was therefore not merely an activity of the knight's youth, but something he needed to keep up with constantly during his adult life. One of the ways in which he could do this was by participating in tournaments – which were, at this time, not the elaborate formal jousts of later years but rather dangerous free-for-alls over large areas in which multiple combatants used real weapons. Contemporary writers were keen to emphasise the benefits of such activity:

No athlete can bring high spirit to the contest who has never trained for it. It is he who has seen his blood flow and felt his teeth crack under another's fist; he who, on being knocked

138

down, has thrown his whole body against his adversary; he who, every time he fell, rose more defiantly, who goes forth to combat with great hopes.[15]

So realistic was the experience that fatalities were not unknown: as we saw earlier, the first cohort of French knights sent over by Louis had engaged in tournaments with their English rebel allies in order to accustom themselves to fighting together, leading to the death of Geoffrey de Mandeville; and King John's elder brother Geoffrey, duke of Brittany, had been killed while participating in a tournament back in 1186. But the danger was all part of the experience, giving knights useful mental as well as physical preparation for war.[16]

One relatively recent innovation meant that knights could at least recognise each other when they were on the field of battle. The uniformity of the plain metallic grey mail armour worn up to the mid-twelfth century had meant that all the combatants wearing it looked very similar to each other, a great problem during an engagement and one that was only compounded by the development of the helm to cover the entire face. But within the last fifty years heraldry had become a recognised system in England and France, with each noble family adopting a specific coat-of-arms, or blazon; the knights on all sides at Lincoln in 1217, therefore, would have had their identity proclaimed by bright surcoats and banners that would be visible even to those wearing helms.[17]

The net result of the combination of the knight's armour, helm, horse and lance was that the ideal environment for him to fight in was flat open ground, where he could gain the necessary momentum for a charge and where he had plenty of space to manoeuvre and not too many obstacles in his way. None of those at Lincoln, on either side, would have had much experience of fighting in the crowded narrow confines of urban streets, and particularly not in streets that were as steep as many of those in the city. Of course, knights were not the only combatants in an army; indeed, they were a minority within it. But those on foot, although they had more freedom of movement due to wearing less armour, still required room to manoeuvre – infantry spears were of little use in confined spaces, and archers and crossbowmen needed room to be able to draw and loose their weapons.

The progression of the forthcoming engagement, and its possible outcomes, were going to depend not merely on the courage and actions of the combatants, but also to a great extent on the location of the fighting. The most significant question was whether the battle would take place inside or outside the city walls, and fortunately our sources provide us with plenty of information on how this was decided.

SOURCES FOR THE BATTLE

At Lincoln, as at Dover, we are fortunate in the survival of numerous medieval texts that can help us put together a complete picture of the action. Most of the chroniclers are those we have met already, although there are a few changes in focus, and the amount of attention each one devotes to each event differs. The Anonymous of Béthune, who narrated the months outside Dover in such detail, was not at Lincoln himself and therefore deals with the engagement only briefly, as do the

Barnwell annalist, Ralph of Coggeshall and the later Matthew Paris in England, and William the Breton over in France. The battle is also mentioned in passing by two other French chroniclers of the later thirteenth century, Philip Mousket and the anonymous (and rather gossipy and amusing) writer known as the Minstrel of Reims.

The two sources that we rely on most heavily for the battle of Lincoln are the biography of William Marshal and the account of Roger of Wendover, a monk of St Albans. The earlier part of Roger's chronicle, later entitled *Flowers of History*, is derivative and based on the work of his predecessors at the abbey, but from 1215 onwards he was writing contemporaneously, and – in contrast to some other monastic chroniclers – with a vibrant energy. He does not appear to have been an eye-witness to the actual battle, but St Albans was a major foundation, one that took its historical writing seriously and, crucially, one that often welcomed important guests who could tell the resident chronicler at first hand of their experiences and memories. At the time of the engagement in May 1217 Roger was the prior of Belvoir, a cell of St Albans located on the border of Leicestershire and Lincolnshire, and thus only some 30 miles south of Lincoln.* Belvoir lay on the direct route between Mountsorrel and Lincoln, so Roger might even have seen the French and rebel reinforcements as they were on the march from the former to the latter. His vivid account can therefore

---

*A cell was a small monastic foundation that was not self-sufficient and relied on a larger abbey, known as the motherhouse, which posted some of its members there either permanently or in rotation. Belvoir was a priory, meaning that it was headed by a prior – a senior monk but one who was subordinate to the abbot of his motherhouse.

be read very usefully in conjunction with the History of William Marshal, and the snippets of information unique to some of the other writers, to give us the full and dramatic story.[18]

ARRIVAL AND RECONNAISSANCE

The royalist army set out from Torksey at or just before dawn on the morning of Saturday 20 May.* It comprised around 400 knights, 250–300 crossbowmen, and an unspecified number of sergeants and infantry. They were in good order and confident, as Roger of Wendover tells us:

> March[ing] against the enemy, only fearing that the latter would take to flight before they reached the city; the crossbow-men all the time kept in advance of the army almost a mile; the baggage waggons and sumpter-horses followed altogether in the rear with the provisions and necessaries, whilst the standards and bucklers glittered in all directions, and struck terror into those who beheld them.[19]

When the host arrived outside Lincoln, approaching from the north-west and still very early in the morning, William Marshal divided it into five parts. Four of these divisions comprised a mixture of mounted knights and foot soldiers; he would lead one himself and the other three were put under the command of Ranulf de Blundeville, the earl of Chester,

---

*Time was measured differently in the thirteenth century to the way it is now: each day was divided into twelve hours from sunrise to sunset, meaning that an 'hour' could vary in length depending on the time of year. But in modern parlance, they set off at around 4 a.m.

William Longespee, the earl of Salisbury, and Peter des Roches, the bishop of Winchester. That a cleric should take an active part in a military engagement might seem unusual, but it depended very much on the cleric in question,[*] and Peter was known to be bellicose, 'a man of knightly rank, and skilled in warfare'.[20] He had also previously been precentor of Lincoln cathedral, and was thus more familiar with the layout of the city than many of his compatriots. Finally, all the crossbowmen were put together in the fifth division under the command of Falkes de Bréauté.

There was an attempt at reconnaissance and communication with the garrison, but unfortunately our sources are confused on the exact course that this took. Roger of Wendover tells us that Nicola de la Haye managed to send out a messenger via the castle's postern, to tell the royalist army that they could enter via that route. The *History of William Marshal* has a different and somewhat self-contradictory story, possibly as a result of the author later being given different recollections of the day by numerous men all wishing to take the credit – indeed, he even notes that 'those who have given me my subject matter do not agree unanimously, and I cannot follow all of them, for that would be wrong of me and I would lose the right road

---

[*]A prevailing custom at this time was for families to donate their 'surplus' younger sons (the ones they could not provide with lands, or for whom they could not arrange an advantageous marriage) to the Church. As this was generally done on the basis of birth order rather than inclination or aptitude, it could lead to some very mismatched vocations. At the battle of Bouvines in 1214 William Longespee, the earl of Salisbury, had been battered into submission and taken prisoner by Philip Augustus's bellicose cousin Philip de Dreux, who was taking an active part in the combat despite being the bishop of Beauvais.

and be less trustworthy'.[21] First he tells us that John Marshal (a nephew of the regent) met a knight of the garrison outside the castle to exchange information, but then he comes up with the rather more implausible tale that Peter des Roches, the bishop of Winchester, somehow made it right into Lincoln, where he was able to wander through the streets and in and out of the castle seemingly at will, meeting with 'that worthy lady [...] who was its castellan and was defending it to the best of her ability', and then finding an old blocked city gate that might allow entry for the army.[22]

Whatever the exact details of the reconnaissance that the royalists were able to carry out, it does seem that the castle had a postern or other means of entrance from the open ground outside the city, but that it was too small to allow for the admittance of a whole army, so the decision was therefore taken that only Falkes de Bréauté and his crossbowmen, on foot, should enter by that route. This would bring them into the castle enclosure itself, where they could reinforce the exhausted garrison, shoot their bolts down from the walls at the French and rebels in the city, and also make a sortie and attempt to open one of the city's main gates from the inside, in order to provide a better point of entry for the mounted parts of the army.

It would appear, then, that Plan A for the royalists was to take the fight inside the city. However, they also had to be ready for the possibility that the French and rebels might make a sortie and seek to engage them on open ground outside the walls. William Marshal had a plan for this too, involving the creation of a slightly gory defensive wall of their

Fig. 1: King John is widely regarded as one of England's worst-ever kings, deposed at the end of his reign and depicted here by thirteenth-century chronicler Matthew Paris with the crown symbolically slipping from his head. (Bridgeman Images)

Fig. 2: In June 1215 King John agreed to the terms of Magna Carta, but he reneged on it almost immediately, with the result that the rebellious barons decided to overthrow him. (British Library MS Cotton Augustus II 106)

Fig. 3: The barons offered the English throne to Louis (later Louis VIII), the eldest son and heir of the French king, Philip Augustus. (Public domain)

Fig. 4: Louis arrived in England in May 1216, but he was not able to organise a coronation for himself: Westminster Abbey, the traditional venue, had closed its doors to him because he had been excommunicated. (Pixabay)

Fig. 5: Louis's first major military target was Dover castle, an impressive fortification with several concentric layers of defence. (Pixabay)

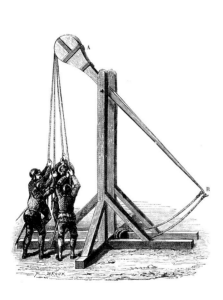

Fig. 6: Up until this point, stone-throwing siege machinery in England had consisted mainly of small engines powered by manual traction, which would be ineffective against the walls of Dover. (Getty Images)

Fig. 7: Louis brought with him a recent innovation: a large counterweight trebuchet, which could throw heavier missiles more accurately over a greater distance. The machine was set up on a hill facing the castle, out of range of the archers and crossbowmen inside, and did great damage. (Getty Images)

Fig. 8: An artist's impression of the progress made by the French and rebels at the siege of Dover during the summer of 1216. The outer barbican and one of the stone towers of the gatehouse were collapsed by French miners. (Getty Images)

Fig. 9: The towers that formed Dover's gatehouse in 1216, showing the steep slope that made any approach difficult and dangerous. This is the exact point where the besiegers made a breakthrough; the beaked tower was added later in order to fill the gap where the original had collapsed. (Julian Humphrys)

Fig. 10: King John's tomb in Worcester cathedral; he was buried there because his preferred locations were at that time in French hands. His death in October 1216 was the best thing that could have happened to the royalist cause. (Alamy)

Fig. 11: After John's death, the royalists immediately crowned his nine-year-old son, Henry, proclaiming him king by hereditary right in order to supersede Louis's claim of election. (The Parker Library, CCCC MS 16ii, f. 60r)

Fig. 12: Henry was too young to rule in person, so a council was formed to support him. William Marshal, earl of Pembroke and Striguil, was appointed his regent and took charge of the military campaign against the French and rebels. (-JvL-, Flickr, CC BY 2.0)

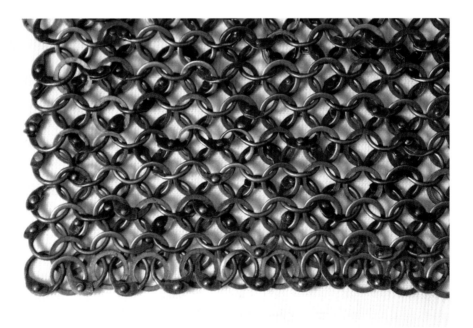

Fig. 13: Both sides included knights in their armies. Contemporary armour was constructed by interlinking and riveting thousands of mail rings, which resulted in protection that was heavy but extremely flexible. (Author's collection)

Above and Opposite Fig. 14–16: Donning armour was a complex business and impossible for a knight to manage on his own. Many parts, including chausses, mittens and coif, had to be carefully fastened with ties so they did not come loose while the knight was in combat. (Author's collection)

Fig. 17: The end result was almost complete bodily protection; defeated knights were far more likely to be captured than killed. Helms were unwieldy and hampered breathing, sight and hearing, so they were only put on at the last possible moment. (Getty Images)

Fig. 18: Lincoln castle had been besieged by the French and rebels over the winter of 1216 and the spring of 1217, but it held out under its castellan, Nicola de la Haye. In May 1217 a royalist army set out to relieve it. (Pixabay)

Left Fig. 19: The royalists were able to get archers and crossbowmen inside the castle to shoot down at the besiegers. There were two principal types of arrowhead: narrow bodkins, intended to pierce the links of mail armour, and wider broadheads that were used against horses. These were very effective, and there were many equine casualties at Lincoln. (Author's collection)

Right Fig. 20: The leader of the French forces at Lincoln was Thomas, the count of Perche. His coat of arms consisted of a white background bearing bright red chevrons, which made him an obvious target for enemy soldiers. (*Sigillographie des anciens comtes du Perche*)

Above Fig. 21: Thomas of Perche rallied his men in the open area in front of Lincoln cathedral, one of the only flat spaces in the city, but he was killed there (reportedly as a result of being stabbed through the eye-slit of his helm) and the French and rebels began to flee. (Pixabay)

Fig. 22: Lincoln's streets were very steep, which had a significant effect on the course of the battle. The royalists had the advantage of facing downhill; the French and rebels were forced to fight while retreating backwards down the slope. (Julian Humphrys)

Fig. 23: Matthew Paris's depiction of the battle of Lincoln: a royalist crossbowman shoots down from the castle, the count of Perche dies from a stab wound to the eye, and the defeated French and rebels flee. (The Parker Library, CCCC MS 16ii, f. 55v)

Fig. 24: The capture of many of Louis's supporters at Lincoln meant that he was in need of reinforcements. These were raised for him in France by his energetic and capable wife, Blanche of Castile. (Bridgeman Images)

Fig. 25: Blanche's fleet was intercepted at sea. One of the English ships described by contemporary chroniclers was a cog – a large, wide vessel that had castles built fore and aft so that it was difficult to board and so that archers could shoot at their opponents from a greater height. (The Stratford Archive)

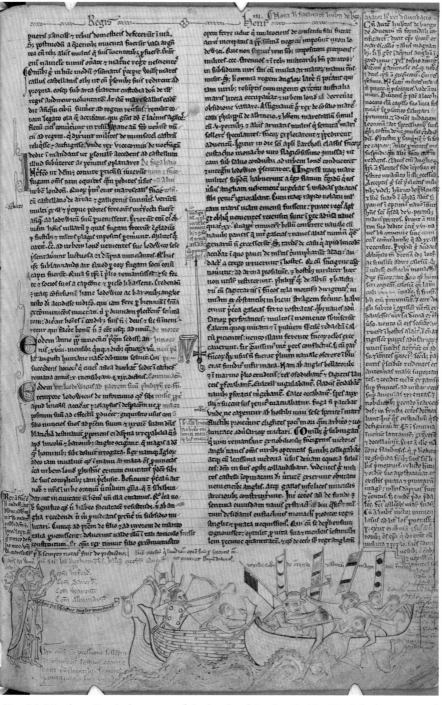

Fig. 26: Matthew Paris's depiction of the battle of Sandwich. The English shoot pots of lime, there is a vicious hand-to-hand fight on the French command vessel, and Eustace the Monk (at the far right) is beheaded. The engagement is witnessed from the shore by various earls and by bishops who declare 'I absolve those who are about to die for the liberation of England'. (The Parker Library, CCCC MS 16ii, f. 56r)

own: he 'asked for two hundred soldiers and ordered them to be ready to kill their own horses with their knives, so as to be able to take shelter behind them, if necessary'. This would provide a makeshift physical barrier, and there was perhaps an unspoken subtext that this would also prevent the newly horseless troops from being able to flee the field, thus stiffening their resolve to fight, even if the combat were brought out to them.[23]

Meanwhile, the French and rebels had been doing some reconnaissance of their own. They did not have a well-defined single leader, being instead commanded by a kind of committee made up of Gilbert de Gant, who had been directing the siege for quite some time, and the newly arrived count of Perche along with Robert Fitzwalter and Saer de Quincy, the earl of Winchester. De Gant had the local knowledge, and Fitzwalter and de Quincy had the experience, but Perche had the most direct line of authority from Louis. The confusion over which one of these men was really in charge was to be their undoing.

It was Fitzwalter and de Quincy who made the first trip outside the city walls to survey the oncoming enemy. They returned with the news that the royalist host was approaching 'in good order, but we are much more numerous than they', and giving their opinion that they should leave the city to engage in battle on open ground, 'for, if we do, we shall catch them like larks'.[24] This type of engagement would give them the best chance of success: they were more numerous than the royalists and had a distinct advantage in having some 600 knights at their disposal, around half again as many as their opponents. An engagement on open ground was therefore their best bet, if battle could not be avoided altogether, as it would give their knights more room to manoeuvre. What they needed to avoid was being trapped in the narrow streets with enemies both in front of and behind them.

The count of Perche, not satisfied with this report, then went outside the walls himself. Technically he was the senior ranking man among the French and rebel barons, but he was also young and inexperienced, and he made a disastrous mistake. As we heard above, in the quote from Roger of Wendover, the royalist army was approaching with its banners flying, displaying the coats-of-arms of those men entitled to them. Each lord or knight owned two of these banners: he kept one with him to announce his place in the host, while the other remained further back in the baggage train. However, with all of them on display at once, Perche was deceived as to the size of the army, thinking it twice as big as it actually was. He therefore deemed it too much of a risk to fight out in the open and ordered the French and rebels to remain inside the city. He and his compatriots then set one part of their force to defend the walls and the gates – thus spreading the available troops far too thinly – and another to continue and intensify the attack on the castle, in a last-gasp attempt to take it. If they could capture and get inside the castle themselves, the situation would change, with the pendulum perhaps swinging back in their favour. However, this manoeuvre was unsuccessful, and the French and rebels ended up in exactly the position they wanted to avoid: that is, trapped between the two enemy forces as the castle stood firm and the relieving royalist host advanced.

FIRST BLOOD

The royalist army now split into its pre-arranged divisions. The earl of Chester (who had insisted on being the one to strike the first blow) attacked Lincoln's north gate, drawing many of the already stretched French and rebels that way and providing space and opportunity for Falkes de Bréauté and his crossbowmen to slip one by one into the castle via the postern. Once inside, they rushed up to the battlements and were able to send a lethal rain of bolts down into the crowded mass below, aiming predominantly at the enemy horses: 'They discharged their deadly weapons against the chargers of the [rebel] barons, levelling horses and riders together to the earth [...] by means of the crossbow-men, by whose skill the horses of the barons were mown down and killed like pigs, the party of the barons was greatly weakened.'[25] The sudden onslaught caused chaos among the French and rebels, with men being thrown from the thrashing, wounded and dying horses, and some of them becoming trapped as a result. The available space became ever more clogged, preventing even those who were unharmed from moving to defend the city gates. This benefited the royalists, and the earl of Chester was able to break through the north gate and engage in combat there; his men 'boldly rushed on the enemy [...] sparks of fire were seen to dart, and sounds as of dreadful thunder were heard to burst forth from the blows of swords against helmeted heads'.[26]

Meanwhile, William Marshal himself, followed by the divisions of the earl of Salisbury and the bishop of Winchester, attacked the city's western gate, which was by now being defended either very badly or not at all. The regent's biographer naturally waxes lyrical about his hero's actions, but even allowing for the expected exaggeration, the subsequent engagement must have been quite some sight to behold. It started, we are told, with a moment of down-to-earth realism: Marshal was so keen to enter the fray that he nearly did so without his helm, only donning it when he was reminded by a subordinate. But, once properly armed, the greatest knight of his age charged into the fray for the final time in his long and distinguished career:

> As swiftly as if he were a bird, a sparrowhawk or an eagle, he pricked the horse with his spurs [...] This man, who had performed so many deeds of valour, plunged into the very thick of them over a distance greater than three spears' length, thinning their ranks by main force and breaking up in his path a press which was very tightly formed and crowding in on him.[27]

The regent was not past it yet, whatever the earl of Chester might think, and he was followed by the earl of Salisbury and by the bishop of Winchester, who shouted 'God is with the Marshal!' as he rode. The royalist troops, cavalry and infantry, poured through the open gate and into the already crowded, dangerous streets.

Let us take a few moments to visualise and understand the nature of this momentous experience for those who were in the middle of the action.

Imagine, for example, a knight. He rose before dawn this morning and ate whatever rations were put in front of him – perhaps calmly, or perhaps forcing it down into a stomach that was already churning. He knows that he'll need to keep his strength up for what is to come, unsure of when or whether he'll get another meal. He confesses his sins and receives absolution from one of the clerics in the host, and then, his anticipation rising, he's armed by his squires. The chausses; the thick, heavy gambeson; the hauberk; the arming cap and coif; the identifying surcoat; all are placed on him, the ties and buckles fastened with precision as he stamps his feet and shakes his arms to ensure everything is secure. The last thing he wants in the midst of battle is for his chausses to fall and become tangled round his feet, or his coif to slip down in front of his eyes. His sword belt is buckled round him and settled comfortably, but he doesn't yet don his great helm. It's heavy, awkward, causes breathing difficulties and restricts his vision, so it will only be set on his head when combat is imminent. For now, he or his squire will carry it.

The order is given to form up and move out, and the knight mounts. So far, this is all familiar: the weight and feel of his armour, the horse he's owned and trained with for some time. He lets himself sink into the rhythm of riding, making a few forced jokes with his companions to take his mind off the knot in his stomach. Because today is different. Today is not a training session, nor even a tournament – it's the day he'll ride into a pitched battle, something he's almost certainly never done before, unless he happens to be one of those unfortunates who were at Bouvines or La-Roche-aux-Moines more than a decade ago.

Lincoln comes into sight. The battle lines are drawn up, and the knight is in the division to be commanded by William Marshal himself. He listens to the instructions, knowing that even the best-laid plans might fall apart in the heat of conflict if matters start to go against them. Then he listens to the regent's oration, and his heart begins to lift a little. He's here to fight for a just cause, and it's too late for nerves, because all around him his companions are forming up.

His squire holds up the helm, and he ducks under it as the boy positions it correctly. All of a sudden, the knight is in his own world, a dim one seen only straight ahead through the narrow eye-slits, and one where all sound is muffled. He checks that his left arm is positioned correctly in the straps of his shield, and that his sword is ready to be drawn at a moment's notice, and then he takes the lance from his squire and tells the boy to fall back.

Under him, the knight's destrier has sensed what is about to happen, and is impatient. Not long now. A brief prayer, said silently. The knight is already sweating, trapped in the many layers of padding and metal that encase him as the sun climbs higher in the sky and the warmth of the spring day is felt. A trickle of moisture runs down his face, but he knows from experience that he must suppress the automatic and useless urge to wipe it away now that he's wearing the enclosed helm. By the time the day is over he'll be drenched, and he'll be lucky if it's only with sweat.

And then they're off. The momentum of the charge builds up, and the knight can see the great, the legendary, William Marshal at the apex of the formation. Pride and exhilaration sweep away any last vestiges of nerves as he urges the destrier on. He might even be shouting out loud; he can hardly tell. He's part of the great rushing charge as it crashes through the city gate, and even amid the noise and the padding over his ears he can hear the cries of 'God is with the Marshal!'. The elation and battle rage reach a crescendo. This is what he's been training for since he was a tiny child. This is what he was born to do.

The first enemies appear in his limited field of vision, and he braces himself for the shock of contact. Battle will be joined, and he's ready for it.

The royalist host was able to take some valuable prisoners almost immediately, because some of the French and rebel knights who had been unhorsed by the volleys of crossbow bolts from the castle were still trapped. It might seem odd that a group of charging combatants would pull up in order to capture, rather than kill, their opponents, but this was standard practice at the time if those opponents happened to be of noble or knightly rank. The lords on both sides of a conflict such as this might well have been related to each other, and they were also all members of an exclusive 'brotherhood' of knights which transcended nationality, allegiance or ideology – it is not really an exaggeration to say that the knights on one side felt they had more in common with the opposing knights than they did with their own common soldiers. Plus, of course, capturing a foe provided the opportunity for gain: if you held a knight prisoner you could claim his valuable horse and armour, and you could keep him in custody until his family or his overlord paid a substantial ransom. The members of the royalist army might have proclaimed and even believed that they were fighting for national pride, but this did not mean they were not sensible of the benefits of personal gain.

Such merciful treatment was only for those of sufficient rank. Enemy soldiers who were lower down the social scale were not worth capturing, as they would bring no ransom. They could also not be sold into slavery, as the practice had long ceased, and moreover they would need feeding if they were to be held captive, thus diverting precious resources. They could therefore expect to be killed, and this is exactly what happened now to the French siege-machine operators who had been continuing the bombardment of the castle even as battle raged around them. The chief engineer was decapitated while in the very act of loading another stone into one of his machines, and the months-long barrage finally ceased, no doubt to the great relief of Nicola de la Haye and the defending garrison.

The walls of Lincoln castle were still standing, and the royalist army was inside the city and fully engaged. The French and rebels were on the point of disaster; they needed a leader to rally around, to inspire and regroup them, if the battle were not to turn into a rout.

DEATH IN THE STREETS

Thomas, the count of Perche, had already seen a great deal of action and taken on a great deal of responsibility in his short life. His county was a place of strategic significance, lying between Normandy and Maine in the heart of the lands once controlled by Henry II, and he had inherited it at the age of just seven, upon the death of his father in 1202 while preparing to embark on the Fourth Crusade. Despite his family ties to the English royal house Thomas was a firm supporter of Philip Augustus throughout the years of conflict with John, and he had fought for the French king at the decisive battle of Bouvines in 1214 while still in his teens. He had continued to champion the Capetians, and upon reaching his majority he had been among those who volunteered to fight for Louis when the English crown was offered to him by the rebel barons.

Thomas was much younger than any of the English rebel commanders at Lincoln,* and possibly more idealistic. He had sworn to uphold Louis's right to the throne and was prepared to fight for his liege lord's cause whatever the consequences. He cut a distinctive and readily identifiable figure: the *History of William Marshal* describes him as 'a very tall, handsome, fine-looking man', and although his looks would have been hidden behind his helm, his height and the unmistakeable surcoat of white emblazoned with three red chevrons ensured that he stood out.[28]

The count of Perche undoubtedly had a talent for military matters, and he could now see the severity of the situation. If panic set in and flight started, it would be very difficult to stop. Taking charge, he was able to rally the French and rebels in the space between the eastern gate of the castle and the western front

---

*Indeed, both Fitzwalter and de Quincy had children older than Perche, which might explain any reluctance on their behalf to cede command to him.

of the cathedral – the only large piece of flat open ground that the city afforded. This action was praised even by an opposing chronicler: he 'put up a very stern defence' and he 'performed many great feats of arms that day', even starting to turn the tide of the battle by his efforts.[29] However, the problem with Perche being a tall and readily identifiable man of rank was that it made him an obvious target, and he was soon surrounded by a multitude of enemies, too many to fight off, and killed.

The French chroniclers, relying on second-hand reports, are uncertain of the exact manner of his death. William the Breton says only that Perche was 'the first among the fallen, before reaching his twenty-second year', and the Minstrel of Reims claims that he 'was killed by a scoundrel who lifted the front of his hauberk and plunged in a knife', though this particular writer is probably trying to make a point about the perfidy of the English, as he does elsewhere in his work.[30] Our two most detailed accounts, however, tally to a great extent, so we can be relatively confident of exactly how the young count died. Roger of Wendover tells us that:

> The king's knights rushed in a close body on the count of Perche, entirely surrounding him; and as he could not withstand their force as they rushed against him, they called on him to surrender, that he might escape with his life. He, however, swore that he would not surrender to the English, who were traitors to their lawful king [i.e., Louis]. On hearing this, a knight rushed on him, and striking him in the eye, pierced his brain, on which he fell to the ground without uttering another word.[31]

The *History of William Marshal* puts its own hero front and centre, but otherwise tells a very similar tale. Marshal reached out to seize Perche's bridle, we are told; this was presumably in an attempt to capture him alive, but all did not go according to plan:

> He [Perche] had been wounded mortally through his eyehole by a cruel thrust of the sword delivered by Sir Reginald Croc, with the point of the sword straight through the eye. When the count of Perche saw the defenders being so pushed back by our men, he immediately let go of his bridle, took his sword in both hands, and dealt the Marshal three consecutive blows on his helmet. The blows were so hard and fierce that the marks could be clearly seen on the helmet. But, immediately after that, he slumped down and fell from his horse [...] Once the blade had been withdrawn from the wound he had received through the eyehole, there was nothing for him but death.[32]

The repetition of the specific detail of the thrust through the eye-slit of Perche's helm adds weight to the idea that this was indeed the cause of his death; the incident was also depicted in a famous image of the battle drawn by Matthew Paris in the margin of the manuscript of his *Chronica Majora*.*[33] If it really was so then Perche was extremely unlucky: helms, as we know, were fully enclosed and provided very good protection at the expense of sight and hearing, so to have been killed by a

*See Plate 23.

(possibly even accidental) thrust in a weak spot was unusual enough to warrant comment.

Interestingly, although Perche was an enemy combatant, William Marshal's biographer treats the young man's death as something to be regretted: 'Once his helmet had been removed, while the Marshal was by his side to see that he was stone dead, the sorrow there was intense [...] It was a great pity that he died in this manner.'[34] Another example, perhaps, of the international brotherhood of knights and the closeness of the lords fighting on both sides of the conflict.

This very obvious and public death of the French leader, the man who had been holding his side together almost single-handedly, spelled the beginning of the end, and the French and rebels started to give ground. With the castle now safe from further bombardment, and the royalist crossbowmen unable to shoot down into the tightly packed melee for fear of hitting an ally, Falkes de Bréauté and his men poured out via the main gate to join the fighting in the streets. Despite the knightly combatants getting more of the contemporary attention and praise, it was this intervention that decisively swayed the course of the engagement. Agile men on foot, armed with their secondary weapons of daggers and clubs, rather than crossbows or long swords or lances, were much better suited to the type of close-quarter combat now being carried out in the cramped, narrow streets. And the direction of the fighting aided them too: as the French and rebels started to give ground towards the south, they were backing away while facing uphill, with the royalists now having the great advantage of fighting facing downhill.

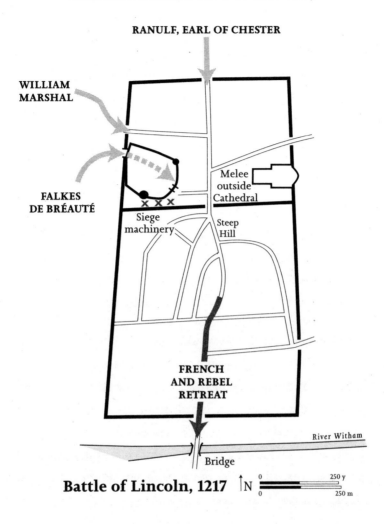

RANULF, EARL OF CHESTER

WILLIAM MARSHAL

FALKES DE BRÉAUTÉ

Melee outside Cathedral

Siege machinery

Steep Hill

FRENCH AND REBEL RETREAT

River Witham

Bridge

Battle of Lincoln, 1217 ↑N

0   250 y

0   250 m

It is difficult to convey just how challenging the situation was for knights on horseback. The streets of Lincoln had an average gradient of 1 in 12, rising to 1 in 4 at the steepest points, making them very difficult to ascend. Underfoot they were cobbled or of mud churned up by the constant passage of people, animals and carts, either of those surfaces making purchase for horses' hooves almost impossible.[35] The roads were narrow even at ground level, and most buildings had an overhanging second storey, which impeded mounted knights even further; they were forced into the centre of the street and are unlikely to have been able to ride more than two abreast. Manoeuvring a lance would have been all but impossible.

However, these were determined men, and the French and rebels made several further attempts to regroup, one of them probably taking place at the top of the aptly named Steep Hill, where there was a slightly more open and more level piece of ground. It must have been absolute chaos, and the *History of William Marshal* gives us a flavour of the combat, not really needing to overdramatise to any great extent:

> Had you been there, you would have seen great blows dealt, heard helmets clanging and resounding, seen lances fly in splinters in the air, saddles vacated by riders, knights taken prisoner. You would have heard, from place to place, great blows delivered by swords and maces on helmets and on arms, and seen knives and daggers drawn for the purpose of stabbing horses [...] The noise there was so great that you would not have heard God thunder.[36]

The French and rebels were slowly pushed backwards down the hill, and once they reached the bottom, and the city's southern wall, they were faced with a huge problem: the Stonebow gate.* This appears to have been of a strange design

---

*This is not the same edifice as the current Stonebow, which dates from around 1520; the gate that was extant in 1217 was demolished in the fourteenth century.

which prevented a mass exodus. Roger of Wendover describes it in quite some detail:

> The flail of the southern gate through which they took their flight had been replaced in a transverse way across the gate, which greatly impeded their flight; for when anyone came up and wished to go out that gate, he was obliged to dismount from his horse and open it, and after he had passed the gate was again closed, and the flail fell across it as before, and thus the gate was a great trouble to the fugitives.[37]

It is not quite clear from the description exactly what Roger means by the 'flail' (*flagellum*) or what the gate looked like – a self-closing bar securing the way, or perhaps something akin to a modern 'kissing gate', which only allows one person to go through at a time? In any case, that a bottleneck was caused by the design of the gate seems certain. William Marshal's biographer, incidentally, has a much more prosaic explanation for the obstruction and delay: he tells us that there was a cow stuck in the gate opening.[38]

The congestion and the lack of opportunity for escape meant that there was a frenetic last stand inside the city's south gate. This did not result in an all-out massacre, though, as the royalists were still intent on taking as many noble prisoners as possible. And this they achieved with almost startling success: forty-six men of baronial rank and above were captured, including the rebel commanding group of Saer de Quincy, Robert Fitzwalter and Gilbert de Gant, along with at least 300 knights.[39] With the count of Perche already dead and the castle relieved, the royalist victory had been complete. Roger of Wendover claims that there were only three fatalities: Perche, the knight Reginald Croc who might or might not have struck the fatal blow (if so, perhaps he was killed in the crowded melee surrounding the count or in the immediate aftermath of the latter's death), and one other whom he does not name. However, what this account means in practice is that there were only three deaths among those of sufficient rank for Roger to bother to note them; there were certainly many others among the common soldiery and the engineers.[40]

Not all of those who escaped the battle lived to tell the tale, either. There was yet another bottleneck caused by the fleeing men having to cross the River Witham in order to reach the suburb of Wigford and then the outskirts of the city and the road to London. Falling in the water was an almost certain death sentence for a man in heavy armour, so there was no chance of swimming, but there was only one bridge, meaning that there was a frantic crush of defeated combatants waiting to cross it. And finally, the roads leading south out of Lincoln ran through or past places where the inhabitants were only too glad to take revenge on the invaders: many of the soldiers in flight, we are told, 'and especially almost all the foot-soldiers, were slain before they got to Louis; for the inhabitants of the towns through which they passed in their flight, went to meet them with swords and bludgeons, and, laying snares for them, killed numbers.'[41] Again, this violence fell more heavily on the infantry; any knight who was still mounted would have had a greater chance of escaping such ambush or pursuit.

As the sounds of battle finally ceased inside the city, and the pursuit of fleeing defeated men could be heard heading off into the far distance, it might have seemed as though peace had finally come to beleaguered Lincoln. But, unfortunately, although the battle was over, the violence was not.

AFTERMATH: THE 'FAIR' OF LINCOLN

The people of Lincoln had become embroiled in the war through no desire and no fault of their own. News of Louis's invasion must have reached their busy and thriving trade hub fairly soon after it happened, but they might have thought they could stay well away from a war they hoped would be confined to the south-east. However, Gilbert de Gant's initial move in the summer of 1216, temporarily halted by Nicola de la Haye, must have set alarm bells ringing, and there was certainly no escape from the concerted attack at the end of that year. The civilian men, women and children stood no chance at all of fighting off a professional army, so all they could do was take shelter and defend their own homes and businesses. Happily there are at least no reports of widespread looting or attacks on citizens during this time, as the French and rebel forces were concentrating their attention on the castle.

The people could not hide forever, though, and once it became clear that the occupation of Lincoln and the assault on the castle were going to last weeks or months, there was nothing for it but to venture out and attempt to live and work as ordinarily as possible under the circumstances – after all, families still needed to eat. Throughout the spring, therefore, a cautious approximation of normality was maintained. There might have been the odd unpleasant interaction with the occupiers, but once again our chroniclers, even the ones who do sometimes take the time to emphasise the plight of England's common people during the war, record no atrocities.

The news that a royalist army was on its way to relieve the siege must have been very welcome: the citizens of Lincoln were to be rescued from their plight. There would be danger during the actual engagement, of course – prudent merchants would barricade and guard their premises, anyone with a nice solid door would shut and bar it, and the streets would be empty. The two sets of combatants would be attacking each other, though, so if the citizens kept their heads down then they should be safe, and once the fighting was over they would, it was hoped, be free to return to their normal lives.

Some of this supposition was true: most of the fighting was between soldiers, with civilians not needing to become involved, and the battle resulted in human (and equine) military casualties rather than destruction of property. But three major factors, none of them under the control of the people of Lincoln, were to come into play. First, the papal legate Guala had cruelly excommunicated the citizens and clergy before the battle; second, although the fighting was over, it was still only mid-afternoon; and third, the victorious soldiers, with plenty of daylight left, were so intoxicated by their victory that they wished to continue their orgy of violence after the enemy combatants were variously defeated, dead or in custody. The words 'adrenaline rush' would have meant nothing to people in the early thirteenth century, but that does not mean that such a thing did not exist.

At first, the actions of the royalist army stayed more or less within the bounds of conventional behaviour, in that they seized the possessions of their defeated opponents. 'No knight eager to win booty or capture knights could fail to do so that day,' says one of our accounts, while another tells us, 'after the battle was thus ended, the king's soldiers found in the city the waggons of the barons and the French, with the sumpter-horses, loaded with baggage, silver vessels, and various kinds of furniture and utensils, all of which fell into their possession without opposition.'[42]

This looting soon spilled over into violence against the citizens and their own property. William Marshal, still bathed in the sweat of his heroic victory but now coldly exhibiting one of the less palatable aspects of chivalry, made no attempt at all to prevent it. This is perhaps surprising, in both a modern and a contemporary context: even disregarding any common humanity and sympathy for the citizens that might have aroused his protective instincts, it was politically a very bad look for the army of the innocent young king – the king who was going to be so different from his father – to perpetrate such outrages. One theory that we might put forward is that Marshal suspected that he would not actually be able to stop the violence even if he tried, because the men were by now so frenzied that they would disregard any orders to restrain themselves, and that in this case it would be better for the regent personally to say that he had authorised it rather than to run the risk of looking as though he could not control his own men. And, of course, he had the perfect get-out-of-jail-free card: the legate's order of excommunication. The citizens were outside the protection of the Church and – if you squinted hard enough – they could be portrayed as collaborators with the enemy who had not put every effort into fighting off the French and rebels.

Lincoln now became a scene of violent mayhem as the city was sacked and plundered. Once all the shops and homes had been broken into and emptied, their owners beaten or killed if they tried to put up a defence, the royalist soldiers invaded the churches. Their excuse here was that the excommunication order had been extended to the clergy:

> Having then plundered the whole city to the last farthing, they next pillaged the churches throughout the city, and broke open the chests and store-rooms with axes and hammers, seizing on the gold and silver in them, clothes of all colours, women's ornaments, gold rings, goblets and jewels. Nor did the cathedral church escape this destruction, but underwent the same punishment as the rest, for the legate had given orders to the knights to treat all the clergy as excommunicated men [...] When they had thus seized on every kind of property, so that nothing remained in any corner of the houses, they each returned to their lords as rich men [...] they ate and drank amidst mirth and festivity.

Violence combined with rapacity and now also with drunkenness had its predictable result, and the men of the royalist army turned their attention to Lincoln's female citizens. It is not clear how many of them suffered, but we do know the tragic fate of some of those who attempted to escape:

> Many of the women of the city were drowned in the river, for, to avoid insult [i.e., rape by the soldiers of the royalist army], they took to small boats with their children, their female servants, and household property, and perished on their journey [...] for the boats were overloaded, and the women not knowing how to manage the boats, all perished.

Although no precise figures are available, when we take into account the number of French and rebels who were captured, rather than killed, it is entirely possible that the sacking of the city in the aftermath of the battle actually resulted in more casualties than the battle itself.

So much booty was seized from the city that the engagement became widely known as 'the Fair of Lincoln' or 'the Battle of Lincoln Fair'.* Many individuals made great gains: the royalist troops from looting and stealing, and their leaders from ransom payments and the appropriation of armour, horses and possessions from the captured enemy knights and lords. William Marshal was made significantly richer by capitalising on his family relationship to the late count of Perche in order to

---

*It is also sometimes known more neutrally as the Second Battle of Lincoln, in order to differentiate it from an earlier engagement in 1141, during the wars between King Stephen and Empress Matilda.

claim the lands that the latter had held in England.[43] Thomas, as an excommunicate, could not officially be buried in hallowed ground, but due to his rank a compromise was fudged, and he was interred in the grounds of the hospital in Lincoln. He had no children and no siblings; he was succeeded as count of Perche by his father's youngest brother, who was a bishop in France and who had no interest in claiming English titles, so Marshal's acquisitiveness went unchallenged. Another who gained was Ranulf de Blundeville: already the earl of Chester, he was named earl of Lincoln shortly after the battle, officially by the king but in practice by his regent, William Marshal, who evidently wanted to bury the hatchet.

Someone who gained nothing from the Fair of Lincoln, and indeed ended up worse off despite her heroics, was Nicola de la Haye. In one of the most astonishing acts of ingratitude imaginable, she was removed from the office of sheriff of Lincolnshire just four days after the battle, the position then given to William Longespee, the earl of Salisbury. The thinking behind this was presumably to offer Salisbury (who was Henry III's uncle) a great reward for having swapped sides and returned to the royalists, while also acting as an incentive to others — such as Warenne and Arundel — who might be persuaded to do the same. In this respect the appointment was successful, but if the idea was additionally to bring peace and stability to Lincolnshire then it failed miserably. Being named sheriff meant that Salisbury was entitled to have charge of the administration of the county, but he seized the city and the castle as well. Nicola had not spent months defending her birthright from enemies only to lose it to an ally, and she fought back by all the litigious means available, resulting in an acrimonious dispute that lasted for years.[*44]

The consequences of the battle for Louis and his campaign were severe, but not fatal. He was 'full of anger and rage' when the 'sad and defeated' uncaptured survivors limped their way to him, declaring that 'it was owing to their flight that their companions had been made prisoners, because if they had remained to fight, they would perhaps have saved themselves as well as their companions from capture and death'.[45] However, the majority of his lords and knights had merely been captured, rather than killed, and once their ransoms were paid he could expect them to return to the fold. Louis also suffered no loss of personal reputation: he had not been defeated himself, and indeed had made progress in other areas during the spring of 1217.

The consequences for the royalists were both practical and symbolic. As William Marshal could report when he rode off to Nottingham shortly after the battle, to see the king and the legate, they had staved off the immediate disaster that would have resulted from the fall of Lincoln castle. Louis would not be able to extend his influence further north, and he had been deprived, at least temporarily, of a large proportion of his army. The victory had also been a big morale booster: the

---

[*] It was Nicola, incidentally, who had the last laugh. As part of an eventual attempt to solve the dispute, Nicola's only surviving relative and heiress, her granddaughter Idonea (the daughter of her late son, Richard), was married to Salisbury's son and namesake, William. As they were both children at the time, Salisbury only had to wait for the elderly Nicola (his senior by some twenty-five years) to die, and then he could control all the estates in their name until they came of age. This never happened, because Nicola outlived him.

forces of the innocent young king, supported by the pope and his legate, had defeated those of the excommunicate would-be usurper. God was on their side. Nonetheless, neither William Marshal nor any of the other experienced heads among the royalists were counting their chickens just yet. The war was by no means over, and there was still an awful lot to do if the claims of Henry III were to supersede those of the putative Louis I of England.

The royalists were also faced with some tough decisions about how they were going to proceed and what they were willing to do. They had already allowed an unchivalrous assault on the civilians of Lincoln — to what extent, exactly, were they prepared to get their hands dirty?

FIVE

Dover, the Weald and France, February to July 1217

WINNING AT ALL COSTS

'What, then, is chivalry?'

This question is posed by none other than the author of the History of William Marshal; and well might he ask, because his hero's actions in early 1217 are very much open to interpretation.[1]

In addition to keeping an eye on developments at Lincoln, the royalist party had, during late 1216, also needed to deal with events elsewhere, with the French and rebels making inroads in several parts of the realm thanks to their tactic of splitting their forces. A truce was agreed over Christmas – something that was not an uncommon occurrence during a long campaign, both in honour of the religious feast and in recognition of the fact that it was very difficult to keep troops in the field during the winter due to the lack of fresh food and fodder, and a dearth of foraging opportunities. This gave both sides something of a breathing space during which they could take stock.

William Marshal knew he did not yet have the resources for a major attack that would push Louis back and out of England;

although some rebels and waverers had returned to Henry III's party following the re-issue of Magna Carta in November, they were still too few in number to turn the tide. The royalists therefore needed more time to consolidate and to encourage further defections. The short Christmas break was not enough, as evidenced by the fact that as soon as the truce expired, on 13 January 1217, Louis leapt straight back into action and took Cambridge castle within a week. Marshal, who was at that point in Oxford – keeping tabs on the situation at Lincoln, while also trying to stay alert for attacks elsewhere and making ready to move towards London, Dover or anywhere else necessary at short notice – asked Louis to prolong the truce. This would give him more time to plan the royalist strategy for the spring and summer, but the request was something of a long shot as Louis was in a better military position and might be reluctant to accede to it. Marshal sweetened the offer by proposing to surrender the royalist-held castles of Norwich, Hedingham, Orford and Colchester as part of the deal, at which point Louis gave his assent and the truce was extended until 23 April, Jubilate Sunday.* The terms were that 'everything was to remain till that time in the same state as it was on the day of the truce being sworn to, with respect both to castles and other possessions'.[2]

Voluntarily offering to surrender four castles might seem like an odd thing to do, and indeed Marshal's biographer was so confused by the idea of his hero performing such an action

---

*The third Sunday after Easter was known as 'Jubilate Sunday' as the psalm for the day began with Jubilate Deo ('Shout with joy to the Lord', now known as Psalm 66). That particular psalm continues with the words 'your enemies dwindle before you; all the earth bows down to you', which both sides in the war would no doubt have liked to take as a favourable omen.

that he tried to suggest, very improbably, that the truce was
arranged without the regent's knowledge. However, the offer
might have represented a strategic recognition on Marshal's
part that the royalists could not defend a large number of
isolated or far-flung strongholds, so they were better off giving
them up and consolidating men and materiel elsewhere. If the
castles in question were handed over peacefully as part of the
negotiated agreement rather than being taken by storm (as was
a distinct possibility if the royalists continued to attempt to hold
them) he would have more control over the way in which their
contents were dispersed. Marshal had – deliberately, we may
assume – not made any specific arrangement that stores were
to be handed over as well as buildings, so when the garrisons
of each castle marched out they took their provisions with
them. This was a great benefit to the royalist party, which was
by now almost broke and was having to pay its knights with the
goods and jewels that were all that remained of John's treasury,
rather than in cash.[3] It seemed evident that Dover was going
to be the focus of a renewed attack by the French and rebels
later in the spring, and there was little money to re-provision it
after the siege of the previous year, so the stores from the four
surrendered castles were transferred there.

It was in early February 1217, while the truce was in force,
that Louis did something unexpected: he decided to use the
fallow period to travel back to France in order to ask his father
for more troops, money and resources. In hindsight this is not
terribly surprising from a financial and logistical point of view,
as we can see that he also lacked the wherewithal to launch
the major push that would win the war, and a long stalemate

beckoned. Nevertheless, it was politically and strategically questionable, showing either a great faith in William Marshal's integrity or a staggering naivety, depending on which way you look at it.

It was not without some difficulty – as we will explore below – that Louis was able to take ship, but eventually he did and he reached Paris at the end of February. He was there for several weeks, during which time he had no success whatsoever in persuading Philip Augustus to help. The French king still appeared to be playing his own game, publicly refusing even to discuss the matter ('King Philip, fearing excommunication, gave no aid to his son […] like the most Christian man he was, he would not speak with him'), while once again not specifically forbidding Louis from raising more troops in a private capacity.[4] Louis was frustrated, but there were some positive outcomes from his temporary visit. He was able to persuade a few more knights and their accompanying retinues to join him, which was better than nothing. He was able to bask in the accomplishment of having ensured the royal succession, meeting for the first time his third son, who had been born the previous September. And, significantly, he could talk to his wife about what else he would need to ensure success for his – their – campaign for the English crown.

The news that Louis had left England might have come as a shock to William Marshal, but he took advantage of it straight away, sending royalist troops fanning out through the east, south-east and south to attack Ely, Rochester, Farnham, Chichester, Portchester, Southampton, Winchester and Marlborough.[5] This meant that he had broken the terms of the agreement; he had reneged on his solemn word, and this was a serious matter.

The declaration of a truce, of course, could only ever be a generally accepted convention rather than an actual law (because there could not be a law that governed warring parties, especially international ones, in such a way), but, self-evidently, once it was declared it involved the cessation of armed conflict.[6] In this case the terms had been laid out clearly to stipulate that everything should remain as it was on the day the truce was agreed until the day it ended, including the possession of castles. It is difficult, therefore, to square Marshal's actions with any modern conception of integrity or chivalry.

Naturally his biographer spins the situation positively, trying to imply that it was Louis who had broken the truce first and that Marshal was merely retaliating:

> Then Louis decided to return to France. Once the Marshal saw and knew that Louis had no intention of keeping the truce, indeed that he had broken it, he said: 'He can know this for a fact, that it will never be kept by our side. We shall never ask him for anything, there will be no further bargaining, and it will be every man for himself.'[7]

As an argument, this is weak: there is a difference between using a period of truce to leave the field and regroup, and using it actually to restart military action while the enemy is absent. It is debatable whether the former 'breaks' the truce, while the latter certainly does, and Marshal (as well as all his contemporaries) would have known this. Indeed, the biographer's comment that 'there will be no further bargaining' might well work both ways, as any current or future opponent of Marshal's would be less likely to negotiate if they thought he would break his word as soon as their back was turned.

The most charitable way to interpret Marshal's actions is to conjecture that he might have believed, or wished to believe, that Louis's withdrawal was permanent. If this were the case then the war was over and the realm of England, *de facto*, was now under the control of Henry III, meaning that members of his administration were therefore free to take whatever action they deemed appropriate. However, although not impossible, it does seem unlikely that this was the case, and Marshal does not seem to have put the idea forward as an excuse. The truce was not vague or indefinite: it was to last specifically until 23 April, at which point all parties expected hostilities to resume.

What seems most likely, then, is that Marshal knew that the truce was only a temporary pause in the war, and that Louis would be back when the agreed period was up, but he decided to break it anyway. 'Chivalry' was as nebulous a concept in the thirteenth century as it is now, capable of being interpreted in many different ways. Marshal had given his word to Louis, but was he bound to keep his pledge to an excommunicate? Was his primary duty to remain honest and honourable, and to keep his promises, or was it to win back the kingdom of England for the boy he recognised as king? If the latter, and given the dire situation in which the royalist party found itself, was he entitled to use any means at his disposal, no matter how 'unchivalrous', to ensure success?

There are many instances in twelfth- and thirteenth-century military accounts of actions being taken that might cause the modern reader to blink, while contemporaries saw them as a perfectly normal part of war. The ravaging of the countryside, for example, or the burning of towns and villages under the control of an opposing lord; the looting of homes, the theft of goods from civilians and non-combatants, or the taking of those same innocent bystanders as hostages; the killing of agricultural workers so that opposing lords could not benefit from their labours in the fields or the taxes they paid. The key thing with all of these, though, is that they were actions taken against those of lower rank, those who mattered less in the eyes of lords and knights and whose individual lives and livelihoods did not need to be taken into account in the big-picture calculations of a war. If we were to take any of the so-called 'rules' of chivalry as being hard and fast, it might be that a knight was expected to keep his word once he had given it to another knight – if only for the maintenance of his own reputation. Even this, however, was subject to interpretation and point of view, and a couple of earlier sections of the History of William Marshal give us an excellent illustration of the way similar acts might be perceived differently depending on whether they were performed by friend or foe.

In 1188 William Marshal was an advisor to Henry II while the latter was in peace negotiations with Philip Augustus. When the talks were finished Philip's troops dispersed, whereupon Marshal had the following to say to Henry: 'Sire, listen to me: the King [Philip] has disbanded his armies, and they have gone off in many directions. I advise you to disband your own troops, but in secret tell them to return to us without fail on a day to be set by you. Then make an incursion into the King of France's domains.' This sounds completely underhand, but Henry's response, as depicted by the text's author, is 'Marshal, you are an excellent man and have advised me very well; it will be done, exactly as you say.'* And yet, at a later point in the text, when Marshal is advising Richard the Lionheart in his dealings with King Philip, the French take the opportunity of a truce to attack a castle, and this is 'a heinous crime' and 'a cowardly act of treachery'.[8] Both of these examples involve the word of a king being given to another king – that is, a peer in the eyes of both God and society – and then broken. But each is presented very differently.

Chivalry, then, appears to be very much in the eye of the beholder: 'we' can do things that would be unacceptable coming from 'them', because our cause is more noble or more important, or simply because we are right and they are wrong. A good case might therefore be made either for or against William Marshal's actions in early 1217, under the prevailing circumstances and depending on your point of view; readers are encouraged to examine the evidence and make up their own minds.[9]

Theory aside, the practical problem for the royalist party was that Louis did intend to return, and when he heard what had been going on in England during his absence, he was furious. This galvanised him and his party, and he was ready to launch

---

* 'You are an excellent man' is the published translation; the original is *molt estes corteis*, which is perhaps better rendered as 'you are very courtly' or even 'you are very chivalrous'.

a renewed attack on Dover as soon as he got back. He had managed to recruit about 140 knights and some additional mercenaries, who were all travelling with him; not sufficient to swing the war definitively in his direction, but certainly enough to cause Marshal and his compatriots more headaches.

However, another faction of the royalist party had also been active, and the French reinforcements were about to encounter an opponent who was even less overtly 'chivalrous' than William Marshal himself. This leader was neither a lord nor a knight, and his position was unofficial, but his methods were brutally effective.

THE REAL ROBIN HOOD?

When narrating the course of the war, our thirteenth-century chroniclers tend to place greatest emphasis on the contributions of the noblemen and knights: they are the ones who are named, whose deaths are recorded, whose actions are recounted in the greatest detail and who are given most of the credit for any success. Some contemporary writers, as we have seen, also mention various groups in passing – for example, crossbowmen, foot soldiers, civilians or clergy – but not with anything like the same attention or degree of individuality. However, occasionally a person of common birth did something so striking that they could not help but come to wider notice, and during the 1216–17 war against the French invaders, such a one was William of Cassingham, also known as Willikin of the Weald.*

---

*And also as William of Casingeham, Cassyngehamme, Kasinghamme, Kensham, Colingeham, de Wans, de Waux, de Vaus, and at least twenty other variants of the toponym, to say nothing of

The Weald was a huge forested area across Kent and Sussex; in 1216 it was about 120 miles from east to west and 30 miles from north to south, much more extensive than the area still known as the Weald today. The woods were dense and the area sparsely populated, containing a few manors and villages but no towns of any size, and the Weald formed a formidable obstacle between the towns of the south-east coast, where the French had first landed, and London.

As we might expect for a man of common birth, we know nothing at all of William's life before he came to prominence in 1216, although we can assume two things. The first is that he was local to the Weald: Cassingham, now the hamlet of Kensham, was a manor in Kent situated about 13 miles north of Hastings, and William demonstrated extensive local knowledge during the war that can only have come from long familiarity. The second is that in 1216 he was probably in his twenties: he is referred to as 'a young man' by contemporaries, and we know that he lived until 1257, the combination of which makes it likely that he was born in the early or mid-1190s.

When the French arrived on the Isle of Thanet* and at Sandwich in May 1216, William took up arms straight away in defence of the royalist cause, attracting many local volunteers to his band. To them the situation was a straightforward war of defence against foreign invasion: the French fleet had landed in their locality, and they wanted to repel the assault. However,

---

the different spellings of the forename. This might be one of the reasons why William is so little known: later researchers might not have realised that all these names referred to the same man.
*Thanet is now a peninsula, but in the thirteenth century it was an island.

this could not be achieved via any sort of pitched battle, due to their lack of knightly resources – these were men of common birth, so they owned no horses, armour, swords or lances. Instead they used the weapon more familiar to them and more appropriate to their status, the bow.

The bow (not yet the larger 'longbow' of later years) was a lightweight and extremely efficient weapon in the hands of a trained archer, who could loose a series of arrows very rapidly with an effective range of around 100–120 metres (330–390 feet), and an absolute range of perhaps twice that. There is a persistent myth, incidentally, that medieval archers were supposed to be able to shoot 'twelve arrows a minute', which has always sounded suspicious – not least because, in a world without clocks, nobody in thirteenth-century England would have had the slightest idea of what 'a minute' was – but happily this has been debunked.[10] The bow could be used in many different types of terrain and avoided the necessity for hand-to-hand combat against a heavily armoured opponent. It was this very effectiveness that had made the nobility initially reluctant to accept its use in warfare: a lord or knight – or his horse – could be killed at a distance by a commoner, with no opportunity to strike back, and this offended knightly sensibilities on several levels. In 1139 the Church, at its Second Lateran Council, had banned the use of bows and crossbows by Christians against other Christians (shooting Muslims and heretics appears to have been fine), but the problem was that as soon as one side in a war used archers, the other side was obliged to do the same if they were not to be at a great disadvantage. By 1216 the ban was being almost universally ignored, and there were archers and crossbowmen in any army, including those of both the royalists and the rebels in the present conflict.[11] The bow was particularly suited to the sort of strategy that William of Cassingham and his unarmoured or lightly armoured men were following, in that they could attack the French with a volley of arrows from a distance, and then either melt away into the woods or follow up with swift hand-to-hand combat while their opponents were still reeling.

The men of the Weald also used their local knowledge to good effect. The vast, dense forest made life very difficult for the invaders (and particularly for heavily armoured, mounted knights), and William was able to engage in guerrilla warfare, setting ambushes and cutting off stragglers. His efforts became well known almost straight away: as early as the summer of 1216 Roger of Wendover wrote of 'a young man named William, refusing to make his fealty to Louis, [who] collected a company of a thousand bowmen, and taking to the woods and forests with which that part of the country abounded, he continued to harass the French during the whole war, and slew many thousands of them.'[12] The Anonymous of Béthune, whom we know to have been in the south of England at that time, also notes William's actions:

In the Weald there was a serjeant who because of his valour was very much lord of the men of the Weald; later he often fought against Louis' troops. His name was Willekins of Cassingham but the French called him Willekins of the Weald, because they could not say Cassingham. He was very well known subsequently among Louis' forces.[13]

In keeping with the nature of William's campaign he was known for executing, rather than imprisoning, any captured enemy troops. As a man of less than knightly rank, he was not bound by any ostensible code of chivalry, and he also had to consider the practicalities: he had no fortified stronghold or fixed base, nowhere secure to incarcerate his captives and no spare supplies with which to feed them. Decapitating any prisoners, therefore (his execution method of choice), got rid of the problem while also striking fear into the hearts of his enemies. He and his men would expect no mercy if they were captured, so why should they show any? The tactic was successful, and the French were harassed and held up at multiple junctures, becoming wary of entering the Weald at all and instead being forced to communicate with London by taking the long route around the coast.

This resistance action taken on his behalf came to the attention of King John, who, in September 1216, wrote a public letter to the men of the Weald to thank them. He also decreed that William of Cassingham should be paid an annual income, both as a reward for his loyalty and to enable him to continue the fight. This appreciation was continued by the administration of the young Henry III following John's death, and in early 1217 William was appointed to the position of Warden of the Seven Hundreds of the Weald.[14]

William and his band made a significant intervention in February 1217 when Louis decided to make his temporary return to France. The French prince headed for Winchelsea and Rye in order to take ship, but the resistance fighters engaged in the classic guerrilla tactics of cutting off his food supplies, destroying mills (so the French could not grind their own corn even if they were able to find any) and demolishing bridges. As informal resistance fighters, and not official members of the royalist party under William Marshal, they did not hold themselves bound by the truce he had agreed – any more than he did himself – and their actions brought admiring praise from Marshal's biographer:

> And then there was Willikin of the Weald. He harassed them fiercely and was of no mind to play games, having many of them beheaded. Thus it was that Louis was harried so that he felt himself in desperate straits. Some thousand of his men were killed there, men who never received confession; all they received were the spears and swords, and these they had in abundance as soon as they strayed from the ranks of the army.[15]

This intervention could actually have ended the war very swiftly. Trapped between the men of the Weald, cutting off the route to London, and the sea blockade formed by the fleet of Philip d'Albini (of whom we shall hear more later in this chapter), the French could easily have starved. If Louis had died of malnutrition or disease, or by the sword in a desperate attempt to break through in either direction, the French would have given up and the remaining English rebels would have had nobody to fight for. Philip Augustus, already seemingly ambivalent about his son's campaign, would hardly choose to continue it in the name of his seven-year-old eldest grandson, and any hope of further help from across the Channel would evaporate.

Unfortunately for the royalists Louis did succeed in getting away – rescued by the skilled commander of his fleet, Eustace the Monk, who managed to evade the blockade – and he made it safely to France. But William of Cassingham and others were ready for him when he came back, and this was to have a further significant impact on the course of the war during the following weeks and months. Louis approached English shores on 22 April (the day before the extended truce expired), intending to sail directly to Dover, where he had left a skeleton force outside the castle to guard the remains of the siege camp that he would need again. However, the now much enlarged resistance got there first:

> Next day, Saturday, they had a fair wind and a calm sea, so that they went as smoothly as if they had been on a pond. In this way they sailed so close to Dover that they had a clear view of their lodges, which were still standing. At this juncture Oliver, King John's bastard son, reached Dover, as did Willekins of the Weald, and with him a strong force. They killed many of the men guarding the lodges, then set fire to these so that they were soon burnt. And when Louis and his men went sailing in towards Dover and saw the smoke from the lodges, they did not dare put in there [...] They sheered off to the right, reached Sandwich and settled there in the town.[16]

The fact that William was now acting in concert with a commander of royal (albeit illegitimate) blood shows just how valuable his contribution to the war effort was, and how it was acknowledged by the powers-that-be. Indeed, it was subsequently also recognised by many others: on the basis that he operated in a forest, was famed for archery, acted as an outlaw and was very quickly given a folk-hero nickname, it has been suggested that William was the original basis for the legends of Robin Hood.* While this can never be proven beyond doubt, his intervention at this crucial point made a great deal of difference to the progress of the war.

Happily for William, and in contrast to the fortunes of Nicola de la Haye, his contribution to the royalist cause was recognised and rewarded once the war was over. He was not ennobled, nor given huge riches (distinctions of rank had to be preserved, no matter how heroic his actions), but he was granted lands in Essex to add to his annual income and his wardenship in the Weald, which was enough to raise him to the level of minor gentry. William died in 1257 after forty years in royal service and, in another sign of appreciation, his widow was then put under the king's protection and given a pension.[17]

William of Cassingham's determined guerrilla campaign, and particularly the action outside Dover in April 1217, meant that Louis was diverted from his planned course. He could not go to Dover straight away, which in turn meant that Hubert de Burgh had plenty of warning that he could expect a renewal of the siege. Hubert had also, thanks to William Marshal's foresight, benefited from the additional stores sent from the surrendered

---

*In fighting for the current crowned king against an invader, William was technically on the right side of the law, but he could be considered an 'outlaw' against the prevailing rule because the south-east was under Louis's control, not John's.

royalist castles, so whenever the French assault came again, he would be ready.

DOVER, REVISITED

Hubert had actually been prepared for quite some time.

When the first phase of the siege had ended, following John's death and the declaration of Henry III as king, Hubert had been able to leave Dover briefly in order to meet with the other royalist leaders at Bristol in November 1216, and had been present when Magna Carta was re-issued in Henry's name. Meanwhile the Dover garrison emerged and 'burnt the houses and buildings which Louis had erected in front of the castle', following this up by 'ravaging the country' in order to secure 'a plentiful supply of necessaries for the garrison', and also to deny the French access to any supplies when they should return.[18] Neither the fact that this broke the local truce that had been arranged, nor that the inhabitants of the surrounding area (regardless of which side in the war they might support) were thereby deprived of nutrition just as the colder months were approaching, appears to have bothered Hubert or been worthy of note by contemporary chroniclers.

Hubert was back at Dover by Christmas, and there was plenty of time over the winter for the breach in the outer wooden barbican to be more properly mended and for other minor repair jobs around the castle to be undertaken (again, seemingly regardless of the agreement that 'everything was to remain till that time in the same state as it was on the day of the truce being sworn to, with respect both to castles and other possessions'). However, the stone gatehouse that had been destroyed by mining could not be rebuilt so quickly, especially at that time of year.* It is likely, therefore, that some temporary wooden fortifications were erected in order to strengthen whatever stonework was possible in the short term, and the garrison would be aware that this weak point in the castle's defences was likely to be the focus of future attacks.

Winter turned to spring and Dover castle remained unmolested, its garrison no doubt cheering when they heard of the travails of the French, at the hands of the men of the Weald, as they attempted to take ship for France. Hubert and his troops could breathe a little more easily once Louis had gone, as it was unlikely that the depleted rebel forces remaining in England during the French prince's absence would seek to besiege them, especially if they had decided that the truce was worth observing. But those at Dover would certainly have kept a good lookout and held the date of 23 April at the forefront of their minds; it would have come as little surprise, therefore, to see and hear on 22 April that the renewed and reinforced French fleet, led by Louis himself, was approaching their position.

It was at this point that William of Cassingham, Oliver Fitzroy and their combined forces prevented the French from landing and attacked the siege camp outside Dover castle. It is not quite clear from the conflicting sources whether this camp was the remains of anything still left standing after the garrison's own

---

*Thirteenth-century stonemasons tended to stop construction over the winter because of the difficulty of setting mortar in cold, wet conditions, instead spending their time cutting and shaping stones ready for use the following spring when the new construction season started. A tall structure such as a gatehouse could not, in any case, be built all at once, as the lower courses of stone needed time to set before the weight of the higher courses was piled on them.

sortie the previous autumn, or whether the French and rebels had in the meantime built new structures in preparation, or whether the various chroniclers had simply got their timelines mixed up and actually the burning of the camp only happened once. In any case Louis and his troops were prevented from landing at Dover, and the garrison would have been able to see his ships turning northwards to head for Sandwich instead.

Hubert and the Dover men stood ready for the next two weeks. During this time the French swept through the south-east of England once again, from Sandwich round to Winchester, regaining all their conquests of the previous year. The war now became even less chivalrous all round: Louis, who had been 'not at all pleased' to find that various castles had been attacked and taken in his absence, had the town of Sandwich burned to the ground in retaliation.[19] He then turned his attention to Winchester, while apparently sending an advance party back to Dover under either the count of Nevers or the latter's marshal.[*]

Dover was once again isolated, the only royalist stronghold in a swathe of land under enemy control, and the garrison could once again expect to be in fear of their lives if their castle should be taken by storm. They began with the same sort of belligerent tactic that had been effective the previous year: a sortie that resulted in bloodshed and the narrow escape from

---

[*]The count of Nevers was Hervé de Donzy, a man with a reputation for duplicity. He had fought for Philip Augustus against John in Normandy in 1204, but then for John against Philip at Bouvines in 1214. Somehow he had subsequently regained such royal favour that his daughter and sole heiress was at this time betrothed to Philip, Prince Louis's eldest son. Had young Philip not later died at the age of nine, Hervé might one day have found himself the father of the queen of France.

death of the count of Nevers's marshal.[20] But then it was time to retreat behind the high walls and await the main French force, in the expectation of another major siege.

It was not, however, the whole of the French and rebel army that arrived. Louis had been obliged to repeat his tactic of the previous year and divide his army: a small group to remain in London while half of the rest, commanded by the count of Perche, the earl of Winchester and Robert Fitzwalter, headed north to Mountsorrel and Lincoln. It was therefore a depleted force that arrived at Dover on 12 May under Louis's personal command. This was the good news; the bad news was that he had brought his mighty trebuchet with him, and this was erected in more or less the same position as it had been the previous year, in order to attack the weakened point of the castle's northern gatehouse. We are told by the Anonymous of Béthune that the machine did 'great damage', although he does not specify exactly what form this damage took. He also notes that the French 'began to put up houses everywhere as fast as they could', thus implying that they were preparing for another long siege, although it is not clear whether the 'houses' (maisons) were fortified positions of some kind or simply buildings for the long-term accommodation of troops.[21]

While the siege engineers were organising the bombardment, the more mobile troops of the French were able to range about the area, and they burned Hythe and Romney, attempts by William of Cassingham to stop them being, for once, ineffective.

Dover's walls were still standing, but Hubert's main concern was that the French besieging party would be reinforced. He was not able to keep up with developments elsewhere, having no means of getting messages in and out of the castle, but he could assume that the northern party that had headed for Mountsorrel and Lincoln would not be back any time soon. There was, though, an ever-present danger that the French would be reinforced by sea. Small parties of knights and common soldiers were beginning to make their way across the Channel, but fortunately for Hubert he had allies both at sea and in the fickle Channel weather, as we will see.

The situation was still under control on 25 May, when Hubert became aware of consternation in the besieging camp: he would not yet have known the details, but news had arrived of the engagement that had taken place five days previously at Lincoln, with such disastrous consequences for the French and rebels. Louis stayed at Dover for a few more days, waiting for reinforcements that never materialised, and then he discontinued the siege, disassembled and packed up his trebuchet, and rode for London, where he arrived on 1 June. The following day marked exactly a year since he had been proclaimed king of England amid such jubilation in the capital, but the resistance of Hubert de Burgh and others meant that he still could not definitively claim the title.

The second siege of Dover had lasted just two weeks. In hindsight it looks easy – and Hubert and his garrison could offer up their heartfelt thanks that the royalist party had been so successful at Lincoln – but, of course, they could have had no possible idea at the time that the battle was taking place. Their stubborn defence was therefore all the more valuable because they had been prepared to continue it for as long as was necessary, and, due to them, Dover remained a defiant stronghold in a prime position in what was otherwise French territory. The French still did not control the whole of the south-east and still did not have an entirely secure foothold, and this gave the royalists some hope.

The arrangement of yet another truce meant that Hubert de Burgh could once more emerge from Dover. The long, light days of June gave him ample opportunity to survey the damage to the local area and to send messengers to the other members of the royalist cause, but he was as aware as anyone that the war was still not over. Louis remained at large and held London, most of the knights and lords from his routed army could be ransomed, and – significantly – a fresh threat was gathering in France. Hubert looked across the Channel and knew that he needed to make preparations for a new and different phase of the war, because the French were about to be greatly reinforced.

THE INIMITABLE BLANCHE OF CASTILE

In the summer of 1217 Blanche of Castile was twenty-nine years old. She had been married to Louis for seventeen of those years and had ample experience of the French royal court and the way in which it functioned. She also had a great deal of influence. Women had to exercise authority in a different way to men, rarely being rulers in their own right and instead having to use what we might now call 'soft power', but Blanche had all the right qualifications. She was the daughter, sister and daughter-in-law of kings. She was the wife of the future king of France and, crucially, the mother of the king after that, having ensured the royal succession by means of her own body. She had given birth to six children, of whom three, all boys, were living. This was the primary duty of a queen consort, and it was of particular importance in France given the fertility problems that had afflicted the previous two generations of kings, and the attendant extreme concern over the future of the royal dynasty.[*]

The respect and the prestige that her position as wife and mother gave to Blanche should not be underestimated, and she was clever enough to use it for her own and her husband's purposes. They would both benefit if his campaign were to be successful: her status would be raised even further if she were to be queen of England long before she could expect to be queen of France, and with her husband deriving his right to the throne from her. This outcome might also, in due course, provide the opportunity for two of her sons to become reigning kings.

When Louis returned to France in February 1217, in search of help for his cause, he had no luck in persuading Philip Augustus to support him by providing either troops or finances. He had no choice but to accept this and return to England, but Blanche was able to plead his cause further after he had departed. In this, she could use her position as a royal female to great effect: intercession was one of the specific

---

[*]Louis VII had been in his mid-forties, on his third marriage, the father of four daughters and despairing of a male heir before Philip Augustus belatedly came along. Philip's own first marriage produced only Louis and a pair of male twins who died shortly after birth; his second no offspring at all; and his third, bigamous, union a daughter and a son who were widely considered to be illegitimate. Blanche's fecundity (she would go on to give birth to ten sons in total, as well as two daughters) therefore calmed many nerves in Paris and put her in a strong position politically.

duties of a queen, so nobody could think it unusual for her to try. Moreover, according to both religious and secular conventions it was understood that Blanche owed loyalty to her husband above all others, so the king could not blame her or be offended by her pleading on Louis's behalf. She thus got much more of a hearing than anyone else would have done on the same subject, and she pressed her advantage as hard as she could.

Blanche was successful. The precise details of how and why she managed to persuade Philip Augustus to hand over some of the contents of his treasury are not clear, but contemporaries agree on the fact that she did, and that this happened to a greater or lesser extent against his will. Most of the French chroniclers are reticent: the Anonymous of Béthune notes briefly that Blanche 'gather[ed] all the men and knights she could get to send to help her lord'; Philip Mousket does not mention her by name, but does make a passing reference to the contribution of 'his [Louis's] wife', and William the Breton does not allude to Blanche at all, simply saying that Philip refused to speak to Louis.[22] Over in England, however, the observers were much more specific:

As the king was afraid to give assistance to his excommunicated son, as he had been often severely rebuked by the pope for granting his consent, he laid the burden of the business on the wife of Louis, who was not slow in fulfilling the duty imposed on her.

*

I can tell you for a fact that his [Louis's] wife rode through all the towns in France to seek assistance in the form of great contingents of men and coffers of money. She went about her task with such energy that she gathered together such a force that, had they arrived in London fully armed, they would have conquered the entire kingdom.[23]

That these chroniclers, who rarely mention women in such contexts, agree among themselves that Blanche was the driving force behind the raising of revenue and reinforcements is a significant indicator that her actions were well known at the time.

The fullest (and, it has to be said, most entertaining) version of the crucial episode is that given by the anonymous thirteenth-century chronicler known only as the Minstrel of Reims, who invents a whole scene of dialogue in order to explain how Blanche persuaded Philip to part with his cash:

He [Louis] sent word to his father to please, for God's sake, help him and send money. The king answered that, by the spear of Saint James, he would certainly not: he would not risk excommunication for him. When my lady Blanche learned of this, she came to the king, her father-in-law, and said, 'Will you thus allow your son to die in a foreign land? Sire, by God! He is to reign after you! Send him what he needs – at least the income on his inheritance!'

'No indeed, Blanche,' said the king; 'I will not do so!'

'No, sire?'

'Truly not,' answered the king.

'In God's name,' said my lady Blanche, 'I know what I have to do!'

'And what is that?' asked the king.

'By the blessed mother of God, I have fine children by my lord; I'll offer them for security! I'll find someone to lend me money for them!'

With that, she ran from the king like a madwoman. Seeing her leave like that, he thought she was serious, so he had her called back and he said, 'Blanche, I shall give you from my treasure whatever funds you want; do with them as you like and whatever you think right – but know this: I will not send him any aid!'

'Sire,' said my lady Blanche, 'thank you very much!'

And then a great treasure was delivered to my lady Blanche, and she sent it to her husband.[24]

Amusing as it might be to think of Blanche threatening to pawn her sons – the king's precious heirs and the future of his dynasty – in order to make money, this depiction makes an important point about how she enjoyed increased influence as the mother of three male heirs. It also emphasises that Philip gave the money to Blanche, not to Louis, thus maintaining a kind of 'plausible deniability' if the pope should enquire about the uses to which his treasure would be put.

Once Blanche had the money, she was at no loss as to how to act. Perhaps realising that mere correspondence would not be enough, she eschewed letter-writing and instead travelled in person throughout northern France in order to persuade, cajole or harangue the lords into making their contributions.

She spent much of the late spring and early summer in the saddle, and her focus on this part of the realm was no accident: Louis was count of Artois in his own right (an inheritance from his long-dead mother and not part of the royal patrimony), so he had personal revenues and allegiances there that were not dependent on Philip Augustus.

This very active part played by Blanche should not surprise us. Despite not featuring very heavily in this context in contemporary accounts, royal and noble women were often involved in military affairs. The most common of these was the sort of defensive situation in which Nicola de la Haye had found herself: wives or widows were left in charge of castles and estates when their husbands had died or were otherwise absent (which might be for months or years if he had gone on crusade). They managed their stores, commanded their garrisons, undertook negotiations, and might even play a more practical role in fending off the attackers.* Military planning, strategy and logistics were also undertaken by women, who would utilise their wealth and property and their organisational skills to support all kinds of campaigns. In all of these roles, women were routinely expected to be knowledgeable, active and capable: in contemporary texts it is taken as read not only that they *could* do all of these things, but also that they *should*, when the need arose.

---

*It was only a year after the events depicted here, in 1218, that the Albigensian Crusade leader Simon de Montfort the elder was killed while besieging Toulouse, struck on the head by a stone launched from a catapult mounted on the walls. An eye-witness noted, without exhibiting any particular shock or surprise, that the machine was being operated by women and girls of the city.

A medieval treatise intended to offer instruction to ladies is clear about how they should act if their husbands were away for any reason:

> His lady and companion stays behind, and she must take his place. Although there may be enough bailiffs, provosts, administrators and governors, there has to be someone in charge of them all, and therefore it is proper that she should take on this responsibility. She should conduct herself with such skill that she may be feared as well as loved [...] Her men should be able to rely on her for all kinds of protection in the absence of their lord, in a situation where anyone would offer to do them harm.

The same text then offers some specific military instruction that might surprise modern readers, but which was seen as perfectly normal at the time:

> She ought to have the heart of a man, that is, she ought to know how to use weapons and be familiar with everything that pertains to them, so that she may be ready to command her men if the need arises. She should know how to launch an attack or to defend against one, if the situation calls for it. She should take care that her fortresses are well garrisoned [...] She should consider what manpower she has and can call upon with confidence if the situation warrants it [...] She should devote some thought to how she will be able to provide for the household until her husband comes back, and what financial resources she has and can find in order

to do this [...] The lady should speak authoritatively and consistently to her people.[25]

This second quote includes the key words 'until her husband comes back', which offers us a strong further hint about appropriate female behaviour in such circumstances: married noblewomen were expected to be proficient in military matters, but they were also expected to act within strictly defined parameters – that is, to act only in support of a male relative and not in their own names. There are numerous instances of medieval women being either praised or vilified on exactly this basis, the most egregious example of double standards being the criticism heaped on Empress Matilda, King John's paternal grandmother, for raising troops and riding with them in support of her own claim to the English throne, while her counterpart Queen Matilda (King Stephen's wife) was praised for doing exactly the same thing at exactly the same time, but on behalf of her imprisoned husband.[26]

In the present instance, Blanche behaved precisely according to contemporary conventions. She acted in the manner expected of a royal female when she interceded with the king on behalf of her husband; she made it clear that she was working in support of her husband (and, by extension, her sons and their future careers); and she demonstrated considerable skill in carrying out complex military-related tasks. The successful prosecution of a war was not just about combat. Combatants could not fight unless they were in the right place at the right time, adequately fed and supplied, and accompanied by their armour, weapons, horses and necessary attendants.[27] As well as raising troops, therefore, Blanche also organised provisions for them and their horses, and money to pay them while they were away. Then there was the question of transport, which in this particular campaign meant assembling a fleet and the crew to sail it; she requisitioned some ships and ordered others to be built.

It was not part of Blanche's remit to lead the army overseas herself. The final way in which she conformed to gendered expectations, therefore, was that once all the preparations were complete she handed over command of the troops she had raised to a man. He was one of France's highest-ranking nobles, Robert de Courtenay, who, although neither particularly rich nor the holder of very extensive lands, was of royal blood, being Philip Augustus's first cousin and a grandson of Louis VI in the male line. He was also, as it happened, Henry III's great-uncle: in another example of how closely the two sides in this war were intertwined, he was the maternal uncle of Isabella of Angoulême, Henry's mother. Robert was at this point in his late forties, and he had a great deal of military and political experience: he had fought loyally for his cousin in Normandy in 1204, had been with Philip at the pivotal siege of Château Gaillard that led to the conquest of the duchy, and had also taken part in the Albigensian Crusade that had started in 1209 and was still ongoing.[*] He would lead the main group of Louis's reinforcements when it was ready to embark, taking it across

---

[*]The Albigensian Crusade was a campaign initiated by the Church under Pope Innocent III, and principally prosecuted by the French crown, against a heretical sect in southern France whose members were known as Cathars.

the Channel and then uniting it with the French and rebel forces already in London.

Blanche's initial tactic, in the spring of 1217, was to send troops over in small parties as soon as they were ready. Her thinking was perhaps that a constant, if modest, supply might be most useful to Louis, rather than making him wait for the main force, but this proved to be one of her few mistakes. The Channel and its unpredictable weather patterns aided the English royalist cause, and the French now also found themselves up against a talented naval commander, whose contribution to the war effort was about to become invaluable.

VIOLENCE AT SEA

'The English guarded the sea, controlling it with their galleys,' says the French chronicler Philip Mousket of this stage of the war.[28] It is noticeable that by this point in his narrative he has given up on any distinction between royalists and rebels, and simply calls the parties 'the English' and 'the French'; this was becoming a struggle between kingdoms and nations rather than a civil war in which one side was aided by foreign allies.

The English were commanded at sea by a knight called Philip d'Albini,* a long-time loyal servant of John who had fought on the English king's side in Normandy back in 1204 and who had later been appointed keeper of the Channel Islands. He had remained loyal to John throughout John's

---

*Philip's surname can be spelled d'Albini, d'Aubigny or (less frequently) Daubeney; I retain d'Albini to avoid any confusion with William d'Aubigny, the earl of Arundel, who was unrelated. Philip was related to the William d'Albini whom we met defending Rochester in Chapter 1, although the exact nature of the relationship is not clear.

travails, and was one of the barons listed in Magna Carta as supporting the beleaguered king. He had been put in charge of the royalist forces in Kent and Sussex – that is, at the sharp end of the defence against invasion – and had naturally transferred his allegiance to Henry III after John's death.[29] Due to the geographical location of his duties, on the south-east coast and in the Channel Islands, he needed to be at sea a great deal, and he soon gained a deserved reputation as a capable naval commander.

Philip's fleet had been patrolling the Channel for some months, and in February 1217 he had successfully blockaded Rye, preventing Louis from taking ship there for his temporary return to France. Instead Louis had been forced to head to Winchelsea and endure the depredations caused by William of Cassingham and the men of the Weald before he was picked up by Eustace the Monk.

Just after Louis arrived to besiege Dover for the second time, on 12 May 1217, an initial fleet of forty ships was sent from France by Blanche, who was no doubt keen to show the fruits of her labours by getting a first party of reinforcements to her husband ahead of the rest. The Anonymous of Béthune, once again our most detailed source for events in the south-east, gives specific details of what followed. 'The sea was rough and the wind high,' he says, 'and it drove all of them together back to Calais, except for five, which together forced their way ashore.' It was another two days before the remaining thirty-five ships could make another attempt, but by that time Philip d'Albini had been alerted and had approached with his own fleet:

On the following Monday the vessels which had gone to Calais returned and came sailing to Dover. Just as they were approaching, Philip [...] arrived from Romney with at least four score ships, large and small, and went towards them. They had a good 20 large ships fortified and ready for battle. Louis' men, who had little ships, did not dare wait for them but fled back towards Calais. But there were 27 which were already so far ahead that they could not turn back but were compelled to force their way on and take the risk. Eight of the 27 were captured and 19 escaped in great alarm. The seamen and sergeants captured in the eight ships were all immediately killed and the knights were thrown captive into the bilges, where they suffered very much. The English then dropped anchor in front of the castle and stayed calmly there, guarding the town so that no provisions or help could reach Louis by sea.[30]

It is noticeable that the Anonymous, too, now refers to the royalists simply as 'the English', as they defend their land from these new foes. War at sea was governed by fewer conventions than on land, and no mercy was shown either to the common soldiers or even to the sailors, who might feasibly have been classed as non-combatants, merely transporting the fighting men. There was no concept of an international brotherhood of the sea, nothing that caused sailors to feel obliged to rescue their counterparts from drowning. This lack of mercy and compassion was of a piece with the greater ferocity being shown in the war since its renewal, and it set the pattern for the naval combat that would follow.

No small fleet would stand a chance of getting through to Louis, but a second one was dispatched only a couple of weeks later. It embarked shortly after the battle of Lincoln, but this was coincidental rather than a direct result of the engagement, news of which could not possibly have reached Blanche in France before she sent the ships off. This fleet neared Dover a couple of days after Louis had heard of the defeat – here, he hoped, were the reinforcements he so needed in order to make up for all the knights who had been captured at Lincoln. However, this small group of ships was easy pickings for Philip d'Albini. Visibility was good that morning, as the Anonymous of Béthune is careful to tell us, and the English fleet could see the approaching French vessels from afar. They made sail themselves and attacked, capturing eight ships and scattering the rest. A paltry eighteen knights and a few sergeants were all that made it through to Louis, at which point he left Dover for London.[31]

These royalist successes, coming hard on the heels of the victory at Lincoln, meant that more and more erstwhile rebels (including, in a coup for William Marshal, the powerful earls Warenne and Arundel) began to defect back from Louis to Henry. Other than a few die-hard rebels, the enemy force was now nearly all French, which meant that there was even greater scope for Marshal and the other royalist leaders to position themselves as the English defending their homeland against an invasion by French foreigners.

Some attempts at negotiations were made during the summer, but no agreement could be reached. The royalists might look as though they now held the upper hand, and indeed the tide was turning in their favour; but all were aware that Blanche's indefatigable efforts had raised a very large new force, and that it would soon be on its way. Philip Augustus might not exactly have sanctioned it, but nobody was under any illusion that he would prevent it from setting sail.

In the absence of any order to the contrary from the French king, of any peace agreement in England or even the declaration of a further truce, Blanche of Castile and Robert de Courtenay made ready their main fleet, one so large that it stood a much better chance of getting past Philip d'Albini's blockade than anything that had gone before. Robert took ship and Blanche waved him off on 20 August, the fleet to be commanded at sea by the experienced captain and infamous monk-turned-pirate Eustace the Monk, who had already been of great service to Louis in his earlier endeavours.

This fresh army was certainly big enough to turn the tide of the war; if it reached Louis, it would swing the pendulum back his way again. The engagements at Lincoln and Dover, and the gritty resistance efforts of the men of the Weald and the garrisons of many other castles, had been steps in the right direction, but all of those gains were now in danger of being lost. It was therefore imperative that the newly raised French army should be stopped before it could reach Louis, and that the two halves of his forces should not be allowed to combine.

The determined and 'unchivalrous' efforts of William Marshal, Hubert de Burgh, William of Cassingham and others had kept the royalist hopes breathing long enough for the war still to be a live cause – just. The resistance fighters now had to step back in favour of the knights, for battle was inevitable once more; however, this time it was to take place neither on an open field nor in cramped city streets, but on the heaving, bucking decks of ships at sea.

Sandwich, August 1217

THE DEVELOPMENT OF THE ENGLISH NAVY

Since the Conquest of 1066 the Anglo-Norman kings of England had been in constant need of ships. With such an expanse of territory to control, divided by the Channel, they could not afford to be long absent from either kingdom or duchy, and were therefore obliged to make frequent crossings in order to maintain their authority on both sides. They could achieve this either by retaining ships and crews of their own, or by hiring or commandeering them where necessary, but in either case their need for vessels was primarily for transport across relatively peaceful waters with friendly ports on both sides for embarking and landing.

All of this changed in 1204 with King John's loss of Normandy to Philip Augustus. The Channel was no longer a sort of internal waterway between territories under his control, but rather the border with an increasingly hostile France. Ships were therefore needed for different purposes: keeping merchant traffic safe on the much longer and more dangerous journey between England and John's remaining French lands in Aquitaine, and guarding England itself against the possibility of invasion. This incentivised John to take a much greater interest in naval affairs, and to ensure that there were a sufficient number of ships under permanent crown control.* Over the next few years various steps were taken: by 1206 there was an official position called 'keeper of the king's ships'; by 1208 John had reserved the right to seize privately owned ships for his own use, should the situation require it; and between 1209 and 1212 twenty new galleys and thirty-four other ships were constructed. All would need to be kept in good repair, and supplied and crewed when necessary.[1]

By 1212 a nascent navy was in fairly good shape, with the crown commanding a fleet of its own and also being able to call on the ships and men of the Cinque Ports (Hastings, Dover, Hythe, Romney and Sandwich), who had owed naval service in lieu of military service on land since the time of William the Conqueror. This service only totalled the use of fifty-seven ships for fifteen days each year, which implies that it was mainly intended for transport purposes, or for defensive patrolling, rather than embarking on long foreign campaigns, but it was sufficient for that purpose.

The different styles of ship being built and used during these first years of the thirteenth century are sometimes difficult to discern, mainly because contemporary chroniclers were no more familiar with naval terms than they were with types of siege machinery. Nevertheless, we can certainly

---

*A case could be made that this was actually shutting the stable door after the horse had bolted – arguably, if John had been in possession of an effective navy earlier, he might have been able to stave off the defeat in Normandy by means of coastal raids and the threat to ports. But that is another story ...

distinguish some broad categories. The *galley* – the type of ship named most often – was a sleek, shallow vessel, single-masted, which used oars as well as a square sail. A galley was relatively expensive to run, as it needed around seventy paid oarsmen (or double that for 'great galleys', very large models that had two rows of oars) as well as a sailing crew, but it was manoeuvrable and could be used in situations where the wind was unfavourable and sail was not possible.* It could carry cargo, but because of the large crew the available space for goods was constrained, so it was more likely to transport people, either passengers or troops. A smaller vessel that was similar to a galley in being streamlined and propelled by oars was the *esnecca* (the name derives from the Old Norse word for 'snake'); these appear to have been valued for their swiftness and agility and might be used at the periphery of a fleet, escorting the larger ships, or perhaps for carrying messages when speed was of the essence.

A *cog*, sometimes also referred to as a *nef* (although *nef* is simply the generic Old French word for 'ship', which is not very helpful) was also single-masted but was a shorter, rounder vessel that sat higher in the water than a galley and which was often used for transporting cargo as well as troops. Tall wooden 'castles' might be added to it both fore and aft, making it more defensible, in that its sides were so high that it would be difficult to board, and the cog's own archers would be able

---

*It is sometimes thought (perhaps based on half-remembered old films about the Roman empire) that a galley's oarsmen were slaves or prisoners, but this was not the case in the thirteenth century: the rowers were paid wages and enjoyed the same rights as other members of the crew.

to shoot downwards (a distinct advantage) at any assailants. A similar large, round ship was the *buss*, though these appear to have been used more for cargo than for fighting men.[2]

Despite their different appearances and uses, all of these types of ship had two things in common. The first was that their fighting strength was based on the men within them (whether crew or troops), and not on the ships themselves. This was a period well before the use of gunpowder weapons in western Europe, so the options for any sort of combat were basically hand-held missile weapons (bows or crossbows) as two ships neared each other, followed by closing for hand-to-hand fighting. Exact numbers would vary, of course, but as a rule of thumb a ship's contingent of fighting men would be around two-thirds archers and/or crossbowmen, and one-third other foot soldiers armed with spears, swords and various sidearms. A separate group of ship's crew had as their primary employment the sailing and control of the vessel, but they might also engage in combat if the situation warranted it, using whatever weapons came to hand, such as knives, cudgels or boarding axes. Occasionally some galleys would be fitted with iron prows so that they could ram an opponent, but in general the aim would be to capture the valuable opposing ship rather than to sink it, so the offensive would be directed at the personnel rather than the vessel itself.

The second common factor was that all these ships required great skill and experience to sail and navigate. The compass, as we know it now, was not yet in use in Europe (though magnetised pins floating in water were not unknown), and navigation was based on the sun and stars, with occasional use of an astrolabe if one was available.* This required good visibility, which meant that it was difficult to sail when it was cloudy, or at all during the winter months. Latitude could be determined, but longitude could not, and reliable maps and charts were few and far between, so the most valuable asset to a ship's captain was a first-hand personal knowledge of the waters to be sailed, and their attendant dangers. It was for these navigational reasons that many sea journeys were made while remaining close to the shore so that landmarks could be sighted, which in turn meant that most naval engagements took place near a port or coast rather than on the open sea.

By 1213 King John was aware that Philip Augustus was planning a full-scale invasion of England. This meant that his naval needs were even greater, so early in that year he 'ordered a list to be made of all the ships in each of the ports of England [...] found capable of carrying six horses or more' and commanded them to muster at Portsmouth 'well-equipped with stores, tried seamen, and good soldiers, to enter into our service'.[3] As we have just noted, it was the men rather than the ships themselves that provided the fighting capacity, so requisitioned merchant ships, possibly with a few minor adaptions, would be just as useful as anything purpose-built as long as they could be packed with combatants.

As it transpired, John's assembled fleet was put to a different purpose. Philip lost the pope's support for his planned campaign and never launched the invasion; and in May 1213

---

*An astrolabe was a kind of hand-held instrument used to calculate astronomical positions. They were very complex devices, which made them both rare and expensive.

the English ships, under the command of John's half-brother William Longespee, the earl of Salisbury, raided Damme in Flanders where the unused French fleet was at anchor. The French troops were at that point inland, leaving only skeleton crews on the ships, and the English army was able to attack and loot at will, capturing many vessels and setting fire to others they could not take away. Such was the destruction that one contemporary says that the burning ships were 'belching forth smoke as if the very sea were on fire'.[4] This was the first real use of offensive naval warfare during John's reign, and it was effective in that the French lost much of their fleet and were unable to continue with any plans for invading England at that time. However, the engagement was not decisive: Philip's losses were not total and he was soon able to rebuild, as was his son. By May 1216 Louis had enough of a fleet to cross the Channel and land unopposed.

As we have seen, English ships under the command of Philip d'Albini enjoyed some success during 1217, and were able to head off the smaller parties of reinforcements sent over by Blanche of Castile in the spring and the early part of the summer. But the main contingent would soon be on the way, and it would be under the command of a man who knew the waters of the Channel very well indeed.

EUSTACE THE MONK AND HIS FLEET

The French fleet was to be led by one of the most notorious figures of the thirteenth century, the sailor, admiral, outlaw and pirate known as Eustace the Monk. His was a name well known in the south-east of England at this time, and one that struck fear into the hearts of every man, woman and child living near the coast.

Eustace was the son of a minor lord in the Boulogne region of Flanders, and had probably been born around 1170. He began his life by training to be a knight before inexplicably deciding to become a Benedictine monk, a vocation for which he was deeply unsuited (he had a reputation for misbehaviour and his abbot apparently called him 'a demon') and one which did not last long. His clerical career was, nevertheless, of sufficient duration to give him the epithet by which he was known both at the time and subsequently, and which is used in the title of a thirteenth-century text written about his life, the *Romance of Eustace the Monk*.*[5] After leaving (or possibly being expelled from) his abbey, Eustace travelled widely for some time before returning to his native land, where he established a bitter lifelong enmity with Renaud de Dammartin, the count of Boulogne, and became an outlaw.

This might all sound like jolly tales of derring-do, but there was a much darker undercurrent, and Eustace was capable of vicious cruelty, especially in his dealings with anybody connected to the count. At one point, his life story tells us, he came across a young serving-boy of Renaud's, whereupon he 'knocked him to the ground, cut out his tongue and sent him [back] to the count'. Eustace later forced another youth to hang himself – without the opportunity to confess his sins

---

*In this context 'romance' merely means a text written in the vernacular Old French (rather than in Latin, like a historical chronicle); it does not contain any overtones of the modern usage of 'romantic'.

first, which would have made the deed all the more heinous at the time – and then set out on a particularly bloodthirsty mission, aiming to find some or any of Renaud's men with the specific intention of mutilating them. When he captured five of the count's men-at-arms he cut off the feet of four of them, leaving the fifth to take a gruesome message back to Renaud.[6]

Eustace was an experienced sailor, and at some point around the year 1200 he left his criminal career on land to begin one at sea, where he continued his reign of violence. He and his band seized the island of Sark, which he then used as a base for his piratical activities; this made him a longstanding foe of Philip d'Albini after the latter was appointed as keeper of the Channel Islands.

In the first years of the thirteenth century Count Renaud of Boulogne was an adherent of Philip Augustus, so Eustace was not averse to taking service with King John, an opportunity offered to him around 1205 or 1206. With John's support and approbation, Eustace made frequent raids on the coast of Normandy (which was by then under French control), as well as attacking shipping in the Channel. However, he seems to have had very few scruples about sticking to his orders or remembering which side he was supposed to be on, and he made violent assaults on towns on the English coast as well – something to which John appears to have turned a blind eye, such was Eustace's value to him. Eustace was feared and loathed throughout south-east England, where the people felt that nobody would protect them from his ravaging. So hated was he that he needed a royal safe-conduct whenever he was obliged to land in England (to see the king in person, for example, or to receive orders), to prevent him from being attacked by irate locals.

In 1212 Count Renaud defected from Philip Augustus to John.[*] This prompted Eustace to make the opposite move and offer his services to the French monarchy, something Philip welcomed – Eustace had a detailed knowledge of the Channel and of John's military and naval organisation, both of which would be of great use to the French king. This new allegiance, of course, gave Eustace even greater licence to attack English shipping and raid English ports, and he became even more hated and feared, a bogeyman in the popular imagination. Parents told their children that Eustace would come to get them if they did not behave. By 1214 Eustace's activities had become so insufferable that Philip d'Albini was dispatched against him, leading a campaign to Sark, but this proved only semi-successful: some prisoners were taken, including one of Eustace's brothers, but Eustace himself remained at large. In 1215 he launched what appears to have been a violent raid on Folkestone that caused King John to express 'anger and indignation' against him in an official document.[7]

When Louis was planning his campaign in the spring of 1216 there was only one real candidate to command the fleet at sea, and Eustace duly saw the French prince safely landed in England. He was on hand several times during the year that followed, most notably getting through the sea blockade in

---

[*]This turned out to be a spectacularly bad move on Renaud's part. He was captured at the battle of Bouvines (along with his co-conspirator, Count Ferrand of Flanders) and then imprisoned by Philip Augustus in harsh conditions, chained to a heavy log and unable to walk more than a couple of steps in any direction. Ferrand was finally released in 1227, thirteen years after the battle, but Renaud was not, leading him to give up all hope and commit suicide later that year.

February 1217 to pick Louis up from Winchelsea in order to make his temporary return to France.

Eustace was the most dangerous man on either side during the war, for the simple reason that he had no fixed allegiance and, from what we can gather, very little conscience. Everyone else had some kind of cause they were fighting for, even if they were sometimes misguided or unsure about exactly what that cause stood for; but he was simply out for what he could get, and did not care how much blood was shed on the way. Even the sober Barnwell annalist was moved to comment on Eustace's lack of loyalty, noting that 'moving from one side to the other as fortune dictated, [he] had greatly disturbed the sea and the shores on both sides'. Other commentators were less restrained, calling Eustace 'a most disgraceful man and a wicked pirate' or noting that he was 'a man who never lost a chance to do whatever harm was in his power [...] never was a more scheming man to be found than this'.[8]

It was Eustace, naturally, who commanded the fleet sent by Blanche to Louis in August 1217. Robert de Courtenay, as we have already noted, was to be in charge of the reinforcing army, but he was no sailor and therefore simply took his place on Eustace's flagship while they were at sea, ready to take over once the troops were again on dry land. The fleet comprised around seventy or eighty ships, of which ten were large vessels carrying combatants and the rest smaller boats transporting supplies. The actual numbers of men are the subject of some debate, but we can settle on somewhere in the region of 300 cavalry (a mixture of knights and mounted sergeants, plus of course the horses themselves), and some 1,000 others, the majority of them foot soldiers and the rest a few crossbowmen plus various attendants and servants.[9]

Eustace was on his flagship, known as 'the great ship of Bayonne', along with Robert de Courtenay, much coin and treasure, and the heavy pieces of a disassembled trebuchet to add to the one Louis already had. Unfortunately for Eustace, he also carried a large number of other high-ranking men who all wanted to have the prestige of being conveyed in the flagship, along with their retinues and horses. The result was a ship so overloaded that it was more difficult than usual to manoeuvre, one which 'could only sit so deep down in the waves that the water almost washed over it'.[10] Eustace had little choice but to go along with the wishes of the nobles, however, so it was in this heavily laden vessel that he set sail for England on 20 August 1217, with the other ships following him across the Channel.

THE ROYALISTS PREPARE

William Marshal and the other royalists knew of the preparations at Calais. The regent had been at Oxford during the second week in August, but he then travelled to the coast, reaching Romney on the 19th. There he summoned representatives of the Cinque Ports, and – in another example of how he was now pragmatically denouncing and reversing the actions of a king whom he had supported in life – he pledged to restore the rights they had lost under John's rule. As an added incentive he also promised them a large share of the spoils to be gained if they were victorious in battle. All of this helped to persuade them, and they assembled their ships at Sandwich and began to make ready:

The Marshal, full of wisdom as he was, spoke with them at such length, gave them so much, and promised them so much in the way of privileges and great wealth that they gladly and willingly steeled themselves to go and face the French [...] Quickly they made straight for Sandwich, and with no reluctance at all. They attended to the preparation of their ships, made ready their ropes, made seaworthy every one of their bowlines, guide-ropes and guys, their sturdy anchors and strong cables.[11]

Marshal also summoned all other loyal men to muster at Sandwich.* It would take some time for everyone to travel and assemble, however, and had the royalists been obliged to fight on 20 August, when the fleet of reinforcements was first sighted, the outcome might have been entirely different. But they now had a stroke of luck (or, as they preferred to think of it, a sign of God's favour): a storm blew up in the Channel and the French ships were forced to return to Calais before they got anywhere near English shores. It was the night of 23–24 August before they could think about sailing again, and the additional three days made all the difference. By the time Eustace and his fleet came into sight again, on the bright clear morning of 24 August, the royalists were fully assembled and ready.

Virtually all of the major royalist players, both secular and clerical, were present: King Henry; the legate Guala; the regent; the bishops of Winchester, Salisbury and Bath; the earls Warenne,

---

*Due to gradual silting over the centuries, Sandwich is now several miles from the coast, but in 1217 it was a sea port.

Salisbury, Hertford and Albemarle; Hubert de Burgh, who had sailed around from Dover; Philip d'Albini, who had already been patrolling the Channel for some time; John Marshal, the regent's nephew; and Richard of Chilham, who was both King John's illegitimate son and Earl Warenne's nephew.[*] Others had contributed ships, knights and men without arriving in person. The fleet comprised thirty-eight vessels in total, of which eighteen were large and twenty of a smaller size. Three of the large ships are singled out for specific mention by our sources: that on which Hubert de Burgh sailed, seemingly a galley; a huge cog belonging to William Marshal, which stood high out of the water and had fore and aft castles; and the ship owned and fitted out by Earl Warenne.

Who would set out on these ships in order to join battle, and who would stay on shore, was the next question. The young king and all the clergymen, as non-combatants, would be of the latter party, but the participation of the others was up for discussion.[†] As we noted earlier, the nature of the forthcoming combat was going to be very different from anything that most lords or knights had experienced before, and the potential combatants now divided themselves into two groups, with the higher nobility – the regent and the

---

[*] Richard was, and was publicly known to be, the child of King John and of Ela de Warenne, one of the earl's sisters, though we do not know how willing a participant the lady had been in the liaison. As John and Ela were cousins (their fathers had been half-brothers), this made Richard John's first cousin once removed as well as his son.

[†] Having said that, we do not know the exact thoughts on this matter of the bellicose bishop of Winchester, who had fought at Lincoln and who might have been inclined to do so again here if given half a chance.

earls — remaining on land. In William Marshal's case this decision was perhaps obvious, due both to his advanced age and to the fact that he was too important a figure in the king's administration to risk, but the reasoning behind some of the other absences is more difficult to fathom. It seems odd, for example, that the earl of Salisbury, who had previous naval experience from his raid on Damme four years earlier, should not take ship; and also that Earl Warenne should not board the expensive vessel he had provided and equipped. Neither of these men was particularly elderly, so this cannot have been an excuse.* The party that would go to sea was made up of the younger nobility such as Richard of Chilham (who would lead the troops on his uncle Warenne's ship), plus experienced naval veterans like Philip d'Albini. The whole would be led by Hubert de Burgh, named commander of the fleet due to his senior position as England's justiciar.

In planning for the battle, great emphasis was laid on the fact that all the enemy were French: as far as the royalists were concerned, this was an English defence of their realm against invasion by a foreign enemy, not (or no longer) a civil war of internal factions. The biographer of William Marshal writes of 'the arrogance of the French' and has his hero give a pre-battle oration which includes the words 'God gave you

---

*Dates of birth were often not precisely recorded, as we have noted previously, so it is not surprising that we do not know the year of Earl Warenne's birth. But, rather unusually for a man of such high rank, in his case we cannot even be sure of which decade he was born in; the most likely estimate is the late 1160s or early 1170s, which would put him somewhere between his mid-forties and mid-fifties at this time. William Longespee was around fifty years of age and thus of a similar vintage.

the first victory over the French on land. Now they return to England to claim the land as theirs, against God's will.' This growing sense of nationalism was also felt by the chronicler Matthew Paris, who included in the manuscript of his *Chronica Majora* an illustration of the battle which he drew himself: it depicts the bishops who remained on shore saying 'I absolve those who are about to die for the liberation of England'.*[12] If we were being cynical, we might also choose to note that the promise of great gains from plunder was surely also a very good incentive, but this was unsurprisingly not at the forefront of the chroniclers' minds as they sought to provide a narrative of heroism and national pride.

The key objective of the English fleet (as we will now call it, rather than continuing to use 'royalist') was to stop the French from landing at all. William Marshal 'knew beyond any doubt that, if the French fleet out there was able to put to shore, then the game would have disastrous results and England would be lost'.[13] If the reinforcements reached Louis in London, the war would be prolonged and the danger of having a Capetian on the English throne in perpetuity would be increased.

The English fleet sailed out from Sandwich on the morning of 24 August, two years to the day since Pope Innocent III had issued the denunciation of Magna Carta that proved to be one of the catalysts for the war. It was St Bartholomew's day, so prayers were said to him as the fleet sailed out to engage the French at sea.

---

*See Plate 26.

SOURCES FOR THE BATTLE

The major sources for the battle of Sandwich, as it would
become known, are those we have already met: the *History of
William Marshal*, which devotes the longest passage to it, along
with Roger of Wendover, the Anonymous of Béthune and the
French royal chaplain William the Breton. The engagement is
also covered briefly by various other monastic chroniclers,
including Ralph of Coggeshall and the Barnwell annalist;
the *Romance of Eustace the Monk* mentions it, but focuses on its
protagonist and his actions rather than giving an overview of
the battle as a whole.

Interestingly, the slightly later thirteenth-century writer
Matthew Paris gives two differing accounts of the engagement.
He starts with a narrative that is predominantly based on
that of Roger of Wendover, but he then adds a whole new
section that focuses on (and is very laudatory of) Hubert de
Burgh. These two men were actually known to each other in
later life, in the decades following the battle, which raises
the intriguing possibility that they might have sat down to
talk about it and that Matthew therefore had access to inside
information not available to the more strictly contemporary
writers. The nature of his content also suggests that if this
chat did happen, Hubert amplified his own role in the
engagement as the years went by:* according to this account
it was he, not William Marshal, who persuaded the men of

---

*There are also indications of this elsewhere in Matthew Paris's text: as we saw in Chapter 3, it
was in his account alone that Hubert gave such a heroic oration when he refused to surrender
Dover castle after King John's death.

the Cinque Ports to fight, while Marshal and the bishop of Winchester both backed away from the action by saying that they were 'not sailors or pirates' and that de Burgh would need to find someone else to help him. This second account of Matthew Paris's ends by declaring Hubert the 'miraculous victor' of the day.[14]

These chroniclers, although keen to record whatever information they could get hold of, were by no means experts in naval matters, which means that some of their details are confused or obscure. Their accounts were analysed in the nineteenth century by naval experts who knew more of the sea, but who were conversely less knowledgeable about the political situation in the thirteenth century (one of them, for example, gives the regent's name as 'Richard' Marshal). These commentators were, however – not surprisingly given the era in which they lived – more than a little jingoistic about an English naval battle against a French foe, and their analyses have in turn been re-examined by subsequent historians.

Reading all of these sources in conjunction with each other means that we can build up a fairly clear picture of what happened off Sandwich on 24 August 1217.[15]

INITIAL MANOEUVRES

At first it looked like the two sides might not actually engage at all.

The French initially headed for Dover, but when they neared the English coast they turned and made their way northwards, parallel with the shore. Their aim was to round the Isle of Thanet, enter the mouth of the Thames and sail directly to London. In the circumstances this was the best option available: why attempt to land on the hostile south-east coast and start a long march, under threat of attack from the men of the Weald, when they could sail all the way to the friendly capital and dock there? As they made their way north they attempted to maintain formation, though it appears to have become looser as time went by. Eustace the Monk's flagship was now right at the back, rather than the front, though it is unclear whether this positioning was by design, in order to protect the rear of the fleet, or whether it was due to the vessel being so overloaded and thus moving more slowly than the others.

The English fleet, led by Hubert de Burgh's ship, now left Sandwich and headed directly out to sea. This course meant that they were sailing into the wind, which was blowing from the south-east, and they passed astern and to the south of the French, who, according to the History of William Marshal, thought they had escaped: 'Sir Hubert de Burgh's ship went sailing ahead of the others. He put on a great pretence of engaging in combat, but, in fact, he sped past at such a speed that there was no question of an engagement.'[16] Contemptuous shouts of 'La hart! La hart!' (a hunting cry) were heard from the French ships, and it now looked as though there was clear water between them and the mouth of the Thames.*

---

*'La hart' was the call given when hunting deer (also sometimes known as 'hart' in English), when the prey was sighted. This would fit with the French thinking that they could capture what they believed to be only a small number of ships. However, the Old French word 'hart' can also be translated as 'noose' (as it is in the published version of the History of William Marshal), which would give an altogether more sinister meaning to their intentions.

Indeed, they underestimated the English numbers and might even have thought that they could capture the ships to double their triumph as they arrived to meet Louis in London.

But all this was merely a ruse. The English sailors were able to bring their ships about swiftly, or at least all the ships except Hubert's, which had got too far ahead of the others and therefore overshot the turn, thus putting him at the rear (he would later claim he had feinted on purpose, in order to lull the French into a false sense of security and persuade them that the English would not be able to fight). Following the turn, the English fleet had in naval terms acquired the weather gage, the upwind position, which meant that they now had both the sun and the wind behind them and were able to approach the French with ever-gathering speed. This was a superb naval manoeuvre. It has sometimes been said that this was the first time that an English fleet had used such a tactic (and Matthew Paris gave the credit to Hubert de Burgh for his cunning), but there is some evidence that the overlooked and underrated Philip d'Albini had done something similar in his attack on the French ships back in May, so it might have been his idea this time too.[17]

Regardless of whose initial plan it had been, the move was extremely effective. The French, who had thought that the English were safely on their way out to sea, possibly even heading for Calais, were taken completely by surprise by the turn and the speed with which the English ships were now approaching them.

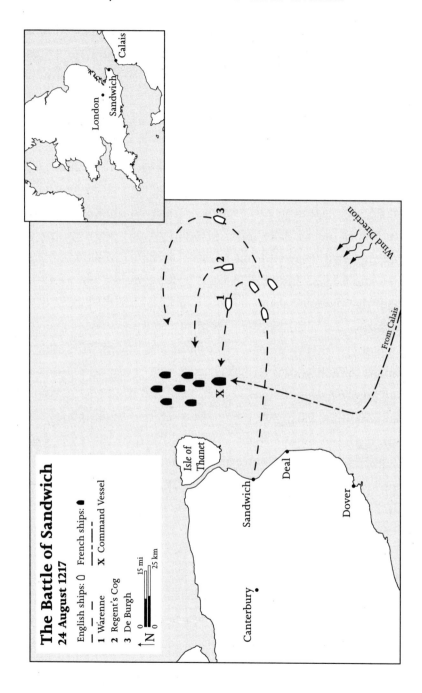

The Battle of Sandwich
24 August 1217

English ships: ◊ French ships: ●
– – – X Command Vessel
1 Warenne
2 Regent's Cog
3 De Burgh

0   15 mi
0   25 km

There is some slight confusion over precisely what happened next, and who made the first move to engage. William the Breton, telling the story from the French perspective, believed that Eustace the Monk would have sought to avoid contact, but that 'Robert de Courtenay ordered his ship to head towards them, thinking they could be easily captured, but the vessels of his companions did not follow.'[18] If this is true then Robert – unfamiliar with naval matters – made a grave error; and if Eustace felt obliged to go along with it, despite his standing orders being to deliver the fleet to London, this is another example of leadership by committee being an inefficient practice. An experienced sea captain should always have complete control over his vessel, regardless of who, or how important, his passengers were.

Robert, in his inexperience, might have thought that the other French vessels would immediately turn and follow him (as might happen in a cavalry charge on land, a form of conflict in which he was much more practised), but they were by this time some way ahead of the great ship of Bayonne, running with the wind, and steering a ship at sea was a very different prospect from reining in and turning a horse. No other vessels moved in support, which meant that Eustace's ship was left to bear the brunt of the attack alone.

Although the biographer of William Marshal makes a predictable general dig at French overconfidence at this point in his narrative, neither he nor any of our other contemporary chroniclers mention this supposed decision by Robert de Courtenay. It is possible that William the Breton was mistaken – perhaps receiving conflicting reports later on – and that the

French flagship was isolated and caught up with first simply because it was behind the others, difficult to manoeuvre and moving very slowly.* Whatever the exact reason, the ships of both sides were now almost close enough to engage, and the English had all the advantage of momentum.

It was at this point that the English used another innovative tactic – and one about which there can be little doubt, because the contemporary witnesses agree to a remarkable extent. As we noted earlier, missile weapons such as bows and crossbows could be used as ships closed on each other and before hand-to-hand combat took place, but now the English used a very different type of missile: lime dust.†

Lime, or quicklime, was not an uncommon substance in the early thirteenth century. It was made by heating limestone of the correct quality to the correct temperature (which, like navigation, was a process that had to be done by eye and experience by skilled practitioners) in a kiln for three days and three nights. When cooled, this produced a powder that could be mixed with a small amount of water to make slaked lime, also known as lime putty, or combined with a greater quantity of water and an aggregate such as sand to make mortar, which was used in the construction of stone walls.[19] The powder would

---

*William the Breton later has Robert Fitzwalter being captured in this engagement (although the latter was not present because he was still in captivity following the battle of Lincoln), which adds credence to the idea that he might not have been in possession of clear and accurate information when he wrote his account.

†The modern word lime has many different uses; in this instance it is nothing to do with either the citrus fruit or the tree, but rather derives from the Latin limus (slime or silt) and the Old English lim (sticky substance, glue).

generally be seen on building sites rather than on ships, and there can therefore be little doubt that on this occasion it had been brought aboard the vessels of the English fleet specifically for offensive purposes. Of particular note was that lime dust was extremely caustic (causing external burns when in contact with the skin, and internal burns if inhaled or swallowed), that it reacted particularly violently to water (causing intense chemical heat), and that the wind was blowing directly away from the English ships towards the French fleet.

As can be seen in Matthew Paris's famous illustration of the battle, the lime was launched by archers and slingers as well as by hand.[20] The effects on the French – as noted, in a rare moment of narrative unity, by virtually all our chroniclers – were devastating:

The English attacked with great energy, hurling stones at them and lime, which blinded them all.

*

They also threw hot lime-dust on the sea, which, being borne by the wind, blinded the eyes of the French.

*

They had big pots of quicklime and hurled them down at those below them, causing them such great harm that they lost their sight and were incapable of seeing a thing.

*

Then they [the English] began to hurl well-ground lime in large pots, which they smashed to pieces on the ship's rails. The powder rose in great clouds, and it was this which caused them [the French] the most damage. After that, they could no longer defend themselves, for their eyes were full of powder. Those who were tormenting them were upwind.[21]

Within a very short space of time the French found themselves blinded, coughing and choking in agony, and were in no state to defend themselves against the imminent physical attack.

The lime had been a masterstroke, and several more decisive factors would now come into play. The French had more vessels in total than their assailants, but many of these were small, while the English had a greater number of large ships of a type suitable for combat. The French were carrying a great deal of cargo, as well as troops, while the English had set out with the specific intention of fighting and had loaded their ships accordingly, making them lighter and more manoeuvrable. The French probably had more knights, but this was not a particular advantage for fighting on a ship, and the English had many more lightly armoured combatants of greater agility. The French benefited from the vast maritime experience of Eustace the Monk, but he was hampered by the need to defer to high-ranking nobles who knew less about the sea than he did, while the other French captains were less familiar with the waters. Meanwhile, many of the English captains and sailors were local men from the Cinque Ports who knew the prevailing conditions well. And finally, the French needed to reach a specific place, London, while the English only needed to prevent them from getting there.

The first English ships reached the great ship of Bayonne.

BATTLE IS JOINED

It was the ship owned by Earl Warenne, with its troops led by Richard of Chilham, that won the race. It rammed Eustace's flagship; most likely not with the intention of sinking it, but rather so that its prow would be embedded in the French vessel in order to impair it and prevent any escape. Shortly behind Richard's ship came the large cog belonging to William Marshal, which sat much higher in the water than the wallowing French vessel, thus allowing the English archers to rain down arrows and crossbow bolts on their already incapacitated opponents. Marshal's biographer, getting into the spirit of the action, could not resist narrating some heroic knightly deeds that would not be out of place in a classic Hollywood film:

Reginald Pain of Guernsey, a brave soldier, with nothing of the coward in him, jumped from the cog to the other ship. His landing was not gentle, for his leap had been such a fearsome one that in his path he knocked down [the renowned French knight] William des Barres, and, without further delay, he knocked down as he fell Sir Robert de Courtenay; that was a fine exploit indeed. He made Sir Ralph de la Tournelle spin round three times as he went; he was unable to take avoiding action at first, but then moved to engage with him. The solider met him with great force and there was a battle royal between them.[22]

Meanwhile, grappling hooks were thrown, ships were lashed together, and English knights and foot soldiers clambered across to engage their enemy. This situation was replicated across the fleet, but the main combat was on the French command vessel, which was soon surrounded by another two ships as well as Warenne's and Marshal's. One of these was that commanded by Philip d'Albini, tactical hero of the hour, whose archers, 'sending their missiles amongst the French, soon caused great slaughter'. The French crews, we are told, 'were struck down by the weapons and arrows of the English sailors, who were used to naval fights, [and who] pierced them with their javelins and arrows, or cut them down with swords and lances'.[23]

More and more boarders arrived on the great ship of Bayonne, and soon the deck was so packed that there was barely room to swing a sword. The combat was vicious: not a series of elaborate duels between specific high-status individuals – as the History of William Marshal depicts, bearing more resemblance to the courtly literature popular at the time than to a real battle – but rather a screaming, seething, hacking mass of brutal close-quarter violence, all made worse by the heaving of the ship on the waves and the fact that half the combatants could neither see nor breathe properly. And with so many bladed weapons in evidence, it was not long before the wooden deck underfoot was slippery with blood, adding to the chaos.

Eustace the Monk, realising that there would be little mercy shown to him if he were defeated, defended himself vigorously and with great improvisation:

Eustace and his men defended themselves by hurling and throwing missiles and firing arrows. They slaughtered a great many Englishmen and defended themselves courageously. Eustace knocked down a good number of them with an oar which he was holding. Some had their arms broken, others their heads smashed. This one was killed and that one laid out; one was knocked down and another wounded, while a third had his collar-bone shattered.[24]

Eventually, though, he was forced back, and at some point he left the deck and disappeared below. Meanwhile, the knights and lords in his party were not able to give as good an account of themselves as they might have wished. Normally, with their superior armour and horses, they would expect to enjoy a distinct advantage over other combatants, but none of that counted for anything on the crowded, unsteady deck of the ship, where they were at the mercy of more lightly armoured sergeants and sailors who were better able to cope with the cramped confines and the many trip hazards.

The battle on the great ship was not a long one, and there was nowhere for the defeated French to flee. They surrendered, and then the cry went up that Eustace the Monk needed to be found. He, more than any of the French invaders, was the real target of the men of south-east England who had seen their towns attacked over and over again, the blood of their friends and family spilled, and they rampaged through the ship in search of him.

It was not long before Eustace was dragged out of his ship's hold and brought up on deck to face summary justice. At first he tried to bargain, but the angry men of the English ports were having none of it:

> [Eustace] offered, to save his life, ten thousand marks, but that could never be: he was confronted by a master too cruel for his good, Stephen of Winchelsea. Stephen told him a fearsome tale, reminding him of the wrongs he had done him both on land and on sea – undeservedly, since he had done him no harm – through his cruel treachery; but now he would put that right.

Ten thousand marks was a ludicrous sum, equal to about a quarter of the English crown's total annual income at the time, and despite all his years of piratical activity it is very unlikely that Eustace would be able to come up with such an amount.* In any case, his enemies made no move to accept or to enter on negotiations, and Eustace was instead offered a simple but gruesome choice: 'The decision would be his as to which he would go for, for there was no secret about it: he

---

*A mark was an accounting unit equal to two-thirds of a pound (i.e. 13s 6d or 160 pennies). Ten thousand marks was thus £6,667 6s 8d, at a time when an earldom might be expected to yield an annual income of between £200 and £400.

would be beheaded there and then, without delay and without reprieve, either on top of the siege engine or on the ship's side.'[25] Unfortunately for us, none of the accounts of the event mentions which choice, if any, Eustace made, but his head left his shoulders there and then. Nobody, not even the writer of his life story, could muster a shred of sympathy: the Romance ends simply with the moral that 'no one who is always intent on evil can live for a long time'.[26]

Eustace the Monk, the terror of the seas and the scourge of coastal towns on both sides of the Channel for so many years, was dead.

BLOOD IN THE WATER

Eustace's summary execution marked the start of a rout – and the fact that this happened so speedily after his demise shows us what an important figure he was in the engagement. Virtually all the ships of both fleets were now in close contact with each other, and the fighting had been fierce, with the French giving as good an account of themselves as they were able, especially when we consider the lime dust they were inhaling. But now, on seeing that their admiral was dead and the command ship captured, many of the French attempted to flee. A small number might have got away, but most did not; their ships had been rammed and then lashed to the English ships, or they had been disabled by having their rigging cut so that the sails fell and the vessels could not be controlled. They were chased, overhauled and boarded.

War at sea was governed by fewer conventions than that on land, and the French sailors and common troops knew they would be shown little mercy. 'Having no hopes of escape,' Roger of Wendover tells us, the French 'threw themselves of their own accord into the waves, that they might not be taken alive by their enemies, for they preferred death to being taken prisoner by the English.' Those who remained on board were beaten and hacked into submission and then thrown overboard, wounded or dead, staining the waters of the Channel red:

> Once they caught up with a ship, I can tell you that they [the English] lost no time at all in killing those they found on board and throwing them into the sea as food for the fish [...] there was many a bounty-seeker who thought he would come by great wealth or a fine scarlet cloth [...] he made to fish it up with a hook, but he was mightily displeased with what he found, and felt that he had been truly robbed; all there was there was congealed blood.[27]

The English were by now so maddened with bloodlust – by the nature of their victory, by the killing that had already occurred, by the idea that they were taking revenge not just for the attempt to land foreign troops, but also for the years of threat and violence to their families – that they could hardly stop themselves. Once the French sailors and common troops had been dealt with, a group of the English turned their attention to the knights and lords, including Robert de Courtenay and thirty-two others on the great ship of Bayonne.*

---

*We have already noted that the great ship of Bayonne was overloaded, but if there really were thirty-three knights on it (including Robert himself), along with all their horses and attendants

The bloodthirsty band was narrowly prevented from engaging in further slaughter by a group of English knights, who stepped in to save their peers. There is a vague possibility that this rescue was prompted by a brotherly feeling towards fellow knights, regardless of nationality, but it seems more likely that the English knights, with William Marshal's pre-battle announcement that booty would be shared still ringing in their ears, had their eye on the valuable ransoms that the French lords would fetch.

The final act of the battle was the belated arrival of Hubert de Burgh. Either he had overshot the turn by quite some way or he had been holding back deliberately – it is difficult to tell – but in either case he now sailed directly into the chaos to seize two French ships himself.

'What more shall I tell you?' asks the Anonymous of Béthune. 'It was a great defeat, and the English pursued them a long way. Then they returned to Sandwich with their prisoners and their plunder, which was great.' Not every commentator was happy with such a succinct summary, and some were keen to link the victory to God's favour. The battle had 'turned out as God had wished'; or, more portentously:

And so the Lord struck down the heads of his enemies, who were coming to scatter the English people, and many were captured with the rest of the ships, and made captive; and the Lord made the waters of the sea fall upon some of them

---

and the pieces of the trebuchet, it is a minor miracle that Eustace was able to sail it across the Channel at all.

who had fled, and they were drowned like lead in the violent waters [...] And thus Almighty God [...] broke the strength of the enemy, and his right hand was glorified among his people.[28]

Again we see the emphasis on French aggression – they were now apparently 'coming to scatter the English people', rather than merely to reinforce a faction of English rebel barons in a civil war – and on the English fightback and victory, which, as a righteous cause, benefited from God's help. In this story, England had repelled an attempted incursion by France, and the transformation of the war from an internal factional struggle to a national defence against foreign invasion was now complete.

'DRESSED IN SCARLET AND SILK'

The victorious English ships, together with their captured vessels and high-ranking prisoners, returned to Sandwich. There they were greeted by the bishops in full regalia, giving thanks to God, and a regent who was so exultant at the outcome that he actually kept his word and allowed all the plunder to be distributed even as he had promised. The gains, as they had been at Lincoln, were great; and at least this time they had been taken from enemy combatants rather than innocent civilians. The English sailors, we are told, 'were able to share out the coins in bowlfuls', and there were also arms, equipment, horses and fine clothes. 'If only you had seen the sailors,' wrote Marshal's biographer, 'rich in clothes and money, walking up and down the road dressed in scarlet* and silk, or rich cloth or samites, vying with each other wherever they happened to be gathered.'

In keeping with the narrative that the victory had been a sign of God's favour upon the English and its young king, Marshal did not forget the Church in his distribution of plunder. He ordered

> a hospital to be founded with the remainder of the money, to commemorate the victory, a hospital in honour of Saint Bartholomew, who, on that day and in that place, had given them the victory [...] the sailors graciously obeyed his command, for they founded that house of great fame and repute to house, sustain and give comfort to God's poor.†29

Nobody, incidentally, thought to note what became of the trebuchet that Eustace's ship was carrying, but − given what a powerful and innovative weapon it was at the time − it seems reasonable to assume that it was added to the English royal arsenal rather than being thrown away or burned. The captured ships were certainly put to use, as evidenced by a summons of 1 September 1217 by the regent to the men of the Cinque Ports

---

*'Scarlet' was a type of cloth, not a colour (though it was often dyed red, hence the later derivation of the word). It was an expensive, high-quality fabric, which explains it being included here alongside silk as a luxury item.

†St Bartholomew's Hospital in Sandwich is still standing, and still in use as an almshouse, although there is some uncertainty over whether it was founded in 1217 or whether it had already existed since 1190 but that a chapel was added to it in 1217 to commemorate the victory.

of Hastings, Dover, Hythe, Romney and Sandwich, in which he instructs them to 'come with all your ships, both those newly won and others'.[30]

But the greatest victory, as far as the common people of the south-east coast were concerned, was not the capture of French knights; it was the death of Eustace the Monk and the knowledge that they were finally free of the threat of attack from him and his violent and vicious band. He was more dangerous than Louis – who would rule them from a distance just as any other king would – and their fear was more immediate, local and personal. Eustace's severed head was fixed on to the end of a spear and was later paraded around Canterbury and other towns in the south-east, to the great joy of the people there.

It was Eustace, not Louis nor any of the French lords or English rebels, whose name lived on in infamy. In the fourteenth century, long after any living memory of this war had faded, a tale, included in two different chronicles, circulated. It told of an evil tyrant called Monachus ('the Monk'), who wished to invade and conquer England because he had heard it was ruled by a child. As he approached England's shores, the brave men of the ports set out in their ships and defeated him at sea, killing him and returning with much plunder. This is quite clearly based on the events of August 1217, but it is noticeable that there is no mention at all of Louis, and that it is 'the Monk' whose invasion is feared.[31] It is no wonder that the people of Canterbury and elsewhere were glad to have irrefutable proof that Eustace's head was no longer attached to his body.

The total French losses from the battle of Sandwich are unclear. It may be that some of the larger French ships made it back to Calais – and one or two of the contemporary accounts suggest this – but it is also possible that the entire fleet was either seized or sunk. There were certainly enough captured vessels for them to be added to the English navy, as we have seen. But the exact number was immaterial, because regardless of whether the ships had been captured or had escaped, the French fleet had spectacularly failed in its objective of providing Louis with reinforcements.

There would still be negotiations to come, but effectively the war was over.

SEVEN

Aftermath

Fame, ever quick off the mark and travelling swiftly, rested neither by night or day, for she came to London before the break of day to give Louis news which he did not find at all pleasing, that his men who were coming to join him had been routed and had suffered a sorry fate at sea, and that all those captured from the ships had been killed, except for the highly prized and high-ranking knights, who, because of their crime, had been taken and were now in prison in Dover, and how those who had escaped did so to their great shame. Louis was very dejected and grieved.

*

This battle was fought on a Thursday, St Bartholomew's day, and the news reached London and Louis very late on the Saturday evening. He was very angry, and rightly so.

*

It seemed useless for them to stay there any longer.[1]

It did not matter how many or how few words contemporaries used to describe Louis's situation following the battle of Sandwich: he knew it was all over. However, he still had a few final cards up his sleeve, and if William Marshal wanted to end the war definitively here and now, without further repercussions, he would need to tread carefully.

The negotiations began on 5 September 1217 when Marshal and Louis met in person for the first time, on an island in the Thames, with Robert de Courtenay (who had been released from captivity for this purpose) standing with Louis, and Hubert de Burgh with the regent. This date was, as it happened, Louis's thirtieth birthday. The large age gap between him and Marshal, of something like forty years – and all the more obvious once they finally came face to face – reminded the regent that Louis would be around long after he himself was gone, so he needed to think carefully of the future of the realm that would have to survive without him sooner rather than later. He also needed to take four significant factors into consideration.

The first issue was that although Louis did not have the reinforcements he needed in order to win the war, he had not actually lost it by being personally defeated in battle, and he still had enough men remaining to cause further trouble if he chose to. Second, and relatedly, Philip Augustus had held off from this conflict up until now, but if he felt that there was any *real* danger to his son and heir – of death, imprisonment or a humiliation that would reflect badly on the Capetian house – he might well decide to throw the entire might of the French crown into the arena, which would be dangerous in the extreme.

The third factor was that when King John had lost Normandy to Philip, barons who held lands both there and in England had been obliged to jump one way or the other, either retaining their Norman estates by throwing in their lot with the French king and withdrawing their allegiance to John, or making the opposite move. Only a handful had managed to retain both sets of lands, of whom by far the most high-profile was William Marshal himself. So although Marshal owed allegiance to John (and now Henry) for his English estates, Philip Augustus was his direct overlord in Normandy ... and Louis was Philip's son and heir. Finally there was the not-insignificant fact that, regardless of the situation in England, Louis would definitely one day be the king of France, with all the riches and resources of the crown at his disposal, so it might not be the best idea to antagonise him too much.

The negotiations were therefore amicable, with Marshal using all his considerable political experience to safeguard the realm's future and avoid making Louis into an implacable enemy. The result was the Treaty of Lambeth, which was agreed on 11 September and sealed a week later. Under its terms Louis would leave England, but he would be paid the vast sum of 10,000 marks to relinquish his claim to the throne (4,000 marks in cash to take away with him, and the rest to follow in instalments). There were further specifics: Louis would release all his secular adherents from their oaths of allegiance to him; his clerical supporters would need to seek absolution from the pope; and all prisoners on both sides were to be released without further ransom payment, although ransoms already received could be kept. The English rebel barons would be restored to their lands if they agreed to swear allegiance to Henry. The overall impression, then, is of a peace treaty between equals rather than a victorious party dictating to a defeated one.[2]

Louis sailed away on 28 September – from Dover, as it happens, where the castle garrison no doubt saw him depart with a polite farewell and a cheery wave. Our contemporary commentators then make an effort to tell us that peace was restored immediately to the whole realm of England, but – as we will not be surprised to hear – this was not quite the case. The Anonymous of Béthune says blithely that 'the barons dispersed. They had the king's peace proclaimed throughout the land and had woodland cleared alongside the roads because of robbers. Then there was great peace in the land and holy Church was greatly feared and greatly honoured.'[3] The fact that the undergrowth around roads needed to be cut back in order to deter criminals demonstrates that there were many in England who had by now grown used to a state of lawlessness, and it would take some while to restore law and order at local and national levels.

There was disquiet among the nobility, with the barons, despite now all appearing to be on the same side and welcomed back into the fold, remaining for some considerable time in three distinct camps: those who had been staunch royalists all along, those who had been consistent in their rebellion, and those who had swapped sides more than once in order to further their own interests. Each of them formed cliques that interacted with each other with varying degrees of unease and suspicion.

The Church was also not one big happy family, with the papal legate Guala taking every opportunity for retaliation against those who had disagreed with him:

> Immediately after Louis's departure from England, the legate sent inquisitors through all the counties of England, to find out all [the clergymen] who were guilty of the slightest implications in the rebellion of whatever order or rank they might be, and after suspending them and depriving them of all benefit [...] he distributed all their benefices amongst his own clerks, and from the losses of others enriched all his own followers.[4]

There was also still potential danger from across the Channel, the threat of which lasted for years. While we know in hindsight that the invasion was not repeated, this was far from sure at the time. Louis succeeded to the French throne as Louis VIII upon Philip Augustus's death in July 1223, and one of his first acts as king was to launch a successful attack on English-held lands in Poitou, expelling Henry III's men and taking the territories under French royal control. He also declined to renew the truce with England when it expired, and the realm might have felt itself in danger once more. However, there was to be a twist of fate: Louis died suddenly in November 1226, still in his thirties and after a reign of only three years. This left his widow, the vastly capable Blanche of Castile, as regent of France for their twelve-year-old son, who became Louis IX.* Blanche, of course, had her own claim to the English throne, but as she had France to govern, had Louis and six other younger children to look after, was pregnant with another, *and* had been left with the Albigensian Crusade situation to sort out, she had too much on her plate to think of a second invasion of England. Her young cousin across the Channel was therefore left in peace.

William Marshal did not live to see any of this; he had died (of natural causes) in May 1219. To the last he was staunchly faithful to the English royal line as a whole, rather than to any particular present holder of the crown – his last words to the young king were apparently a hope that he would grow up to be a 'worthy man', but that 'if it were the case that you followed in the footsteps of some wicked ancestor, and that your wish was to be like him, then I pray to God, the son of Mary, that He does not give you long to live and that you die before it comes to that'. We might consider this a rather inappropriate and possibly nightmare-inducing thing to say to an eleven-year-old already overawed by being in the presence of a dying man, but Henry apparently merely replied with 'Amen'.[5]

Due to his tender age Henry III was still unable to rule in his own name, but the post of regent was not invested in another individual: instead there would be a regency council

---

*Louis VIII died of dysentery, a common cause of mortality for soldiers, while engaged in the Albigensian Crusade in the south of France. His eldest son, Philip, had pre-deceased him, but he and Blanche had so many children that the succession was in no danger; their next son, Louis, acceded and would go on to be one of France's greatest kings.

made up of three men. This triumvirate comprised Pandulf Verraccio, the papal legate to England;[*] Peter des Roches, the bishop of Winchester; and Hubert de Burgh. In order to confirm his hereditary kingship and pre-empt any accusations of irregularity in his original coronation, Henry was crowned again in 1220 – this time at Westminster Abbey and by the archbishop of Canterbury – and he went on to enjoy a long reign, albeit one that was by no means trouble-free. In a strange turn of Fortune's wheel he and Louis IX of France (who also reigned for many years) became not only great friends but also brothers-in-law when they married two sisters, and through the middle years of the thirteenth century England and France enjoyed a long period of peace.[†]

Henry III became the first king since the Conquest to be seen as a real 'English' king of England – which is odd, when we come to think about it, given that he was mostly of French descent himself.[‡] What this shows is that in the 150 years since William the Conqueror brought his Normans over to defeat and overthrow the old Anglo-Saxon royal line, attitudes had

---

[*]Pandulf, as we noted in Chapter 1, had been listed as a supporter of John in the text of Magna Carta back in 1215. He had been relegated in importance following the arrival in England of the higher-ranking cardinal legate Guala in 1216 but had resumed his position as the pope's representative in England in 1218, following Guala's departure.

[†]Louis and Henry married Margaret and Eleanor of Provence, respectively. As it happens, Henry's younger (legitimate) brother Richard and Louis's youngest brother Charles went on to marry the two younger sisters of Margaret and Eleanor, which knitted the families together even more tightly and made for some interesting Christmas gatherings in the 1250s.

[‡]All four of Henry's grandparents (Henry II, Eleanor of Aquitaine, Count Aymer of Angoulême and Alice of Courtenay) and seven of his eight great-grandparents had been French; even the eighth, Empress Matilda, had been of Anglo-Norman stock.

changed about who was 'English' and who was not. Some of this stemmed from decades of intermarriage; as early as the 1170s a contemporary was able to note that 'nowadays, when English and Normans live close together and marry and give in marriage to each other, the nations are so mixed that it can scarcely be decided [...] who is of English birth and who of Norman'.[6] The situation had developed further by 1216, with much of the idea of 'Englishness' now due to King John's loss of Normandy. This meant that Henry had no business in the duchy and spent nearly all his reign in England, and that the barons were becoming accustomed to holding lands on only one side of the Channel. Memories of the old Anglo-Norman realm would slowly fade as those who had known it died out, as estates originally divided between brothers passed into the hands of cousins and then second cousins, the lines diverging.

Finally, the idea of Henry as an 'English' king also came about in great part because of the appeals to national feeling by William Marshal, and others, during the war; the royalists intending to put Henry on the throne and keep him there were fighting not for the rights of one boy, but *pro patria*. It has often been thought that true national identity did not develop until much later, and that loyalties at this time were predominantly to individuals or families, but it is clear from the evidence of this war that nationhood and pride in one's nation were at least in early development in the first quarter of the thirteenth century.[7]

Another significant factor in this equation was Magna Carta, which was re-issued in Henry's name in the autumn of 1216, at the very beginning of his reign, in order to placate the rebellious barons and entice them back into the fold. It would be re-issued again in 1217 and 1225 in order to demonstrate Henry's and his regime's public commitment to it, so nobody could raise against Henry the same complaints they had made about John. Magna Carta was a uniquely English document, and its subsequent long-lasting influence both on the kingdom's legal system and in folk memory was profound.[*]

Henry would go on to embrace his Englishness even further, naming his two sons Edward and Edmund after his favoured Anglo-Saxon saints rather than after any of their Norman or Angevin predecessors, the first post-Conquest king to do so. His rule was not without its problems, especially in later years, but as far as his subjects were concerned it was at least his own rule and not that of Louis VIII or his sons. England had not been subsumed into France in the same way that Normandy had; and when Henry's barons, led by Simon de Montfort, rebelled against him in the 1250s and 1260s there were no calls to replace him on the throne with a French king or prince. By this time the principle of hereditary accession was firmly established, so there could be no possible replacement for Henry on the throne except his elder son and heir Edward (who supported his father), meaning that the barons had to seek reform rather than attempting an overthrow, as their predecessors had done with King John. The principle has never been rescinded, and

---

[*]This is not always positive: more than two decades into the twenty-first century there is still an unfortunate tendency to misquote Magna Carta in support of various issues related to 'freedom'. Only two clauses remain law at the time of writing: Clause 39 ('No free man shall be seized, imprisoned, dispossessed, outlawed, exiled or ruined in any way, nor in any way proceeded against, except by the lawful judgement of his peers and the law of the land') and Clause 40 ('To no one will we sell, to no one will we deny or delay right or justice').

every subsequent monarch of England (and later Great Britain) has been a direct descendant of Henry III.

It was the military victories in the 1216–17 war that made all of this possible. Although the major engagements we have examined took place over the course of more than a year, and were spread out in different geographical locations, they all fitted together as part of an overall defensive campaign, and influenced each other. The dogged defence of Dover castle through the early phase of the war in the summer and autumn of 1216 meant that the French did not control the whole of the south-east or the Channel, and thus had no secure foothold. If Hubert de Burgh and the garrison had not held out so effectively for so long, Louis might have been able to send a much greater force to Lincoln, resulting in the capture of the castle there and opening up opportunities further north. In turn, the equally resolute defence of Nicola de la Haye and her men during the siege of Lincoln, followed by victory in battle there, meant that Louis was also not able to commit the level of resource to Dover that he would need in order to take it.

Meanwhile, William of Cassingham and the men of the Weald were preventing the French and rebels from ever having a firm base in the south-east; Louis and his followers could have no confidence either in their own safety or in the possibility that they could land much-needed reinforcements to push their cause towards victory. William Marshal's simultaneous grim determination to do whatever was necessary, regardless of any considerations of 'chivalry', kept the royalist fires burning throughout the difficult early months of 1217, as did Philip d'Albini's patrolling of the Channel. Finally, the victory at Sandwich prevented a large new influx of fresh troops and thwarted what really could, by now, be termed as a foreign invasion that would have left England in the hands of the French royal house.

In terms of national defence, the naval victory at Sandwich is genuinely comparable in importance to the battle of Trafalgar in 1805 or the defeat of the Spanish Armada in 1588 under the leadership of Elizabeth I, Henry III's eight-times great-granddaughter.* It almost beggars belief that the engagement is so little known, the major reason in all probability being that later historians, in attempting to develop some kind of 'great island story', did not want to dwell too heavily on a period when a French prince had been invited, welcomed with open arms and declared king of England. Given that many of these eighteenth- and nineteenth-century historians were themselves writing at a time when Britain was at war with France, the whole 1216–17 interlude was simply a huge embarrassment that had to be swept under the carpet. The war is therefore not as well known as it should be, given its

---

*In fact Elizabeth I was also Henry III's ten-times great-granddaughter, as she was descended from his great-great-grandson Edward III twice. Heredity became such an important factor in the transmission of the crown in the centuries that followed Henry's reign that it was not unknown for members of different royal lines to marry each other to bolster their claims, leading to some insanely complicated family trees. In a headache-inducing relationship, Elizabeth's great-great-grandfather Richard, duke of York, was actually his own second cousin twice removed.

lasting consequences.[8] Its heroes are not household names: William Marshal might have accrued his fair share of fame over the subsequent centuries, but how many people could now name Hubert de Burgh, Nicola de la Haye, William of Cassingham or Philip d'Albini?

In gaining their various victories, these protagonists were helped by a number of factors outside of their control. Most notable among these were the fortuitous death of John, Louis's decision not to have himself crowned when he entered London in triumph, the weather in the Channel and the lack of support for Louis from Philip Augustus – if the French king had backed the enterprise with all the resources at his disposal, the outcome might have been different. But the English royalists could only fight what was put up against them, and this they did with determination, with excellent strategic and tactical ability, and with great success. Some of the deeds they performed were unorthodox and unchivalrous, in both modern and contemporary eyes. However, these actions prolonged the war, which enabled the battles to take place, which in turn meant that the war could be won – or, at least, could be brought to an acceptable and peaceful conclusion.

King John was a disaster, and there seems to be very little question that he was both an unpleasant individual and a hopeless king. But John was not England, and John's fall did not have to mean England coming under the jurisdiction of a foreign power. To be fair to Louis, he might well have made a better king than John, but if he had succeeded in becoming the undisputed King Louis I of England, the course of England's future as an independent kingdom might have been very different. This is what William Marshal and his fellow royalists were fighting for: not the person of the current wearer of the crown, but rather the continuity and independence that the existing royal line represented. Marshal made his feelings on this point abundantly clear through his actions and his words: he had been devoutly loyal to John while John was alive and was the crowned and anointed king, but he then spent much of the last part of his career after John's death making promises and arrangements to amend the 'bad' laws and customs that he had presumably supported at the time. Marshal then did everything that he could to secure the throne for Henry III, before telling the young boy that he hoped he would die rather than become a tyrant.

In doing all this, Marshal shifted the popular consciousness of the war, so that it came to be seen as a defence of the realm against foreign invasion, rather than as a civil war caused by an internal rebellion against an unjust monarch. He took advantage of the fact that John had previously been criticised for having 'more confidence in foreigners than in his own', and that the rebels had forfeited any right to complain about or to seek redress for John's injustices at the moment they offered the crown to Louis.[9] The French, according to Marshal's biographer, 'were so full of arrogance that they said that England was theirs, and that the English should vacate the land, for they had no right to it; the French, they say, would have it for their own profit'.[10] While this is an exaggeration (nobody was seriously claiming that the French wanted to overrun England to the extent that the current inhabitants should leave), it helped Marshal push the narrative that the

French were coming as invaders and needed to be stopped. In so doing, and in altering the perception of the war, he helped foster a burgeoning sense of national identity, meaning that the battles and sieges we have examined here really did help to save England, both as a kingdom and as a concept in thirteenth-century hearts.

Chronology

1200

May The Treaty of Le Goulet results in the marriage of Louis of France, Philip Augustus's son, to Blanche of Castile, King John's niece. This gives Louis a tenuous hereditary claim to the English crown in his wife's name.

1203–1204

John loses Normandy, which is conquered by Philip Augustus and subsumed into the French royal domain. Those barons who hold lands in England and in Normandy are obliged to choose between them, with the result that some family holdings are split.

June 1204–June 1205

Hubert de Burgh holds out in John's name in Chinon castle for an entire year, but John sends no help and Hubert is captured in a last-gasp attempt to break out of the siege. He will remain in captivity for two years.

1206

Despite John's feeble attempt to stop him, Philip also conquers much of Anjou, Maine and Poitou. John continues to sink in the estimation of his barons, and exacerbates the situation by unreasonable financial demands and erratic behaviour.

Eustace the Monk enters John's service, but acts indiscriminately, attacking English towns and ships as well as French.

1208–9
John finds himself in dispute with the Church due to his continuing refusal to accept the appointment of Stephen Langton as archbishop of Canterbury. England is put under an interdict and John is excommunicated. He responds by confiscating Church lands and incomes.

1212
Eustace the Monk switches his allegiance from John to Philip; his raids on English towns and shipping intensify.

1213
May Philip assembles a fleet with the intention of invading England, but cancels his plans after John gains papal approval by ceding England as a papal fief. The interdict on England is finally lifted. The French fleet is burned at Damme by William Longespee, the earl of Salisbury.

1214
July In an unsuccessful attempt to regain his family's former lands in France, John is routed by Louis at La-Roche-aux-Moines, while his allies are simultaneously defeated by Philip at the battle of Bouvines.

1215
January–April Crisis point is reached in England between the royalist and rebel factions. Armed conflict ensues and the rebel barons take London.
June Under pressure from the rebel barons, John sets his seal to Magna Carta.

August Pope Innocent III declares Magna Carta to be null and void. John uses this as justification to launch violent raids against the rebel barons, who decide that their only remaining option is to overthrow him.

October–December John besieges and captures Rochester castle, which is being held by the rebel barons. He then moves on to plundering other rebel lands, but makes no attempt to retake London.

The barons send a delegation to France to offer the English crown to Louis, who is keen to accept.

December An initial cohort of French knights arrives in England.

1216

January–February John continues his campaign of devastation, moving north as far as Berwick before turning back to the English midlands. Simultaneously, his other forces, under the command of William Longespee and Falkes de Bréauté, make brutal raids in the east of England.

April The Assembly of Melun takes place, at which Louis puts forward to the French nobles his claim to the English crown. They support him but Philip Augustus does not – or, at least, not officially. This means that Louis is unable to call on the resources of the French crown and is obliged to recruit privately.

May Louis and his supporters sail for England and land on the Isle of Thanet before mustering at Sandwich. John initially considers resisting him at the coast, but chooses instead to withdraw, so the landing is unopposed.

June Louis reaches London, where he is welcomed and proclaimed king but not crowned. He embarks on a military campaign in southern England while John flees westwards. John orders various castles to be re-supplied and their garrisons strengthened.

July Louis begins a siege of Dover castle, which is defended by Hubert de Burgh and a garrison of 140 knights and other men-at-arms.

A party of French and rebels moves to Lincoln, where Nicola de la Haye, hereditary castellan of Lincoln castle, is able to purchase a temporary truce.

William of Cassingham and his band of men cause trouble for the French in the Weald, in south-east England.

August King Alexander of Scots pays homage to Louis for his English lands.

August–September The French forces break through the Dover barbican and collapse one of the gatehouse towers, but they are beaten back by the garrison.

September John reaches Lincoln, where he meets with Nicola de la Haye and tasks her with continuing to defend the castle in his name. He also writes a public letter to the men of the Weald to thank them for their efforts on his behalf.

October A truce is agreed at Dover, and Louis returns to London. King John dies; the royalists proclaim his nine-year-old son Henry III king, on the grounds of hereditary right, and crown him in an irregular ceremony at Gloucester cathedral. William Marshal is named regent and Peter des Roches, the bishop of Winchester, as the king's personal guardian; both will act under the authority of the papal legate Guala.

November A council of Henry III's supporters is held, as a result of which they re-issue Magna Carta in his name.

Hubert de Burgh leaves Dover to attend the council; the Dover garrison emerge to burn the remains of the French siege camp and ravage the surrounding countryside in search of supplies.

French and rebel forces begin a siege of Lincoln. The city falls to them, but the castle, with its separate defences, holds out.

December A Christmas truce is agreed between Louis and William Marshal; it is later extended to 23 April 1217.

1217

February Louis attempts to return to France but is hindered by the guerrilla activities of William of Cassingham and by Philip d'Albini's naval blockade. He is eventually picked up by Eustace the Monk, who manages to evade the blockade.

While Louis is absent, William Marshal breaks the truce and attacks a number of French- and rebel-held castles in the south of England.

April Louis returns to England, having been unsuccessful in his attempts to persuade King Philip to support him with money or troops. He is prevented from landing at Dover by the actions of William of Cassingham and Oliver Fitzroy, giving Hubert de Burgh more time to prepare to withstand a second siege.

Blanche of Castile succeeds in obtaining money from Philip, and she begins to raise reinforcements to send to Louis.

May The French besiege Dover for a second time.

A second French and rebel force moves north to Mountsorrel and thence to Lincoln, joining their compatriots who have been besieging the castle there since the end of the previous year. The combined army is defeated in battle by the royalists, led by William Marshal. The count of Perche is killed, numerous French and rebel leaders are taken prisoner, and the city is sacked by the victorious army, resulting in many civilian deaths. Hearing of the defeat at Lincoln, Louis arranges another truce at Dover and returns to London. Small groups of French reinforcements sent by Blanche are prevented from landing in England by Philip d'Albini and his fleet.

June Attempts at peace negotiations prove to be unsuccessful.

August The main fleet of French reinforcements raised by Blanche sets sail from Calais, but it is defeated at sea in what becomes known as the battle of Sandwich. The French military leader Robert de Courtenay is captured, and the naval commander Eustace the Monk is executed. Eustace's severed head is paraded around Canterbury and other towns in the south-east of England.

September William Marshal and Louis meet for peace negotiations. The resulting Treaty of Lambeth brings an end to the war, and Louis returns to France.

1219

May William Marshal dies. The regency is split between Hubert de Burgh, Peter des Roches and the papal legate Pandulf.

1223

July The death of Philip Augustus and the accession of Louis to the French throne as Louis VIII raises the possibility that the war will be renewed. Louis takes some English-held lands in Poitou and declines to renew the truce with England, but he does not make a further invasion attempt at this stage.

1226

November The unexpected early death of Louis VIII and the accession of the twelve-year-old Louis IX puts an end to any further danger of invasion from France. Henry III and Louis IX later become friends and brothers-in-law, ushering in a sustained period of peace.

1272

November Henry III dies while his elder son and heir, Edward, is out of England. Although the latter does not return for nearly two years, the hereditary principle enshrined during the war means that no challenge arises to his kingship. He is considered King Edward I from the date of his accession, rather than that of his coronation, and this custom has continued ever since.

Notes

Full references to all works cited here may be found in the bibliography. Translations of quotes from works published only in languages other than English are my own, except where otherwise stated.

CHAPTER 1

1. *Innocent*, p. 216. The pope's condemnation of the charter is also noted by contemporary chroniclers; see, for example, AB, *Dukes*, p. 148; RW, pp. 330–3.
2. More detail on King John's activities in the first fifteen years of his reign may be found in the relevant chapters of (among other works), Church, *King John*; Morris, *King John*; Warren, *King John*; McGlynn, *Blood Cries Afar*. The conquest of Normandy by King Philip Augustus of France is covered in detail in Powicke, *The Loss of Normandy*.
3. A thorough and very readable analysis of the charter and its context is Carpenter, *Magna Carta*. An English translation of the complete text has been made available online by the British Library: see https://www.bl.uk/magna-carta/articles/magna-carta-english-translation.
4. The French chronicler Philip Mousket was adamant that John's ceding of England to the pope, and his not-entirely-good-faith taking of the cross (both of which meant that the pope would be on his side), were the major factors in the eventual French defeat (PM, p. 393).

5 MP, *Historia*, vol. 2, p. 611.

6 AB, *Dukes*, p. 148.

7 Innocent, pp. 217–18 (quotes from his letter to the barons) and 220 (on Langton's suspension). On the archbishop's suspension, see also RW, pp. 346–8.

8 Numerous books on King Philip and his reign are available, including two important works in English: Bradbury, *Philip Augustus*; Baldwin, *The Government of Philip Augustus*.

9 GW, p. 719.

10 More on the Treaty of Le Goulet may be found in Hanley, *Two Houses, Two Kingdoms*, pp. 162–3; Powicke, *The Loss of Normandy*, pp. 200–5. The full text of the treaty is given (in French) in Rigord, pp. 148–53.

11 For more on Arthur and Eleanor of Brittany, see their chapter in Andrews, *Lost Heirs*, pp. 62–76.

12 More on this abortive campaign of 1213 may be found in Hanley, *Louis*, pp. 46–51; McGlynn, *Blood Cries Afar*, pp. 88–93.

13 For more on Otto and his career (in German), see Hucker, *Otto IV*. Brief biographical details in English may be found in Sean McGlynn, 'Otto IV', *OEMW*, vol. 3, pp. 94–5; Andrews, *The Families of Eleanor of Aquitaine*, pp. 65–6.

14 AB, *Dukes*, p. 153; see also PM, p. 385.

15 WB, *Vie*, p. 321 and AB, *Rois*, p. 770, respectively.

16 The motivations of the rebel barons are explored in greater depth in Holt, *The Northerners*, and Carpenter, *Magna Carta*, pp. 274–338.

17 More on the siege of Rochester may be found in RW, pp. 335–9; Steven Isaac, 'Rochester, Siege of (1215)', *OEMW*, vol. 3, pp. 182–3; McGlynn, *Blood Cries Afar*, pp. 143–8.

18 Quote from AB, *Dukes*, p. 157. For more on King Alexander and his participation in the war, see Stringer, 'Kingship, Conflict and State-Making in the Reign of Alexander II'.

19 Brief further details of Marshal's activities during the autumn and winter of 1215–16 may be found in Crouch, *William Marshal*, pp. 122–3.

20 HWM, pp. 253 and 257–9, respectively. One cannot help suspecting that the biographer might have been protesting about Marshal's unwavering loyalty a little too vociferously.

21 RW, p. 351. For more on John's campaign in the north during the winter of 1215–16, see AB, *Dukes*, pp. 155–7; McGlynn, *Blood Cries Afar*, pp. 153–6; Warren, *King John*, pp. 249–51. On the atrocities, see McGlynn, *By Sword and Fire*, pp. 222–33.

22 RC, p. 178.

23 RW, p. 349.

24 On Geoffrey's death, see AB, *Dukes*, p. 157. For more on Isabelle of Gloucester, see Andrews, *The Families of Eleanor of Aquitaine*, pp. 205–13; Spong, 'Isabella of Gloucester and Isabella of Angoulême'; Spong, 'Isabella of Gloucester: Heiress, Lord, Forgotten Consort'; Vincent, 'A Rebel Queen in London'; Robert B. Patterson, 'Isabella, *suo jure* countess of Gloucester (c. 1160–1217)', ODNB.

25 The pope's letter quashing Simon Langton's appointment to the see of York may be found in full in *Innocent*, pp. 210–11.

26 For a detailed account of the Assembly of Melun, see RW, pp. 361–4; Hanley, *Louis*, pp. 77–85.

27 For a summary of why medieval commanders avoided pitched battles where possible, with further references to secondary literature on this point, see Hanley, *War and Combat*, pp. 20–1. On the engagement at La-Roche-aux-Moines, see WB, *Vie*, pp. 270–3; WB, *Philippide*, pp. 290–7; AB, *Dukes*, p. 142; Sivéry, *Louis VIII*, pp. 121–6; Hanley, *Louis*, pp. 55–6. On the battle of Bouvines, see WB, *Vie*, pp. 274–95; WB, *Philippide*, pp. 320–49; John France, 'Bouvines, Battle of', OEMW, vol. 1, pp. 163–5; Bradbury, *Philip Augustus*, pp. 295–311; Baldwin, *Government of Philip Augustus*, pp. 215–19; McGlynn, *Blood Cries Afar*, pp. 102–17. The engagement is the subject of two dedicated books, both in French: Duby, *Le dimanche de Bouvines*, and Barthélemy, *La bataille de Bouvines*.

28 Quotes from AB, *Rois*, p. 771; AB, *Dukes*, p. 162; RW, p. 364; WB, *Vie*, p. 324, respectively.

29 RW, pp. 364–5.

30 RW, p. 365. McGlynn calculates that Albemarle, Salisbury, Arundel and Warenne between them switched 430 knights and thirteen castles from John's side to Louis's (*Blood Cries Afar*, p. 171).

31 For more on the importance of coronations at this time, see Hanley, *Two Houses, Two Kingdoms*, pp. 227–8; Hanley, *Louis*,

pp. 243–6. There is charter evidence that Louis, while in England, continued to style himself 'eldest son of the king of France' rather than 'king of England': see ibid., p. 96 and plate 9.

32 For more on the campaign of June and early July 1216, see AB, *Dukes*, pp. 165–8; AB, *Rois*, pp. 771–2; RW, pp. 365–6; Hanley, *Louis*, pp. 101–8; McGlynn, *Blood Cries Afar*, pp. 170–3.

33 MP, *Chronica*, vol. 3, p. 28.

CHAPTER 2

1 For more on the strategic importance of castles and fortifications, see Steane, *The Archaeology of Power*; Hanley, *War and Combat*, pp. 15–17; Jones, 'Fortifications and Sieges', pp. 163–4; DeVries and Smith, *Medieval Military Technology*, pp. 227–33; Oliver Creighton, 'Castles: 500–1100' and Michael Thompson, 'Castles: 1150–1350', in *OEMW*, vol. 1, pp. 336–9 and 339–42 respectively. On the specific subject of the use of castles during the barons' war against King John, see Spencer, *The Castle at War*, pp. 86–104.

2 Quote from OV, vol. 2, p. 181.

3 See the detailed breakdowns of royal expenditure per year per castle in Brown, 'Royal Castle Building', pp. 379–98.

4 More on the history and fabric of Dover castle may be found in Brindle, *Dover Castle*; Humphreys, *Dover Castle*; Goodall, *The English Castle*, pp. 139–44; Hodgson, 'An Introduction to the Defences of Dover'; Michael W. Thompson, 'Dover Castle', *OEMW*, vol. 1, pp. 548–9. The Gatehouse project has compiled many historical references to the site, and these may be found online at http://www.gatehouse-gazetteer.info/English%20sites/1612.html.

5 The fullest contemporary description of the siege of Chinon is (in Latin) RC, pp. 152–5. The engagement and John's refusal to send help are also mentioned in RW, pp. 214–15; GC, vol. 2, p. 98; WB, *Vie*, pp. 237–8.

6 Quote from MP, *Chronica*, vol. 2, p. 664. More on Hubert de Burgh's life and career up until this point may be found in West, *The Justiciarship in England*, pp. 212–24; F.J. West, 'Burgh, Hubert de, earl of Kent (c. 1170–1243)', ODNB; Weiss, 'The Castellan'.

7 The relevant primary sources are AB, *Dukes*, pp. 169–71; RW, pp. 374–5; RC, p. 182; MP, *Chronica*, vol. 2, pp. 664–5; Barnwell,

pp. 230–1; WB, *Vie*, p. 325; PM, pp. 389–90. The siege is also discussed in various secondary sources: see, among others, Hanley, *Louis*, pp. 109–14 and 148–52; McGlynn, *Blood Cries Afar*, pp. 177–80 and 203–4; Humphrys, *Enemies at the Gate*, pp. 49–55; Church, *King John*, pp. 245–6; Spencer, *The Castle at War*, pp. 98–9.

8 For more on the demographics of England at this time, see Hanley, *Louis*, pp. 66–7; Mason, 'Portrait of Britain, AD 1200'; Russell, 'The Clerical Population of Medieval England'.

9 AB, *Dukes*, p. 169.

10 The document in which Peter is confirmed in possession of his family lands is Patent Roll 17 John (National Archives C66/14), which has not been digitised. See also Webster's note on Peter's identity in AB, *Dukes*, p. 163 n.711.

11 The image in question is from Walter de Milemete's *De nobilitatibus, sapientiis, et prudentiis regum* of c. 1326 (Oxford, Christ Church College, MS 92, fol. 78v); it is available to view on the Bodleian Library website, at https://digital.bodleian.ox.ac.uk/objects /b4d2880c-6267-4ad1-923b-fa323c58052b/surfaces /64f1661a-e6eb-4508-8a5b-8a94ab4f1f58/. For more discussion on the absence of torsion machinery in the twelfth and thirteenth centuries, see Purton, 'The Myth of the Mangonel'; Fulton, 'Anglo-Norman Artillery'; Chevedden, 'Artillery in Late Antiquity'.

12 For these calculations and more, see the tables in Fulton, *Artillery in the Era of the Crusades*, pp. 455–7. The chapter dedicated to the mechanics of siege machinery (ibid., pp. 39–58) gives copious further details.

13 For more on siege machinery of the early thirteenth century, see DeVries and Smith, *Medieval Military Technology*, pp. 117–29; Bradbury, *The Medieval Siege*, pp. 241–95; Bennett et al., *Fighting Techniques of the Medieval World*, pp. 192–8; Bachrach and Bachrach, *Warfare in Medieval Europe*, pp. 236–40; Hanley, *War and Combat*, pp. 18–20.

14 AB, *Dukes*, p. 169.

15 For more on the mental aspects of medieval siege warfare, see the chapter on 'War Games, Psychology and Morale' in Hindley, *Medieval Siege and Siegecraft*, pp. 110–24. On the psychology of

medieval warfare more generally, see Rees, Hurlock and Crowley (eds), *Combat Stress in Pre-modern Europe*.

16 RW, p. 338.

17 For more on bows and crossbows, see, among others, Strickland and Hardy, *The Great Warbow*; Roth, *With a Bended Bow*; Loades, *The Longbow*; DeVries and Smith, *Medieval Military Technology*, pp. 34–46; Bachrach and Bachrach, *Warfare in Medieval Europe*, pp. 230–6; Bachrach, 'Origins of the Crossbow Industry in England'.

18 RW, p. 375.

19 RW, p. 375.

20 Quotes from AB, *Dukes*, p. 169 and RW, p. 376, respectively. For more on Alexander's feat, unique for a king of Scots in the Middle Ages, see Stringer, 'Kingship, Conflict and State-Making in the Reign of Alexander II', pp. 128–9.

21 Our supposition that this Peter was a member of the de Craon family of Mayenne in Anjou is given greater weight by the fact that in late 1216 Constance de Craon, daughter of Maurice II, made a donation to a local abbey 'for the soul of my brother Peter', which implies that he had recently died. More on the family may be found in the relevant entry at the Foundation for Medieval Genealogy, at https://fmg.ac/Projects/MedLands/anjounob.htm#MauriceIICraondied1196A.

22 See Humphreys, *Dover Castle*, pp. 36–8; Humphrys, *Enemies at the Gate*, pp. 51–2.

23 For an in-depth examination of medieval siege conventions, see Bradbury, *The Medieval Siege*, pp. 296–334.

24 AB, *Dukes*, p. 170.

25 AB, *Dukes*, p. 170.

26 AB, *Dukes*, p. 171; Barnwell, p. 232.

27 RW, p. 377.

CHAPTER 3

1 RW, p. 376.

2 Barnwell, p. 231.

3 Quote from RW, p. 378. The rumour that John was poisoned first appears in a work called the *Brut Chronicle*, written decades later towards the end of the thirteenth century, at a time when

John's reputation as the very worst of kings was becoming enshrined in popular belief. The story seems highly unlikely, not least because the *Brut* says that a monk of Swineshead was the murderer, and the more contemporary chronicles all agree that John was already ill by the time he left Lynn.

4   RW, p. 378.
5   *HWM*, p. 259, and RC, p. 184, respectively.
6   The full letter may be found (in Latin) in *Guala*, pp. 105–6 (quotes from p. 106).
7   An English translation of John's will appears in Warren, *King John*, p. 255. On the subject of John's deathbed repentance, one of his modern biographers notes rather acerbically that although the king wished 'to give reparation to God in sufficient quantity to make amends for the damage he had done to the Church during his lifetime', it was 'unlikely [...] that there was enough money in the king's coffers to meet such a huge demand on its resources' (Church, *King John*, p. 248).
8   Barnwell, p. 232.
9   For a discussion on this point, see Carpenter, *The Minority of Henry III*, p. 13.
10   *HWM*, p. 265.
11   *HWM*, p. 267.
12   *HWM*, p. 269.
13   RW, p. 380.
14   *HWM*, p. 269. This text contains the most detailed account of the coronation, but it is also mentioned in *Guala*, pp. 28–9; RW, pp. 379–80; MP, *Chronica*, vol. 3, pp. 1–2; RC, p. 184; Barnwell, pp. 233–4.
15   For a discussion of the extent to which Isabella 'abandoned' Henry or was driven out against her will, see Hanley, *Two Houses, Two Kingdoms*, p. 235; Wilkinson, 'Maternal Abandonment'.
16   *HWM*, p. 275.
17   The quote is from Patent Roll 3 Henry III (1218), at the top of membrane 6; see https://www.british-history.ac.uk/cal-pat-rolls/hen3/vol1/pp177-184. The translation appears in Bartlett, *Blood Royal*, p. 121.
18   *HWM*, p. 287.

19 AB, *Dukes*, p. 173.
20 RW, p. 381.
21 MP, *Chronica*, vol. 3, pp. 3–4. This variant is also given as a foot-note in RW, p. 373 (oddly, at a point in the text before John has actually died), from where the translation has been taken.
22 On this re-issue of Magna Carta, see *Guala*, pp. 29–31; Carpenter, *Magna Carta*, pp. 406–11; Holt, *Magna Carta*, pp. 378–82; Carpenter, *The Minority of Henry III*, pp. 22–4.
23 RW, p. 380.
24 RW, p. 385.
25 PM, p. 389. His actual comment about Hubert is amusingly reluctant: *n'es gardoit pas comme vilains*, or 'there was nothing of the villein about the way he defended [the castle]'.

CHAPTER 4

1 More on medieval sheriffs and their duties may be found in Morris, *The Medieval English Sheriff*; Sabapathy, *Officers and Accountability in Medieval England*, pp. 83–134; Bartlett, *England Under the Norman and Angevin Kings*, pp. 149–51 and 159–77.
2 RD, p. 31. The English translation given in this edition of the work is that Nicola's 'heart was not that of a woman', but the Latin is *nichil femineum cogitans*, for which I prefer the translation 'not thinking about anything womanly', as given in Wilkinson, *Women in Thirteenth-Century Lincolnshire*, p. 17.
3 This is detailed in Barnwell, p. 230, where the author specifi-cally notes that Lincoln is held by a 'matron' named Nicola. The Anonymous of Béthune knew that Lincoln castle 'was defended by a lady known as Lady Nicola who had inherited the duty of defence there, and very faithfully did she defend it' (AB, *Dukes*, p. 173).
4 This scene was detailed in the local Hundred Rolls about sixty years later, described either by those who remembered it them-selves or who had been told of it by their parents. I have not been able to consult the original rolls, but their evidence for this episode is quoted in Wilkinson, *Women in Thirteenth-Century Lincolnshire*, p. 19; Hill, *Medieval Lincoln*, p. 199; and Susan M. Johns, 'Haie, Nicola de la (d. 1230)', ODNB.

5 Quote from AB, *Rois*, p. 774. More on Nicola de la Haye and her career up until this point may be found in Johns, 'Haie, Nicola de la (d. 1230)', ODNB; Hill, *Medieval Lincoln*, pp. 199–201 and 205–6; Wilkinson, *Women in Thirteenth-Century Lincolnshire*, pp. 13–21. Wilkinson also wrote a short and accessible online biography of Nicola for the 800th anniversary of Magna Carta in 2015, which is freely available online, at https://magnacarta800th.com/schools/biographies/women-of-magna-carta/lady-nicholaa-de -la-haye/.

6 For more on Lincoln castle and its defences, see Hill, *Medieval Lincoln*, pp. 82–106. A compilation of historical references compiled by the Gatehouse project is available online at http://www.gatehouse-gazetteer.info/English%20sites/1835.html.

7 On the French and rebel march to Mountsorrel and the (lack of) engagement there, see RW, pp. 389–91. HWM, p. 307 adds the detail that the besiegers thought Louis was coming against them in person and that this hastened their retreat.

8 RW, p. 391.

9 RW, p. 392.

10 HWM, pp. 309–11 (my emphasis).

11 RW, pp. 392–3.

12 The rather complicated process of donning all this can be diffi-cult to visualise. A complete step-by-step photographic guide to arming a knight in the early thirteenth century may be found at http://www.catherinehanley.co.uk/historical-background/arming-a-knight-in-the-13th-century/.

13 There is a vast literature available on armour and weapons during the twelfth and thirteenth centuries. For a start, see Nicolle, *Arms and Armour of the Crusading Era*; Nicolle (ed.), *A Companion to Medieval Arms and Armour*; DeVries and Smith, *Medieval Military Technology*, pp. 66–74; Hanley, *War and Combat*, pp. 29–34; Robert Douglas Smith, 'Armor, Body', OEMW, vol. 1, pp. 67–73; Robert Douglas Smith, 'Helmets', OEMW, vol. 2, pp. 250–4. On the specific point of 'having one's helm laced' indicating imminent combat, see Hanley, *War and Combat*, pp. 61–2; Jones, *Bloodied Banners*, pp. 115–19.

14 For more on horses and their use in war at this time, see Ayton, *Knights and Warhorses*; Ayton, 'Arms, Armour and Horses';

C.M. Gillmor, 'Horses', OEMW, vol. 2, pp. 271–5; C.M. Gillmor, 'Horsemanship', OEMW, vol. 2, pp. 269–71. On the specific point of the destrier's average stature, see Ameen et al., 'In Search of the "Great Horse"'. Full details of the fascinating warhorse research project may be found online at https://medievalwar-horse.exeter.ac.uk/.

15 RH, pp. 166–7.

16 For more on tournaments, see Barber and Barker, *Tournaments*; Barker, *The Tournament in England*; Michael Prestwich, 'Tournaments and Jousts', OEMW, vol. 3, pp. 367–70.

17 On the development of heraldry and its display on banners and surcoats, see DeVries and Smith, *Medieval Military Technology*, pp. 73–4; Hanley, *War and Combat*, pp. 32–3; Adrian Ailes, 'Heralds and Heraldry', OEMW, vol. 2, pp. 263–5.

18 The primary works are HWM, pp. 315–55; RW, pp. 391–8; AB, *Dukes*, pp. 181–2; Barnwell, p. 237; RC, p. 185; MP, *Chronica*, pp. 20–5; WB, *Vie*, pp. 326–7; PM, p. 391; MR, pp. 155–6. Further discussion in secondary works may also be found in Carpenter, *Minority of Henry III*, pp. 36–40; McGlynn, *Blood Cries Afar*, pp. 208–16; Hanley, *Louis*, pp. 156–65; France, *Medieval France at War*, pp. 152–5; Hill, *Medieval Lincoln*, pp. 201–5; Spencer, *The Castle at War*, pp. 99–102; Brooks and Oakley, 'The Campaign and Battle of Lincoln 1217'.

19 RW, p. 393. Our two major sources tally very well on the subject of numbers. Roger of Wendover (p. 392) says there were 400 knights, 250 crossbowmen and 'an innumerable host' of others, while the *History of William Marshal* (p. 315) gives the numbers as a very precise 405 knights and 317 crossbowmen. As one of Marshal's modern biographers points out, it is not impossible that the author of the latter had access to the actual muster rolls (Crouch, *William Marshal*, p. 129).

20 RW, p. 214 (as part of Roger's account of Peter's appointment to the see of Winchester in 1205). For more on this very martially inclined bishop of Winchester, see Vincent, *Peter des Roches*; Nicholas Vincent, 'Roches, Peter des [Peter de Rupibus] (d. 1238)', ODNB.

21 HWM, p. 323.

22 RW, p. 394 and HWM, pp. 323–9 (quote p. 327), respectively. Two later detailed analyses of the bishop's supposed walkabout, cross-referenced with what is known of the layout of the city at the time, show that the exploit is almost certainly apocryphal (Brooks and Oakley, 'The Campaign and Battle of Lincoln', pp. 303–5; Tout, 'The Fair of Lincoln', pp. 247–52).

23 Quote from HWM, p. 319. For more on medieval battle commanders acting in the expectation that the men under their command would feel fear and potentially demonstrate cowardice, see Isaac, 'Cowardice and Fear Management'; Morillo, 'Expecting Cowardice'.

24 RW, p. 393.

25 RW, pp. 394–5.

26 RW, p. 395.

27 HWM, p. 333.

28 Quote from HWM, p. 337.

29 HWM, pp. 337–9.

30 WB, Vie, p. 326 and MR, p. 127, respectively.

31 RW, p. 395.

32 HWM, pp. 339–41.

33 Matthew Paris's manuscript illustration of the battle is Parker Library, Corpus Christi College, MS16, fol. 55v; the image is available online at https://parker.stanford.edu/parker/catalog/qt808nj0703.

34 HWM, p. 341.

35 Some, but not all, of Lincoln was cobbled at this time. I am very grateful to the Survey of Lincoln group, who attempted to find out exactly which streets were cobbled by May 1217, so I might work out whether this could have had an effect on the battle, but the information proved elusive despite their best efforts.

36 HWM, p. 347.

37 RW, p. 395.

38 HWM, p. 349.

39 Here we have slightly differing accounts, with Roger of Wendover (p. 396) giving the figure of 300 knights while the Barnwell annalist says 380 (pp. 237–8).

40 RW, p. 396. Ralph of Coggeshall disagrees with Roger, noting that the count of Perche was killed 'along with many others' (RC, p. 185).

41 RW, p. 397.

42 HWM, p. 353, and RW, p. 396, respectively. The following quotes about the aftermath of the battle are all from RW, pp. 396–7; the looting of churches is also mentioned in Barnwell, p. 238.

43 Marshal's claim to Perche's English lands is discussed further in Crouch, *William Marshal*, pp. 137–8.

44 On Nicola's career after the battle until her death in 1230, see Carpenter, *Minority of Henry III*, pp. 66–7; Johns, 'Haie, Nicola de la (d. 1230)', ODNB.

45 HWM, p. 355; WB, *Vie*, p. 327; and RW, p. 398, respectively. The Anonymous of Béthune names some of those who made it back to Louis (AB, *Dukes*, pp. 181–2).

CHAPTER 5

1 HWM, p. 345.

2 RW, p. 387.

3 The finances of the royalist party at this juncture are discussed in more depth in Carpenter, *Minority of Henry III*, pp. 25–7.

4 WB, *Vie*, p. 326.

5 HWM, pp. 297–305; AB, *Dukes*, pp. 176–8.

6 There was a kind of moral and theological framework for war, and when it could be considered 'just', but again this had no official legal standing. For discussion on this point see Hanley, *War and Combat*, pp. 41–50; Titterton, *Deception in Medieval Warfare*, pp. 171–5; Bliese, 'The Just War as Concept and Motive'; Ben Lowe, 'Just War, Just Motive', OEMW, vol. 2, pp. 455–7. More in-depth, full-length works on the concept of the just war are Johnson, *Just War Tradition*, and Russell, *The Just War in the Middle Ages*.

7 HWM, pp. 289–91.

8 Quotes from HWM, vol. 1, p. 397; HWM, p. 27. These and other examples are discussed in Hanley, *War and Combat*, pp. 65–6, and Titterton, *Deception in Medieval Warfare*, pp. 30 and 139.

9 A great deal has been written on the concept of chivalry and its development over the centuries, much of it contradictory

and with no firm single definition ever having been agreed upon. For a brief introduction, see Maurice Keen, 'Chivalry: Overview', OEMW, vol. 1, pp. 374–85. Full-length works include Keen, Chivalry; Barber, The Knight and Chivalry; Kaeuper, Chivalry and Violence in Medieval Europe; Strickland, War and Chivalry; Vale, War and Chivalry; Jones and Coss (eds), A Companion to Chivalry. On the specific topic of William Marshal and chivalry, see Gillingham, 'War and Chivalry in the History of William the Marshal'. One of King John's biographers notes that Marshal's reputation for having 'an unimpeachable record of honourable service' is 'not always deserved' (Church, King John, p. 251), while one of the regent's own modern biographers notes succinctly that 'the kingdom would not be regained by the Marshal sitting still and waiting for Louis to go away' (Crouch, William Marshal, p. 128).

10 Recent research by Jonathan Dean has traced the origin of the 'twelve arrows a minute' myth and has found that the first recorded use of the phrase was in an article published in the United Service Journal in September 1832. I am very grateful to him for bringing this to my attention in a personal communication.

11 There is a large body of work available on medieval archery, both on the practicalities and on the way in which the practice was perceived. For a start, see Heath, Archery; Loades, The Longbow; Strickland and Hardy, The Great Warbow; Roth, With a Bended Bow; Bradbury, The Medieval Archer.

12 RW, p. 366.

13 AB, Dukes, p. 172.

14 The 1216 letter from John to the men of the Weald, and the note that William is to receive an annual income of 30 marks, may be found in Patent Roll 18 John (National Archives C66/15), which has not been digitised. The 1217 entry in the patent rolls confirming the appointment of Willelmo de Casingeham to the position of warden may be found in the transcription online (in Latin) at https://www.british-history.ac.uk/cal-pat-rolls/hen3/vol1/pp51-82#p38, towards the end of Membrane 7.

15 HWM, p. 293. For details of the guerrilla activities at this time, see also AB, Dukes, pp. 173–4; AB, Rois, p. 774.

16 AB, Dukes, p. 177.

17 On the specific point of William's link to the Robin Hood legend, see McGlynn, *Robin Hood*, pp. 77–89. For more on William and his career more generally, see Stephens, 'A Note on William of Cassingham'. A more widely accessible, if slightly overblown, mini-biography (including a map of the extent of the Weald at this time) may be found at https://thefreelancehistorywriter .com/2016/08/12/willikin-of-the-weald-a-forgotten-hero-of -england-a-guest-post-by-michael-long/.

18 RW, p. 381.

19 *HWM*, p. 305.

20 AB, *Dukes*, p. 180.

21 AB, *Dukes*, p. 180.

22 AB, *Dukes*, p. 184; PM, p. 390; WB, *Vie*, p. 326, respectively.

23 RW, pp. 398–9; *HWM*, p. 359, respectively.

24 MR, pp. 128–9.

25 Quotes from CP, pp. 128–9 and p. 129.

26 For more on women and their participation in war at this time, see Valerie Eads, 'Women as Combatants', OEMW, vol. 3, pp. 454–6; McLaughlin, 'The Woman Warrior'; Truax, 'Anglo-Norman Women at War'; Blythe, 'Women in the Military'; Verbruggen, 'Women in Medieval Armies'; Cassagnes-Brouquet, *Chevaleresses*. For examples of double standards being applied to male and female combatants by contemporary chroniclers, see Hanley, *War and Combat*, pp. 86–90; and on the specific example of Empress Matilda, see Hanley, *Matilda*, pp. 240–1.

27 A detailed examination of military logistics throughout the Middle Ages (including exact calculations on human and animal food consumption, and information on food sources, transport, foraging, etc.) may be found in Bachrach and Bachrach, *Warfare in Medieval Europe*, pp. 154–212.

28 PM, p. 392.

29 A brief biography of Philip is Nicholas Vincent, 'Aubigny, Philip d' [Philip Daubeney] (d. 1236)', ODNB.

30 AB, *Dukes*, p. 180.

31 AB, *Dukes*, p. 182.

CHAPTER 6

1   On John's navy-building and his use of ships at this time, see Rose, *England's Medieval Navy*, pp. 35–6 and 44–5; Stanton, *Medieval Maritime Warfare*, pp. 227–30; Warren, *King John*, pp. 120–5.

2   For more on ships and naval warfare in the thirteenth century, see Rodger, *Safeguard of the Sea*, pp. 50–72; DeVries and Smith, *Medieval Military Technology*, pp. 301–9; Bachrach and Bachrach, *Warfare in Medieval Europe*, pp. 309–14; Fernández-Armesto, 'Naval Warfare after the Viking Age'. A useful pictorial representation of various ship types of this era may be found online at the Naval Encyclopaedia: https://naval-encyclopedia.com/medieval-ships.php.

3   RW, pp. 261–2.

4   HWM, p. 233; the engagement is also described by RW, pp. 272–3.

5   Quote from *Eustace*, p. 53. A short factual biography may be found in the introduction to the modern translation of the work: *Eustace*, pp. 7–40. For more, see McGlynn, 'Eustace the Monk'; Lehr, 'Eustace the Monk'; D.A. Carpenter, 'Eustace the Monk (c. 1170–1217)', ODNB.

6   All of these episodes appear in *Eustace*, pp. 58–9.

7   Eustace's attack on Folkestone is noted in Patent Roll 18 John (National Archives C66/15), which has not been digitised. I am very grateful to Susan Brock and Andrew Buck for deciphering the many abbreviations in the passage and translating it for me.

8   Barnwell, pp. 238–9; RW, p. 399; HWM, p. 361, respectively.

9   All the chroniclers give different figures; for an examination of this inconsistency and of the probable real numbers, see McGlynn, *Blood Cries Afar*, p. 225.

10   HWM, pp. 371–3.

11   HWM, pp. 361–3.

12   Quotes from HWM, pp. 363 and 369, respectively. Matthew Paris's manuscript illustration of the battle is Parker Library, Corpus Christi College, MS16, fol. 56r; the image is available online at https://parker.stanford.edu/parker/catalog/qt808nj0703.

13   HWM, p. 365.

14 See the primary source accounts in RW, pp. 399–401; *HWM*, pp. 361–81; AB, *Dukes*, pp. 185–6; Barnwell, pp. 238–9; RC, p. 185; WB, *Vie*, p. 327; *Eustace*, pp. 77–8; MP, *Chronica*, vol. 3, pp. 26–9 (quotes from pp. 28 and 29).

15 The two nineteenth-century accounts of the battle of Sandwich are Laird Clowes, vol. 1, pp. 186–90; Nicolas, vol. 1, pp. 177–84. A detailed early twentieth-century study is Cannon, 'The Battle of Sandwich and Eustace the Monk'. More recent secondary analysis may also be found in Sean McGlynn, 'Sandwich, Battle of', *OEMW*, vol. 3, pp. 219–20; Stanton, *Medieval Maritime Warfare*, pp. 236–40; Rose, *England's Medieval Navy*, pp. 125–9; Rodger, *Safeguard of the Sea*, pp. 54–7; France, *Medieval France at War*, pp. 155–8; and the introduction to the translation of *Eustace*, pp. 36–40.

16 *HWM*, p. 371.

17 A naval historian notes that this displayed 'a precocious grasp of naval tactics [...] which was hardly equalled by any other English admiral before the sixteenth century' (Rodger, *Safeguard of the Sea*, p. 55).

18 WB, *Vie*, p. 327. MP, *Chronica*, vol. 3, p. 28 also thinks that Eustace would have let them pass.

19 A summary of the historical use of lime for building purposes can be found on the website of the Natural Environment Research Council, at https://nora.nerc.ac.uk/id/eprint/18088 /1/A_Short_History_of_the_Use_of_Lime_as_a.pdf. A series of videos showing how lime was made in the thirteenth century has been produced at the French archaeological and education site at Guédelon; the first one may be viewed at https:// www.youtube.com/watch?v=0xcimgg4IBM, with the others following.

20 See the link above, in note 12 to this chapter.

21 Quotes from AB, *Dukes*, p. 186; RW, pp. 399–400; *HWM*, p. 373; *Eustace*, p. 78, respectively.

22 *HWM*, p. 373. McGlynn, in his analysis of the battle, describes Reginald's actions here as being akin to those of a 'medieval Errol Flynn' (*Blood Cries Afar*, p. 231).

23 RW, pp. 399 and 400.

24 *Eustace*, p. 78.

25 Both quotes from *HWM*, p. 375.

26 *Eustace*, p. 78.

27 RW, p. 400 and *HWM*, p. 377, respectively.

28 Quotes from AB, p. 186; *HWM*, p. 377; RC, pp. 185–6, respectively.

29 All of these quotes on plunder are from *HWM*, p. 379.

30 This entry in the patent rolls may be found in the online transcription (in Latin) at https://www.british-history.ac.uk/cal-pat-rolls/hen3/vol1/pp83-106, at the very beginning of membrane 3: *veniatis cum toto navigio vestro, tam nuper lucrato quam alio.*

31 WH, pp. 260–1; HK, pp. 205–6.

CHAPTER 7

1 Quotes from *HWM*, pp. 381–3; AB, p. 186; RW, p. 402, respectively.

2 The details of the Treaty of Lambeth are laid out in full (in French) in WB, *Vie*, pp. 328–31, and in summary in English in AB, *Dukes*, pp. 187–8; *HWM*, pp. 387–9; RW, pp. 402–4.

3 AB, *Dukes*, p. 188.

4 RW, p. 403.

5 *HWM*, p. 407.

6 *Dialogus*, p. 53.

7 *Pro patria* is the original Latin phrase used by Roger of Wendover, translated in the English edition as the royalists fighting 'for their country' (RW, p. 392). A great deal has been written in recent years on the development of nationhood and national identity in the Middle Ages, and how it might have developed rather earlier than was previously thought. See, for example, Forde et al., *Concepts of National Identity in the Middle Ages*; Davies, 'Nations and National Identities in the Medieval World'; the section on national identity in Gillingham, *The English in the Twelfth Century*; McGlynn, '"Pro patria": National Identity and War in Early Medieval England'.

8 To date the only thorough analysis of the 1216–17 war as a whole is McGlynn, *Blood Cries Afar*, which can be supplemented by Hanley, *Louis* and by relevant chapters in more general works such as Carpenter, *Minority of Henry III* and various biographies of William Marshal.

9 Quote from Barnwell, p. 232.

10 *HWM*, p. 257.

Bibliography

PRIMARY SOURCES AND ENCYCLOPAEDIAS

AB, Dukes Anonymous of Béthune, *History of the Dukes of Normandy and the Kings of England*, trans. Janet Shirley, with historical notes by Paul Webster (Oxford: Routledge, 2021)

AB, Rois Anonymous of Béthune, *Chronique des rois de France*, ed. L. Delisle, in *Recueil des Historiens des Gaules et de la France*, vol. 24 (Paris: Imprimerie Nationale, 1904), pp. 750–75

Barnwell Chronicle of the Barnwell annalist, vol. 2 of *Memoriale Walteri de Coventria*, ed. William Stubbs (London: Longman, 1873)

CP Christine de Pisan, *The Treasure of the City of Ladies: Or, the Book of the Three Virtues*, trans. Sarah Lawson (Harmondsworth: Penguin Classics, 1985)

Dialogus *Dialogus de Saccario: The Course of the Exchequer*, ed. and trans. Charles Johnson (London: Nelson and Sons, 1950)

Eustace *The Romance of Eustace the Monk*, in *Two Medieval Outlaws: Eustace the Monk and Fouke Fitz Waryn*, trans. Glyn S. Burgess (Woodbridge: D.S. Brewer, 2009), pp. 3–87

GC Gervase of Canterbury, *The Historical Works of Gervase of Canterbury*, ed. William Stubbs, 2 vols (London: Rolls Series, 1879–80)

Guala *The Letters and Charters of Cardinal Guala Bicchieri, Papal Legate in England 1216–1218*, ed. Nicholas Vincent (Woodbridge: Canterbury and York Society, 1996)

GW Gerald of Wales, *Instruction for a Ruler: De Principis Instructione*, ed. and trans. Robert Bartlett (Oxford: Oxford University Press, 2018)

HK Henry Knighton, *Chronicon Henrici Knighton, vel Cnitthon, monachi Leycestrensis*, ed. Joseph Rawson Lumby (London: Eyre and Spottiswoode, 1889)

HWM Volume 2 of the *History of William Marshal*, ed. and trans. A.J. Holden, S. Gregory and D. Crouch, 3 vols (London: Anglo-Norman Text Society, 2002–6)

Innocent *Selected Letters of Pope Innocent III Concerning England (1198–1216)*, ed. and trans. C.R. Cheney and W.H. Semple (London: Nelson and Sons, 1953)

MP, Chronica Matthew Paris, *Matthæi Pariensis Chronica Majora*, ed. Henry Richards Luard, 7 vols (London: Rolls Series, 1872–83)

MP, Historia Matthew Paris, *Matthæi Pariensis Historia Anglorum*, ed. F. Maddern, 3 vols (London: Rolls Series, 1866–9)

MR Minstrel of Reims, *Tales of a Minstrel of Reims in the Thirteenth Century*, trans. Samuel N. Rosenberg, annotated by Randall Todd Pippenger, with an introduction by William Chester Jordan (Washington DC: Catholic University of America Press, 2022)

ODNB *Oxford Dictionary of National Biography*, online edition, available at www.oxforddnb.com

OEMW *Oxford Encyclopaedia of Medieval Warfare and Military Technology*, ed. Clifford J. Rogers, 3 vols (New York: Oxford University Press, 2010)

OV Orderic Vitalis, *The Ecclesiastical History of Orderic Vitalis*, ed. and trans. Marjorie Chibnall, 6 vols (Oxford: Clarendon, 1968–80)

PM Volume 2 of Philip Mousket, *Chronique rimée de Philippe Mouskes*, ed. le Baron de Reiffenberg, 2 vols (Brussels: M. Hayez, 1836–8)

RC Ralph of Coggeshall, *Radulphi de Coggeshall Chronicon Anglicanum*, ed. J. Stevenson (London: Rolls Series, 1875)

RD Richard of Devizes, *The Chronicle of Richard of Devizes of the Time of King Richard the First*, ed. and trans. John T. Appleby (London: Thomas Nelson and Sons, 1963)

RH Volume 2 of Roger of Howden, *Chronica Magistri Rogeri de Houedene*, ed. William Stubbs (London: Longman, Green and Co., 1869)

Rigord Rigord, *Vie de Philippe Auguste*, ed. F. Guizot, in *Collection des Mémoires relatifs à l'histoire de France*, vol. 11 (Paris: Brière, 1825), pp. 9–180

RW Volume 2 of Roger of Wendover, *Roger of Wendover's Flowers of History*, trans. J.A. Giles, 2 vols (London: Henry G. Bohn, 1849; facsimile repr. Felinfach: Llanerch, 1995–96)

WB, Philippide William the Breton, *La Philippide*, ed. F. Guizot, in *Collection des Mémoires relatifs à l'histoire de France*, vol. 12 (Paris: Brière, 1825), pp. 1–390

WB, Vie William the Breton, *Vie de Philippe Auguste*, ed. F. Guizot, in *Collection des Mémoires relatifs à l'histoire de France*, vol. 11 (Paris: Brière, 1825), pp. 181–354

WH Volume 1 of Walter of Hemingburgh, *Chronicon Domini Walteri de Hemingburgh*, ed. Hans Claude Hamilton, 2 vols (London: Sumptibus Societatis, 1848–9)

All of the pre-1900 editions listed are freely available for consultation on the Internet Archive website, at archive.org

SECONDARY SOURCES

Abels, Richard, 'Cultural Representation and the Practice of War in the Middle Ages', *Journal of Medieval Military History*, 6 (2008), 1–31

Abels, Richard P. and Bernard S. Bachrach (eds), *The Normans and their Adversaries at War: Essays in Memory of C. Warren Hollister* (Woodbridge: Boydell, 2001)

Allmand, Christopher, 'War and the Non-Combatant in the Middle Ages', in *Medieval Warfare: A History*, ed. Maurice Keen (Oxford: Oxford University Press, 1999), pp. 253–72

_____ 'The Reporting of War in the Middle Ages', in *War and Society in Medieval and Early Modern Britain*, ed. Diana Dunn (Liverpool: Liverpool University Press, 2000), pp. 17–33

Ameen, Carly, Helene Benkert, Tamsyn Fraser et al., 'In Search of the "Great Horse": A Zooarchaeological Assessment of Horses from England (AD 300–1650)', *International Journal of Osteoarchaeology*, 31 (2021), 1247–57

Andrews, J.F., *Lost Heirs of the Medieval Crown: The Kings and Queens Who Never Were* (Barnsley: Pen & Sword, 2019)

_____ *The Families of Eleanor of Aquitaine: A Female Network of Power in the Middle Ages* (Cheltenham: The History Press, 2023)

Asbridge, Thomas, *The Greatest Knight: The Remarkable Life of William Marshal, the Power Behind Five English Thrones* (London: Simon and Schuster, 2015)

Aurell, Martin, *L'Empire des Plantagenêt* (Paris: Tempus, 2017; orig. 2004)

Ayton, Andrew, *Knights and Warhorses* (Woodbridge: Boydell, 1994)

———— 'Arms, Armour and Horses', in *Medieval Warfare: A History*, ed. Maurice Keen (Oxford: Oxford University Press, 1999), pp. 186–208

Bachrach, Bernard, 'Medieval Siege Warfare: A Reconnaissance', *Journal of Military History*, 58 (1994), 119–33

Bachrach, Bernard and David Bachrach, *Warfare in Medieval Europe c. 400–c. 1453* (London and New York: Routledge, 2017)

Bachrach, David, 'Origins of the Crossbow Industry in England', *Journal of Medieval Military History*, 2 (2004), 73–88

Baldwin, John W., *The Government of Philip Augustus: Foundations of French Royal Power in the Middle Ages* (Berkeley: University of California Press, 1986)

———— *Aristocratic Life in Medieval France* (Baltimore and London: Johns Hopkins University Press, 2000)

———— 'Master Stephen Langton, Future Archbishop of Canterbury: The Paris Schools and Magna Carta', *English Historical Review*, 123 (2008), 811–46

———— *Paris, 1200* (Stanford: Stanford University Press, 2010; orig. Paris: Editions Flammarion, 2006)

Bandel, Betty, 'The English Chroniclers' Attitude Toward Women', *Journal of the History of Ideas*, 16 (1955), 113–18

Barber, Richard, *The Knight and Chivalry* (London: Longman, 1970)

Barber, Richard and Juliet Barker, *Tournaments* (Woodbridge: Boydell, 1989)

Barker, Juliet, *The Tournament in England 1100–1400* (Woodbridge: Boydell, 1982)

Barley, M.W., 'Town Defences in England and Wales after 1066', in *The Plans and Topography of Medieval Towns in England and Wales*, ed. M.W. Barley, Council for British Archaeology, CBA Research Report no. 14 (1976)

Barthélemy, Dominique, *La bataille de Bouvines* (Paris: Perrin, 2018)

Bartlett, Robert, *England under the Norman and Angevin Kings, 1075–1225* (Oxford: Oxford University Press, 2000)

———— *Blood Royal: Dynastic Politics in Medieval Europe* (Cambridge: Cambridge University Press, 2020)

Bates, David and Anne Curry (eds), *England and Normandy in the Middle Ages* (London: Hambledon, 1994)

Bautier, Robert-Henri (ed.), *La France de Philippe Auguste — Le temps des mutations* (Paris: Editions du CNRS, 1982)

Beem, Charles (ed.), *The Royal Minorities of Medieval and Early Modern England* (New York: Palgrave Macmillan, 2008)

Benham, Jenny, *Peacemaking in the Middle Ages: Principles and Practice* (Manchester: Manchester University Press, 2007)

Bennett, Judith, *Medieval Women in Modern Perspective* (Washington, DC: American Historical Association, 2000)

Bennett, Matthew, 'The Myth of the Military Supremacy of Knightly Cavalry', in *Medieval Warfare 1000–1300*, ed. John France (Abingdon: Ashgate, 2006), pp. 171–84

Bennett, Matthew, Jim Bradbury, Kelly DeVries et al., *Fighting Techniques of the Medieval World, AD 500–AD 1500* (Staplehurst: Spellmount, 2005)

Bennett, Matthew and Katherine Weikert (eds), *Medieval Hostageship c.700–c.1500: Hostage, Captive, Prisoner of War, Guarantee, Peacemaker* (Oxford and New York: Routledge, 2016)

Berrou, Oliver, *The Contribution of Louis VIII to the Advancement of Capetian France* (Saarbrücken: Lambert Academic Publishing, 2013)

Bliese, John, 'The Just War as Concept and Motive in the Central Middle Ages', *Medievalia et Humanistica*, 17 (1991), 1–26

Blumberg, Arnold, 'Fleets of King John', *Medieval Warfare* 1.1 (2011), 19–23

Blythe, James M., 'Women in the Military: Scholastic Arguments and Medieval Images of Female Warriors', *History of Political Thought*, 22 (2001), 242–69

Bradbury, Jim, *The Medieval Siege* (Woodbridge: Boydell, 1992)

——— *The Medieval Archer* (Woodbridge: Boydell, 1996)

——— *Philip Augustus* (London and New York: Longman, 1998)

——— 'Philip Augustus and King John: Personality and History', in *King John: New Interpretations*, ed. S.D. Church (Woodbridge: Boydell, 1999), pp. 347–61

——— *The Routledge Companion to Medieval Warfare* (London: Routledge, 2004)

——— *The Capetians: Kings of France 987–1328* (London: Continuum, 2007)

Brindle, Steven, *Dover Castle* (London: English Heritage, 2012)

British History Online, at https://www.british-history.ac.uk/

Brooks, F.W. and F. Oakley, 'The Campaign and Battle of Lincoln 1217', *Associated Architectural Societies' Reports and Papers*, vol. 26, part 2 (1922)

Brown, R. Allen, 'Royal Castle Building in Early Angevin England, 1154–1216', *English Historical Review*, 70 (1955), 353–98

———— 'The Norman Conquest and the Genesis of English Castles', *Château Gaillard*, 3 (1969) 1–14

———— 'Dover Castle', *The Archaeological Journal*, 126 (1970), 205–13 and 262–5

Cannon, Henry, 'The Battle of Sandwich and Eustace the Monk', *English Historical Review*, 27 (1912), 649–70

Carpenter, David, 'Kings, Magnates and Society: The Personal Rule of King Henry III, 1234–1258', *Speculum*, 60 (1985), 39–70

———— *The Minority of Henry III* (London: Methuen, 1990)

———— *The Reign of Henry III* (London: Hambledon, 1996)

———— *Magna Carta* (London: Penguin Classics, 2015)

———— *Henry III: The Rise to Power and Personal Rule, 1207–1258* (New Haven and London: Yale University Press, 2020)

Cassagnes-Brouquet, Sophie, *La vie des femmes au Moyen Âge* (Rennes: Ouest-France, 2012)

———— *Chevaleresses: Une chevalerie au féminin* (Paris: Perrin, 2013)

Cassard, Jean-Christophe, *1180–1328: L'âge d'or capétien* (Paris: Bellin, 2011)

Cazel, Fred A., 'The Legates Guala and Pandulf', in *Thirteenth-Century England II: Proceedings of the Newcastle-upon-Tyne Conference 1987*, ed. P.R. Coss and S.D. Lloyd (Woodbridge: Boydell, 1988), pp. 15–21

Cheney, Christopher, 'The Alleged Deposition of King John', in *Studies in Medieval History Presented to Frederick Maurice Powicke*, ed. R.W. Hunt, W.A. Pantin and R.W. Southern (Oxford: Clarendon, 1948), pp. 100–16

———— 'King John's Reaction to the Papal Interdict in England', *Transactions of the Royal Historical Society*, 4th series, 21 (1949), 129–50

———— *Pope Innocent III and England* (Stuttgart: Hiersemann, 1976)

Chevedden, Paul, 'Artillery in Late Antiquity: Prelude to the Middle Ages', in *The Medieval City Under Siege*, ed. Ivy Corfis and Michael Wolfe (Woodbridge: Boydell, 1995), pp. 131–76

1217 — THE BATTLES THAT SAVED ENGLAND

Church, Stephen, 'The Earliest English Muster Roll,
18/19 December 1215', *Historical Research*, 67 (1994), 1–17
_____ 'King John's Testament and the Last Days of his Reign',
English Historical Review, 125 (2010), 505–28
_____ *King John: England, Magna Carta and the Making of a Tyrant*
(Basingstoke: Macmillan, 2015)
Church, Stephen (ed.), *King John: New Interpretations* (Woodbridge:
Boydell, 1999)
Clanchy, M.T., *England and its Rulers, 1066–1272* (London: Wiley-
Blackwell, 1983)
_____ *From Memory to Written Record: England 1066–1307*, 2nd ed.
(Oxford: Blackwell, 1993; orig. 1979)
Contamine, Philippe, *La guerre au Moyen Âge* (Paris: Presses
Universitaires de France, 1992)
_____ *War in the Middle Ages*, trans. Michael Jones (Oxford:
Blackwell, 1992)
_____ *Histoire militaire de la France, tome 1: Des origines à 1715*, 2nd ed.
(Paris: Presses Universitaires de France, 1997; orig. 1992)
Coss, Peter, *The Knight in Medieval England 1000–1400* (Stroud: Sutton,
1993)
_____ *The Lady in Medieval England 1000–1500* (Stroud: Sutton, 1998)
Coulson, Charles, *Castles in Medieval Society: Fortresses in England, France and
Ireland in the Central Middle Ages* (Oxford: Oxford University Press,
2003)
Crouch, David, *William Marshal: Court, Career and Chivalry in the Angevin
Empire 1147–1219* (Harlow: Longman, 1990)
_____ 'Baronial Paranoia in King John's Reign', in *Magna Carta and
the England of King John*, ed. Janet S. Loengard (Woodbridge: Boydell,
2010), pp. 45–62
_____ 'The Complaint of King John against William de Briouze',
in *Magna Carta and the England of King John*, ed. Janet S. Loengard
(Woodbridge: Boydell, 2010), pp. 168–79
_____ *The English Aristocracy 1070–1272: A Social Transformation* (New
Haven and London: Yale University Press, 2011)
Danziger, Danny and John Gillingham, *1215: The Year of Magna Carta*
(London: Hodder, 2003)
Davies, Rees, 'Nations and National Identities in the Medieval World:
An Apologia', *Journal of Belgian History*, 34 (2004), 567–79

Delorme, Philippe, *Blanche de Castille* (Paris: Pygmalion, 2002)

DeVries, Kelly, Martin J. Dougherty, Iain Dickie et al., *Battles of the Medieval World, 1000–1500: From Hastings to Constantinople* (New York: Barnes and Noble, 2006)

DeVries, Kelly and Robert Douglas Smith, *Medieval Military Technology*, 2nd ed. (Toronto: University of Toronto Press, 2012; orig. Peterborough, Ontario: Broadview, 1992)

Duby, Georges, *Le dimanche de Bouvines* (Paris: Gallimard, 1985; orig. 1973)

Duncan, A.A.M., 'John King of England and the Kings of Scots', in *King John: New Interpretations*, ed. S.D. Church (Woodbridge: Boydell, 1999), pp. 247–71

Dyer, Christopher, *Making a Living in the Middle Ages: The People of Britain 850–1520* (New Haven and London: Yale University Press, 2009; orig. 2002)

Eales, Richard, 'Castles and Politics in England, 1215–1224', in *Thirteenth-Century England II: Proceedings of the Newcastle-upon-Tyne Conference 1987*, ed. P.R. Coss and S.D. Lloyd (Woodbridge: Boydell, 1988), pp. 23–43

Erler, Mary and Maryanne Kowaleski (eds), *Women and Power in the Middle Ages* (Athens, GA: University of Georgia Press, 1988)

Facinger, Marion, 'A Study of Medieval Queenship: Capetian France 987–1237', *Studies in Medieval and Renaissance History*, 5 (1968), 1–48

Favier, Jean, *Les Plantagenêts: origines et destin d'un empire XIe–XIVe siècles* (Paris: Fayard, 2015; orig. 2004)

Fawtier, R., *The Capetian Kings of France: Monarchy and Nation 987–1328* (Basingstoke: Macmillan, 1960)

Fernández-Armesto, Felipe, 'Naval Warfare after the Viking Age, c. 1100–1500', in *Medieval Warfare: A History*, ed. Maurice Keen (Oxford: Oxford University Press, 1999), pp. 230–52

Fleiner, Carey and Elena Woodacre (eds), *Virtuous or Villainess? The Image of the Royal Mother from the Early Medieval to the Early Modern Era* (New York: Palgrave Macmillan, 2016)

Forde, Simon, Lesley Johnson and Alan V. Murray, *Concepts of National Identity in the Middle Ages* (Leeds: Leeds Studies in English, 1995)

The Foundation for Medieval Genealogy, at http://fmg.ac/Projects/MedLands/index.htm

France, John, *Western Warfare in the Age of the Crusades 1000–1300* (London: University College London Press, 1999)

———— *Medieval France at War: A Military History of the French Monarchy, 885–1305* (Leeds: Arc Humanities Press, 2022)

Fulton, Michael S., 'Anglo-Norman Artillery in Narrative Histories, from the Reign of William I to the Minority of Henry III', *Journal of Medieval Military History*, 14 (2016), 1–31

———— 'The Myth of the Hybrid Trebuchet', *Viator*, 48.2 (2017), 49–70

———— *Artillery in the Age of the Crusades* (Leiden: Brill, 2018)

———— 'Overlooked Ordnance: Artillery Projectiles of the Crusader Period', in *Crusading and Archaeology*, ed. Vardit Shotten-Hallel and Rosie Weetch (Abingdon: Routledge, 2020), pp. 300–27

Galbraith, V.H., *Roger Wendover and Matthew Paris* (Glasgow: University of Glasgow, 1970; orig. 1944)

———— 'Good and Bad Kings in History', *History*, 30 (1945), 119–32

The Gatehouse project, at http://www.gatehouse-gazetteer.info/home.html

Gillingham, John, 'War and Chivalry in the *History of William the Marshal*', in *Thirteenth-Century England II: Proceedings of the Newcastle-upon-Tyne Conference 1987*, ed. P.R. Coss and S.D. Lloyd (Woodbridge: Boydell, 1988), pp. 1–13

———— *The English in the Twelfth Century: Imperialism, National Identity and Political Values* (Woodbridge: Boydell, 2000)

———— *The Angevin Empire*, 2nd ed. (London: Bloomsbury, 2001; orig. 1984)

———— 'At the Deathbeds of the Kings of England, 1066–1216', in *Herrscher- und Fürstentestamente im Westeuropäischen Mittelalter*, ed. Brigitte Kasten (Cologne, Weimar and Vienna: Böhlau-Verlag, 2008), pp. 509–30

———— 'The Anonymous of Béthune, King John and Magna Carta', in *Magna Carta and the England of King John*, ed. Janet S. Loengard (Woodbridge: Boydell, 2010), pp. 27–44

Given-Wilson, Chris, *Chronicles: The Writing of History in Medieval England* (London and New York: Hambledon and London, 2004)

Given-Wilson, Chris and Alice Curteis, *The Royal Bastards of Medieval England* (London: Routledge and Kegan Paul, 1984)

Gobry, Ivan, *Louis VIII, fils de Philippe II, 1223–1226* (Paris: Pygmalion, 2009)

Goodall, John, 'Dover Castle and the Great Siege of 1216', *Château Gaillard*, 19 (2000), 91–102

—————— *The English Castle* (New Haven and London: Yale University Press, 2011)

Gransden, Antonia, *Historical Writing in England, vol. I: c. 550–c. 1307* (London: Routledge and Kegan Paul, 1974)

Grant, Lindy, 'Blanche of Castile and Normandy', in *Normandy and its Neighbours, 900–1250: Essays for David Bates*, ed. David Crouch and Kathleen Thompson (Turnhout: Brepols, 2011), pp. 117–34

—————— *Blanche of Castile: Queen of France* (New Haven and London: Yale University Press, 2016)

Hallam, Elizabeth M. and Judith Everard, *Capetian France 987–1328*, 2nd ed. (Harlow: Pearson, 2001; orig. London: Longman, 1980)

Hanley, Catherine, *War and Combat 1150–1270: The Evidence from Old French Literature* (Woodbridge: D.S. Brewer, 2003)

—————— *Louis: The French Prince Who Invaded England* (New Haven and London: Yale University Press, 2016)

—————— *Matilda: Empress, Queen, Warrior* (New Haven and London: Yale University Press, 2019)

—————— *Two Houses, Two Kingdoms: A History of France and England, 1100–1300* (New Haven and London: Yale University Press, 2022)

Hattendorf, J. and R. Unger (eds), *War at Sea in the Middle Ages and Renaissance* (Woodbridge: Boydell, 2003)

Heath, Ernest, *Archery: A Military History* (London: Osprey, 1980)

Hill, J.W.F., *Medieval Lincoln* (Cambridge: Cambridge University Press, 1948)

Hindley, Geoffrey, *Medieval Sieges and Siege Craft* (Barnsley: Pen & Sword, 2009)

Hodgson, N., 'An Introduction to the Defences of Dover', *Fort*, 6 (1978), 38–60

Holt, J.C., *The Northerners: A Study in the Reign of King John* (Westport, CT: Greenwood Press, 1981; orig. Oxford: Oxford University Press, 1961)

_____ *Magna Carta and Medieval Government* (London: Hambledon, 1985)

_____ *Magna Carta*, 2nd ed. (Cambridge: Cambridge University Press, 1992; orig. 1965)

_____ 'The *Casus Regis*: The Law and Politics of Succession in the Plantagenet Dominions, 1185–1247', in *Colonial England, 1066–1215, Essays by J.C. Holt* (London: Hambledon, 1997), pp. 307–26

Housley, Norman, 'European Warfare, c. 1200–1320', in *Medieval Warfare: A History*, ed. Maurice Keen (Oxford: Oxford University Press, 1999), pp. 113–35

Howard, Michael, *War in European History* (Oxford: Oxford University Press, 1977)

Hucker, Bernd, *Otto IV: Der wiederentdeckte Kaiser: Eine Biographie* (Frankfurt am Main: Insel-Verlag, 2003)

Humphreys, Roy S., *Dover Castle: England's First Line of Defence* (Stroud: The History Press, 2010)

Humphrys, Julian, *Enemies at the Gate: English Castles Under Siege from the 12th Century to the Civil War* (Swindon: English Heritage, 2007)

Isaac, Stephen, 'The Problem with Mercenaries', in *The Circle of War in the Middle Ages: Essays on Medieval Military and Naval History*, ed. Donald J. Kagay and L.J. Andrew Villalon (Woodbridge: Boydell, 1999), pp. 101–10

_____ 'Cowardice and Fear Management: The 1173–74 Conflict as a Case Study', *Journal of Medieval Military History*, 4 (2006), 50–64

Johnson, James Turner, *Just War Tradition and the Restraint of War* (Princeton: Princeton University Press, 1981)

Jones, Richard, 'Fortifications and Sieges in Western Europe, c. 800–1450', in *Medieval Warfare: A History*, ed. Maurice Keen (Oxford: Oxford University Press, 1999), pp. 163–85

Jones, Robert W., *Bloodied Banners: Martial Display on the Medieval Battlefield* (Woodbridge: Boydell, 2010)

Jones, Robert W. and Peter Coss (eds), *A Companion to Chivalry* (Woodbridge: Boydell, 2019)

Kaeuper, Richard, *Chivalry and Violence in Medieval Europe* (Oxford: Oxford University Press, 1999)

Keen, Maurice, *Nobles, Knights and Men-at-Arms in the Middle Ages* (London: Hambledon, 1996)

———— *Chivalry* (New Haven and London: Yale University Press, 2005; orig. 1984)

Knowles, David, 'The Canterbury Election of 1205–6', *English Historical Review*, 53 (1938), 211–20

Kosto, Adam J., *Hostages in the Middle Ages* (Oxford: Oxford University Press, 2012)

Lachaud, Frédérique, *Jean sans Terre* (Paris: Perrin, 2018)

Laird Clowes, W., *The Royal Navy: A History from the Earliest Times to the Present*, 7 vols (London: Sampson Low, Marston and Company, 1897–1903)

Legge, M. Dominica, *Anglo-Norman Literature and its Background* (Oxford: Clarendon, 1963)

Lehr, Peter, 'Eustace the Monk: Piracy and the Limits of State Authority in the High Middle Ages', *Journal of Historical Sociology*, 34 (2021), 479–90

Leyser, Henrietta, *Medieval Women: A Social History of Women in England 450–1500* (London: Weidenfeld & Nicolson, 1995)

Loades, Mike, *The Longbow* (Oxford: Osprey, 2013)

Loengard, Janet S. (ed.), *Magna Carta and the England of King John* (Woodbridge: Boydell, 2010)

Luchaire, Achille, 'La Condamnation de Jean Sans-Terre par la cour de France', *Revue Historique*, 27 (1900), 285–90

The Magna Carta Project, at https://magnacartaresearch.org

Mason, Emma, 'Portrait of Britain, AD 1200', *History Today*, 50.5 (May 2000), 39–45

McDougall, Sara, *Royal Bastards: The Birth of Illegitimacy, 800–1230* (Oxford: Oxford University Press, 2017)

McGlynn, Sean, 'Roger of Wendover and the Wars of Henry III, 1216–1234', in *England and Europe in the Reign of Henry III, 1216–1272*, ed. Björn K.U. Weiler and Ifor W. Rowlands (Aldershot: Ashgate, 2002), pp. 183–206

———— *By Sword and Fire: Cruelty and Atrocity in Medieval Warfare* (London: Weidenfeld & Nicolson, 2008)

———— *Blood Cries Afar: The Forgotten Invasion of England 1216* (Stroud: Spellmount, 2011)

_____ 'Eustace the Monk: Scourge of the Seas', *Medieval Warfare*, 2.6 (2013), 48–51, available online at https://www.medievalists .net/2014/01/eustace-the-monk-scourge-of-the-seas/

_____ *Robin Hood: A True Legend* (London: Sharpe Books, 2018)

_____ '"*Pro patria*": National Identity and War in Early Medieval England', in *Nationalism, Patriotism, Ancient and Modern: An Interdisciplinary Approach*, ed. Alexander Peck (forthcoming)

McLaughlin, Megan, 'The Woman Warrior: Gender, Warfare and Society in Medieval Europe', *Women's Studies*, 17 (1990), 193–209

Menant, François, Hervé Martin, Bernard Merdrignac et al., *Les Capetiens, 987–1326* (Paris: Tempus, 2018; orig. 2008)

Meuleau, Maurice, *Histoire de la chevalerie* (Rennes: Ouest-France, 2014)

Morillo, Stephen, 'Expecting Cowardice: Medieval Battle Tactics Reconsidered', *Journal of Medieval Military History*, 4 (2006), 65–73

Morris, Marc, *King John: Treachery, Tyranny and the Road to Magna Carta* (London: Hutchinson, 2015)

Morris, William A., *The Medieval English Sheriff to 1300* (Manchester: Manchester University Press, 1927)

The Naval Encyclopedia, at https://naval-encyclopedia.com

Nicholson, Helen, *Medieval Warfare: Theory and Practice of War in Europe, 300–1500* (London: Palgrave, 2003)

Nicolas, Nicholas Harris, *A History of the Royal Navy from the Earliest Times to the Wars of the French Revolution*, 2 vols (London: Richard Bentley, 1847)

Nicolle, David, *French Medieval Armies 1000–1300* (London: Osprey, 1991)

_____ 'Warfare and Technology', *Medieval World*, 6 (1992), 49–54

_____ *Medieval Warfare Source Book*, 2 vols (London: Brockhampton Press, 1998)

_____ *Arms and Armour of the Crusading Era, 1050–1350* (London: Greenhill, 1999; orig. 1988)

_____ (ed.) *A Companion to Medieval Arms and Armour* (Woodbridge: Boydell, 2002)

Norton, Elizabeth, *England's Queens: The Biography* (Stroud: Amberley, 2012)

Orme, Nicholas, *From Childhood to Chivalry: The Education of the English Kings and Aristocracy 1066–1530* (London: Methuen, 1984)
_____ *Medieval Children* (New Haven and London: Yale University Press, 2001)
Painter, Sidney, *William Marshal: Knight Errant, Baron and Regent of England* (Baltimore: Johns Hopkins University Press, 1933)
_____ *French Chivalry: Chivalric Ideals and Practice in Medieval France* (Baltimore: Johns Hopkins University Press, 1940)
_____ *Medieval Society* (Ithaca: Cornell University Press, 1951)
Papin, Yves D., *Chronologie du Moyen Âge* (Paris: Editions Jean-Paul Gisserot, 2001)
Parfitt, Keith, 'A Lost Earthwork near Dover Castle', *Kent Archaeological Review*, 121 (1995), 10–11
Pattison, Paul, Steven Brindle and David M. Robinson (eds), *The Great Tower of Dover Castle: History, Architecture and Context* (London: Historic England, 2020)
Petit-Dutaillis, Charles, *Étude sur la vie et le règne de Louis VIII 1187–1226* (Paris: Bibliothèque de l'Ecole des Hautes Etudes, 1894)
_____ *The Feudal Monarchy in France and England from the Tenth to the Thirteenth Century*, trans. E.D. Hunt (London: Routledge & Kegan Paul, 1966; orig. 1936)
Power, Daniel, 'King John and the Norman Aristocracy', in *King John: New Interpretations*, ed. S.D. Church (Woodbridge: Boydell, 1999), pp. 117–36
_____ *The Norman Frontier in the Twelfth and Early Thirteenth Centuries* (Cambridge: Cambridge University Press, 2004)
Powicke, F.M., *The Loss of Normandy (1189–1204): Studies in the History of the Angevin Empire* (Manchester: Manchester University Press, 1913)
_____ *The Thirteenth Century, 1216–1307* (Oxford: Clarendon, 1953)
Prestwich, J.O., 'Military Intelligence under the Norman and Angevin Kings', in *Law and Government in Medieval England and Normandy*, ed. G. Garnett and J. Hudson (Cambridge: Cambridge University Press, 1994), pp. 1–30
_____ *The Place of War in English History 1066–1214* (Woodbridge: Boydell, 2004)
Prestwich, Michael, *Armies and Warfare in the Middle Ages: The English Experience* (New Haven and London: Yale University Press, 1996)

_____ 'The Garrisoning of English Medieval Castles', in *The Normans and Their Adversaries at War*, ed. Richard Abels and Bernard S. Bachrach (Woodbridge: Boydell, 2001), pp. 185–200

Pryor, John H. (ed.), *The Logistics of Warfare in the Age of the Crusades* (Aldershot: Ashgate, 2006)

Purton, Peter, 'The Myth of the Mangonel: Torsion Artillery in the Middle Ages', *Arms and Armour*, 3 (2006), 79–90

_____ *A History of the Early Medieval Siege, c. 450–1200* (Woodbridge: Boydell, 2009)

_____ *A History of the Late Medieval Siege, 1200–1500* (Woodbridge: Boydell, 2010)

_____ *The Medieval Military Engineer: From the Roman Empire to the Sixteenth Century* (Woodbridge: Boydell, 2018)

Rees, Owen, Kathryn Hurlock and Jason Crowley (eds), *Combat Stress in Pre-modern Europe* (Cham, Switzerland: Springer Nature, 2022)

Richardson, H.G., 'Letters of the Legate Guala', *English Historical Review*, 48 (1933), 250–59

_____ 'The Coronation in Medieval England: The Evolution of the Office and the Oath', *Traditio*, 16 (1960), 111–202

Rodger, N.A.M., 'The Naval Service of the Cinque Ports', *English Historical Review*, 111 (1996), 636–51

_____ *The Safeguard of the Sea: A Naval History of Britain, Volume One 660–1649* (London: HarperCollins, 1997)

Rose, Susan, *England's Medieval Navy, 1066–1509* (Barnsley: Seaforth Publishing, 2013)

Roth, Erik, *With a Bended Bow: Archery in Mediaeval and Renaissance Europe* (Stroud: Spellmount, 2012)

Russell, Frederick, *The Just War in the Middle Ages* (Cambridge: Cambridge University Press, 1975)

Russell, Josiah, 'The Clerical Population of Medieval England', *Traditio*, 2 (1944), 177–212

Sabapathy, John, *Officers and Accountability in Medieval England, 1170–1300* (Oxford: Oxford University Press, 2014)

Salch, Charles-Laurent (ed.), *Dictionnaire des châteaux et des fortifications du moyen âge en France* (Strasbourg: Editions Publitotal, 1987)

Sanders, Ivor John, *English Baronies: A Study of Their Origin and Descent, 1086–1327* (Oxford: Clarendon, 1960)

Saul, Nigel, *A Companion to Medieval England 1066–1485*, 3rd ed. (Stroud: Tempus, 2005; orig. 1983)

Saxtorph, Niels M., 'Technical Innovations and Military Change', in *War and Peace in the Middle Ages*, ed. Brian Patrick McGuire (Copenhagen: C.A. Reitzels Forlag, 1987), pp. 216–26

Sayers, Jane E., *Innocent III: Leader of Europe, 1198–1216* (London: Longman, 1994)

Seabourne, Gwen, 'Eleanor of Brittany and her Treatment by King John and Henry III', *Nottingham Medieval Studies*, 51 (2007), 73–111

———— *Imprisoning Medieval Women: The Non-Judicial Confinement and Abduction of Women in England, c. 1170–1509* (Farnham: Ashgate, 2011)

Sivéry, Gérard, *Blanche de Castille* (Paris: Fayard, 1990)

———— *Louis VIII le Lion* (Paris: Fayard, 1995)

———— *Philippe Auguste* (Paris: Perrin, 2003; orig. Librairie Plon, 1993)

Smith, J. Beverley, 'The Treaty of Lambeth, 1217', *English Historical Review*, 94 (1979), 562–79

Spencer, Dan, *The Castle at War in Medieval England and Wales* (Stroud: Amberley, 2018)

Spong, Sally, 'Isabella of Gloucester and Isabella of Angoulême: Queenship and Female Lordship in England and France, 1189–1220', unpublished PhD thesis, University of East Anglia, 2022

———— 'Isabella of Gloucester: Heiress, Lord, Forgotten Consort', in *English Consorts: Power, Influence, Dynasty. Volume 1: Early Medieval Consorts* (Basingstoke: Palgrave Macmillan, forthcoming)

Stanton, Charles D., *Medieval Maritime Warfare* (Barnsley: Pen & Sword, 2015)

Staunton, Michael, *The Historians of Angevin England* (Oxford: Oxford University Press, 2017)

Steane, John M., *The Archaeology of Power* (Stroud: Tempus, 2001)

Stephens, G.R., 'A Note on William of Cassingham', *Speculum*, 16 (1941) 216–23

Strickland, Matthew, 'Against the Lord's Anointed: Aspects of Warfare and Baronial Rebellion in England and Normandy, 1075–1265', in *Law and Government in Medieval England and Normandy*, ed. George

Garnett and John Hudson (Cambridge: Cambridge University Press, 1994), pp. 56–79

_____ War and Chivalry (Cambridge: Cambridge University Press, 1996)

Strickland, Matthew and Robert Hardy, The Great Warbow: From Hastings to the Mary Rose (Stroud: Sutton, 2005)

Stringer, K.J., 'Kingship, Conflict and State-Making in the Reign of Alexander II: The War of 1215–17 and its Context', in The Reign of Alexander II, 1214–49, ed. Richard Oram (Leiden: Brill, 2005), pp. 99–156

Tilley, Arthur (ed.), Medieval France (Cambridge: Cambridge University Press, 1922)

Titterton, James, Deception in Medieval Warfare: Trickery and Cunning in the Central Middle Ages (Woodbridge: Boydell, 2022)

Tout, T.F., 'The Fair of Lincoln and the Histoire de Guillaume le Maréchal', English Historical Review, 18 (1903), 240–65

_____ France and England: Their Relations in the Middle Ages and Now (London: Longmans, Green & Co., 1922)

Truax, Jean A., 'Anglo-Norman Women at War: Valiant Soldiers, Prudent Strategists or Charismatic Leaders?', in The Circle of War in the Middle Ages: Essays on Medieval Military and Naval History, ed. Donald J. Kagay and L.J. Andrew Villalon (Woodbridge: Boydell, 1999), pp. 111–25

Turner, Ralph V., Eleanor of Aquitaine: Queen of France, Queen of England (New Haven and London: Yale University Press, 2009)

_____ 'England in 1215: An Authoritarian Angevin Dynasty Facing Multiple Threats', in Magna Carta and the England of King John, ed. Janet S. Loengard (Woodbridge: Boydell, 2010), pp. 10–26

Unger, Richard, The Ship in the Medieval Economy, 600–1600 (Montreal: McGill-Queen's University Press, 1980)

Vale, Malcolm, War and Chivalry (London: Duckworth, 1981)

_____ The Ancient Enemy: England, France and Europe from the Angevins to the Tudors (London: Bloomsbury Academic, 2009)

Verbruggen, J.F., The Art of Warfare in Western Europe in the Middle Ages, trans. Sumner Willard and S.C.M. Southern (Oxford: North-Holland, 1977)

_____ 'Women in Medieval Armies', trans. Kelly DeVries, *Journal of Medieval Military History*, 4 (2006), 119–36

Vincent, Nicholas, *Peter des Roches: An Alien in English Politics, 1205–1238* (Cambridge: Cambridge University Press, 1996)

_____ 'Isabella of Angoulême: John's Jezebel', in *King John: New Interpretations*, ed. S.D. Church (Woodbridge: Boydell, 1999), pp. 165–219

_____ 'A Queen in Rebel London, 1215–17', in *'A Verray Parfit Praktisour': Essays Presented to Carole Rawcliffe*, ed. Linda Clark and Elizabeth Danbury (Woodbridge: Boydell, 2017), pp. 23–50

Volkmann, Jean-Charles, *Généalogies complètes des rois de France* (Paris: Editions Jean-Paul Gisserot, 1999)

Warner, Philip, *Sieges of the Middle Ages* (London: Bell and Sons, 1968)

Warren, John, *The Past and its Presenters* (London: Hodder & Stoughton, 1998)

Warren, W.L., *The Governance of Anglo-Norman and Angevin England, 1086–1272* (Stanford: Stanford University Press, 1987)

_____ *King John*, 2nd ed. (New Haven and London: Yale University Press, 1997; orig. 1961)

Weiss, Michael, 'The Castellan: The Early Career of Hubert de Burgh', *Viator*, 5 (1974), 235–52

West, F.J., *The Justiciarship in England, 1066–1232* (Cambridge: Cambridge University Press, 1966)

Wheatley, Abigail, *The Idea of the Castle in Medieval England* (York: York Medieval Press, 2015; orig. 2004)

Wilkinson, Louise, 'Women as Sheriffs in Early Thirteenth-Century England', in *English Government in the Thirteenth Century*, ed. Adrian Jobson (Woodbridge: Boydell, 2004), pp. 111–24

_____ *Women in Thirteenth-Century Lincolnshire* (Woodbridge: Boydell, 2007)

_____ 'Maternal Abandonment and Surrogate Caregivers: Isabella of Angoulême and Her Children by King John', in *Virtuous or Villainess? The Image of the Royal Mother from the Early Medieval to the Early Modern Era*, ed. Carey Fleiner and Elena Woodacre (New York: Palgrave Macmillan, 2016), pp. 101–24

Woodacre, Elena and Carey Fleiner (eds), *Royal Mothers and their Ruling Children: Wielding Political Authority from Antiquity to the Early Modern Era* (New York: Palgrave Macmillan, 2015)

Woosnam-Savage, Robert and Kelly DeVries, 'Battle Trauma in Medieval Warfare: Wounds, Weapons and Armor', in *Wounds and Wound Repair in Medieval Culture*, ed. Larissa Tracy and Kelly DeVries (Leiden: Brill, 2015), pp. 27–56

Index